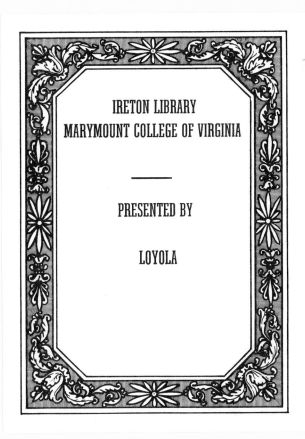

Predicting
Executive
Success

Predicting Executive Success

WHAT IT TAKES TO MAKE IT
INTO SENIOR MANAGEMENT

MELVIN SORCHER

JOHN WILEY & SONS
New York · Chichester · Brisbane · Toronto · Singapore

Copyright © 1985 by Melvin Sorcher
Published by John Wiley & Sons, Inc.

All rights reserved. Published simultaneously in Canada.

Reproduction or translation of any part of this work
beyond that permitted by Section 107 or 108 of the
1976 United States Copyright Act without the permission
of the copyright owner is unlawful. Requests for
permission or further information should be addressed to
the Permissions Department, John Wiley & Sons, Inc.

This publication is designed to provide accurate and
authoritative information in regard to the subject
matter covered. It is sold with the understanding that
the publisher is not engaged in rendering legal, accounting,
or other professional service. If legal advice or other
expert assistance is required, the services of a competent
professional person should be sought. *From a Declaration
of Principles jointly adopted by a Committee of the
American Bar Association and a Committee of Publishers.*

Library of Congress Cataloging in Publication Data

Sorcher, Melvin.
  Predicting executive success.

  Includes index.
  1. Executive ability.   2. Executives—Recruiting.
I. Title.
HD38.2.S67   1985   658.4'09   85-3293
ISBN 0-471-81565-9

Printed in the United States of America

10 9 8 7 6 5 4 3 2 1

This book is for three people who judged me during the early part of my career. They were also my teachers, but in different ways. I cannot imagine anyone better and I am deeply indebted to them.

To the memory of Dr. George G. Stern, my major professor and doctoral advisor, who encouraged me and made a path for me when the obstacles took up more room than the clear space. His intellect and humanism were incredible. I remember him and I miss him.

To Dr. Charles L. Wood, who gave me air cover and understanding at all the right times. He made it possible for me to do what I wanted. He was always behind me and he taught me why it is important to have confidence in people.

To Dr. Herbert H. Meyer, whose management and integrity taught me how people should be treated and motivated. His openness and willingness for me to satisfy my curiosity are gifts that I try to pass on to others.

Preface

The experiences and opinions described in this book were obtained from my own observations in hundreds of situations and from very senior executives in a variety of businesses and corporate cultures: manufacturing, engineering, consumer products, corporate utilities, high technology, communications, real estate, banking, and financial services. These executives are chairmen, CEO's, presidents, senior vice presidents and executive vice presidents who are among the most respected people in their company and their industry. In a few cases, the executives had recently retired but remain active on the boards of companies or in other business interests. In all cases, these executives graciously responded to my questions.

While a number of individuals are quoted and companies cited, some executives did request anonymity for themselves and their company. In addition, I took the liberty of disguising identities, even when not requested, if it seemed appropriate. Nevertheless, it is inevitable, because of the nature of this material, that some readers may perceive similarities to situations or persons they know. I have, however, changed each example so it cannot be identified.

Perhaps the most surprising observation is that almost all the executives with whom I talked think alike about what they look for—and reject—in candidates for senior positions: they just say it differently. They have different ways of getting answers to their questions. But the actual decisions come down to the same issues. These views have been presented in a framework built on sound and pragmatic management principles. My own opinions are, I believe, supported by the bulk of the research of my professional colleagues and by the experience of executives who operate in corporate society. I also want to acknowledge the invaluable comments on the manuscript by Michael A. Sorcher.

I hope readers will enjoy the book and—more than that—find it useful for their own purposes.

MELVIN SORCHER

Trumbull, Connecticut
January 1985

Contents

Predicting
Executive
Success

— 1 —

The Basis of Prediction

WHAT THIS BOOK IS ABOUT

This is a book about prediction. Wall Street analysts predict. Fortune tellers predict. Odds-makers predict. Scientists predict. People even predict weather. Nevertheless, with few exceptions, people who predict events cannot influence outcomes. Most do not even try. Among those who do, however, business executives are surely most persistent in their attempts to make the future resemble their vision of it.

Senior corporate executives, especially the chairmen, board members, and presidents of major organizations, are almost always in some stage of planning for management succession. They try to identify executives who are most promising, who have the greatest potential for accomplishment and good leadership, and who are most likely to move the organization towards its goals. They try to predict which individuals will achieve corporate objectives—they do not want to leave the future to chance. Sometimes, however, "prediction" dissolves to "best guess." It is very difficult to predict with great confidence which of two or more executives will be the most effective corporate leader.

Most of this book will focus on the identification and evaluation of candidates for chief and senior executive positions. Whether they become chairmen, CEOs, vice presidents, or senior executives with other titles, they will be "The chiefs" of either an entire enterprise or a significant portion of it. Most organizations have several chiefs. As much as physicians and lawyers and teachers, these future chiefs will ultimately be responsible for the fortunes, the welfare, and the lives of the people who depend on the organization for income, for security, and for their dreams. Understandably, the selection of a new chief is a lengthy and stressful process for the people who must make the decision or contribute to it.

Many readers of this book will either want to pick a chief or be one. While our focus is on better ways to identify and evaluate candidates for more dependable prediction of performance outcomes, perhaps the most valuable aspects of this book are the behavioral guidelines and criteria which should be used to select the best candidates for senior management succession. This information can be especially useful for individuals who include the position of chief among their important personal objectives. For those who pick—and for those who aspire—there are too many ways to make mistakes and too few opportunities for second tries. This book may help.

THE NEED FOR MORE CARE

Consider the senior executives who run corporations, especially the mid-sized and large ones—or major segments of them. Was each one the best choice among the candidates? This is difficult to determine in retrospect, but, based on performance, perhaps one-third of them would not be selected again. Could this estimate be verified? Probably not, since it is not an opinion that would be volunteered or candidly expressed by corporate chairmen, boards, or presidents who select and supervise chiefs. Could the performance of these chiefs—the effective ones and the less effective ones—have been predicted more accurately? Probably, if more cohesive, multi-dimensional, and better-balanced elements of evaluation were used. Prediction is a lot like navigation: If you use several reliable instruments that give overlapping information, take frequent readings at different times and from different perspectives, you are much more likely to end up exactly where you want to be and when you want to be there. Using only a compass is not likely to be enough to get you from one point to another each time you need to go somewhere, especially when you cannot affort to get lost or delayed along the way.

If an estimate of one-third less-than-desirable effectiveness among senior executives is not far from reality, it may not be unreasonable to estimate that another one-third is extremely effective in meeting the organization's highest expectations. The people who picked this latter group are either very careful or lucky. If the history of chief selection in an organization reveals an almost continuous string of chiefs who meet all or most corporate objectives, the corporation has apparently developed a process which works for it. Following these assumptions, another one-third of the chiefs are doing reasonably well but are not meeting the organization's full expectations.

Somehow the number of surprises—in executive performance and executive expectation—seem to have increased. Stability of tenure among chiefs is no longer as certain as it was 10 or 20 years ago. An article in *Business Week* discussed the issue and made a prediction.

> Turnover at the top is hitting levels without precedent in recent history. . . .It is now at a point where corporate leaders and consultants flatly predict that the jobs of chief executive and chief operating officer *will never be as secure as they once were.*[1]

The article also prescribes:

> To cope, managers perceive a need to scrap old ways of doing things.[2]

Recognizing a need to do things differently is difficult, especially for senior executives who have developed ways of managing that have worked successfully for them. It is not easy to find the incentive and

[1]"*Turnover at the Top*," *Business Week*, December 19, 1983, p. 104.
[2]*Ibid.*

the ability to change strongly reinforced behaviors. Many chiefs part with their companies because of pressure to change. The number of disenchantments for both chiefs and companies can be reduced by the use of more predictive identification and evaluation processes. The core of the issue centers on either or both the quality of candidates from which a final selection is made and on the process of evaluation. Even if an estimate of two-thirds not fully effective is high, the quality of effort put into chief selection cannot be second-rate. Even a small number of chiefs have fate control over an enormous amount of capital and tens or hundreds of thousands of lives. Their effect, for good or for bad, extends well beyond their tenure.

But what happens to the rest of the corporate executive population who are sizing up their chances of becoming chiefs? While most of this book addresses the process of selecting chiefs, many readers may find that they learn a great deal about the behaviors and images that will advocate their own strong candidacy. The *raison d'etre* for this book is chief succession: the planning and the choice.

FRAME OF REFERENCE

It is important for readers to know that the opinions and recommendations in this book are based on the involvement and personal observations of a number of very senior executives in a wide variety of succession situations. These opinions account only for the dimensions of behavior that are directly tied to simultaneously motivating an organization and demonstrating one's potential to be a chief. The opinions of others actively involved in selecting chiefs were sought and included. By careful watching, listening, participating, and questioning, the patterns of executive behavior became evident. In fact, they are so consistent that they are even predictable. While the processes of evaluation and prediction of chief potential are within the context of behavioral science, this book is not an exposition of the scientific method applied to the selection or making of a chief. The spirit of scientific inquiry has instead guided how the observations were interpreted, how inferences and suppositions were developed, how questions were formed to test assumptions, and how additional observations were integrated with the accumulating evidence behind each inference or conclusion.

From this book, readers involved in chief selection will find ways to increase their confidence in their predictions. Executive succession is not a lofty, quantifiable activity that draws its energy and direction only from facts. Instead, it is an activity that grasps for elusive, intangible evidence, stumbles over contradictions, and fills in ambiguity with assumptions and wishes. What a way to pick a Chief! Imagine the consequences if a substantially higher proportion of senior executives *fully* met expectations.

Readers looking toward senior management as an objective will learn which aspects of their behavior need to be shaped or expressed differently. They will also learn which strengths to build and how to apply them. Mistakes and behaviors which can be avoided will become more apparent. Implicit guidelines on how, when, and on what issues to take strong initiative will also be highlighted.

Readers who do not have the drive or ability to be chief will not be able to use this information as a cookbook. It isn't one. It is a compilation of observations and opinions that some readers will absorb, redefine to fit with their individuality, and then apply thoughtfully—and probably successfully.

For both kinds of readers, the role of chief deserves the most careful attention. It is a worthy position, with many opportunities to cause useful things to happen. Those responsible for selecting new chiefs must improve the quality of their selection process, or if they do not, the kind of candidates who would make the best senior executives may be discouraged from trying. That would be a very sad outcome.

REDUCING THE ISSUES TO HUMAN SIZE

When faced with the question of chief succession, people who make the decisions rarely ask which candidate will do better in a proxy fight, or which candidate will get the best return on assets invested, or even which candidate is the smartest. These questions are too general—and the benchmarks for judging the answers have the reliability of an elastic yardstick! Characteristically, the people who make selection decisions tend to ask questions about candidates that go to the center of essentially behavioral and philosophical issues, not to financial or technical ones. Boiling it down, the fundamental question is, "Can he or she run things the way we want them run?"

In virtually any organization, candidates for senior positions have the common characteristic of high intelligence. They have also demonstrated their abilities in typically operational roles. They have already run things. Management succession decisions, therefore, are generally not made on the candidates' technical or financial abilities, since it is often difficult to distinguish among competent people on these aspects. Further, these abilities are often less important in chief positions. Instead, most of the important questions about candidates center about personal values and behavior. This is probably why Andrew Sigler, chairman of Champion International Corporation and a member of the board of directors of several major enterprises said,

> In the broad sense—and not just in a profit sense—you'd better perform or the board is going to get rid of you.[3]

CHOOSING THE RIGHT CANDIDATE

When the time comes to identify the best candidates for a senior executive opening that has occurred or is anticipated, those responsible for the decision raise several questions. How these questions are framed is influenced by how long and how well a candidate is known by a selection committee or hiring executive. There seems to be a strong negative correlation between familiarity with a candidate and the quality of questions raised about him or her. Familiarity causes assumptions and inferences to form the basis for prediction. Typically, questions are less searching and ambiguities or uncertainties are not probed.

A halo often surrounds a familiar candidate. For example, (1) an executive who has contributed solid service, who is articulate, whose decisions have been consistent with corporate values, and who is socially acquainted with other senior executives and his organizational superiors vs. (2) an executive in a distant organizational component who has equally long service and sound accomplish-

[3]Ibid.

ments, but who is not personally known by his organizational superiors.

When a decision must be made between the two candidates in this example, the decision-makers must be very careful. Poor decisions are often made because the wrong questions are asked, or because inference, not reality, provides the answers to the right questions. There is less anxiety about the more familiar executive because it is assumed he or she will continue to operate consistently and with the same predictable results as before. The less familiar executive is often viewed as more threatening to predictability because he or she is not located near the corporate headquarters and, of necessity, has developed an operating style without influence from his or her organizational superiors. The individual responsible for selection often moves away from the less familiar person because it cannot simply be assumed he or she will act predictably. It is much easier to assume predictable behavior with a familiar person.

The major problem with these kinds of assumptions is that behavior required for effectiveness on the part of the chief is very different from the behaviors which have brought a person to the candidacy for it. It is dangerous to assume that successive previous responsibilities will assure subsequent success as a chief. This assumption takes the edge from questions, limits explanation of the link between a candidate's past and how he or she would move in the future, and provides a basis for rationalization of weaknesses that often float like icebergs with only the tips showing.

TYPICAL QUESTIONS

One question that is almost always asked is, "Can he lead?" Other typical questions include: "Can he change things so we go where we should?"; "Can he tighten up the organization and make it more efficient?"; "Is he a mature business person?"; and "Will he keep us out of trouble?"

There is nothing wrong with concerns of this kind, but they are only the basis for developing questions which generate more specific information. Questions that are too broad usually provide only general answers—and make it easy to rationalize virtually any bias or preconception from the answers. People who often ask questions that are too general provide much of the answers from their own imaginations or opinions.

The questions outlined in the previous paragraph are not throwaways. They serve as the basis for what you want to know about someone and how that person will perform in a range of specified circumstances. However, as a general rule, questions about the characteristics or qualities of potential chiefs should not be randomly or spontaneously asked. They must be carefully formulated and developed because questions should not simply seek answers. They must seek information. Information is a great deal more than bias, preconception, expectation, presumption, or generalization. Poor questions will not provide the information needed to more accurately predict the effectiveness of candidates for chief.

For example, if information about leadership is sought, questions such as these will generate better information on which to base predictions: "To what degree will he trust his operating staff to make decisions?"; "In the past, what has been the balance between good staff advice and self-reliance?"; "What events or changes has she caused to happen because of her personal conviction—and how did other people in her organization react to these?"; "Does he discuss work with subordinates with a tone of optimism or suspiciousness or uncertainty?"; "What kind of teamwork has he built under him and how independent are these teams or the individuals on them?"; "What is the compatibility of values between the candidate and the person to whom she will report?" These questions, of course, are only illustrative of how to minimize assumption and get better information. Chapters 3 and 5 will describe how to form questions and how to evaluate the usefulness of the information they provide.

ASKING BETTER QUESTIONS

Better information will make those involved in the selection process more confident in their choice. There is so much ambiguity, contradiction, bias, and wishful thinking in the process of selecting chiefs that the tendency to ask broad but simple questions is under-standable. After all, if no guide or principles are available for developing, asking, and evaluating questions and information it is easy to rely on subjective information. That is what happens in most organizations.

The following examples outline how some candidates convey information about themselves, how their behavior is perceived and judged by others, how assumptions and inferences are developed by people who select chiefs, and how post-selection problems could have been anticipated. Each of these cases is described from the point of view of the people who select chiefs in these organizations.

First Case

Background.   L.O. was the chief operating officer of a well-known, very successful clothing company. At that time he was a candidate for the position of president, reporting to the chairman of the board.

L.O. joined the company 22 years ago, just after receiving an MBA. He started as a salesperson and moved quickly into merchandising and marketing responsibilities. He is an extremely articulate man with a sharp and active intellect. Most people in the company expected him to be the next president, although not everyone thought he was well-suited to it.

L.O. was promoted often, each time after only two or three years in a position. He continued to impress his organizational superiors with his conceptual fluency, his sense of propriety and strategy, and his strong sense of (and preference for) command.

L.O. thoroughly enjoyed deep discussions of managerial issues and how to influence people. He became deeply involved in the functions for which he was responsible and exercised his authority and opinions in each of them. L.O. did not hesitate to develop his own concepts for how things should work and then ask for them to be implemented.

He always tried to surround himself with the best staff and operating executives, using them as extensions of himself. To accomplish this, he removed a few individuals along the way who were not likely to focus totally on meeting his needs.

His long and broad experience in the company had given him a familiarity with it to the point where his comments and behavior indicated a strong feeling of ownership—although in reality he was an officer and employee of the company, not a principal. For example, in reference to decisions made by the president or chairman, he often said things like "If I were him, I would not buy a designer jeans business—we have enough to do with our primary lines," or "I can tell you that if I were running this place, I sure would not put up with. . . ."

The Decision.   L.O.'s career had shown strong forward movement. Answers to questions like, "Can he lead?," "Is he a mature business-person?," or "Can be bring us into new businesses?" brought resounding cries of "Yes!" from his company's board. Such a positive reaction to these questions, combined with a long familiarity with L.O. and his successive promotions through the organization, would warm the hearts of most selection committees or individuals who pick chiefs. L.O.'s background, in fact, gave confidence to his company's board that L.O. was the best candidate for president. No need, they said, to ask better questions, no need for more information—the candidate is well-known.

This was a mistake. Not a terrible mistake, just a mistake that cut the company's ability to compete and grow.

Analyzing the Decision.   But was L.O. capable of running the company in a manner that would enable the company to stay ahead of competitors in design, merchandising, and sales? The board made a mistake by not even considering L.O.'s primary values. They judged him only on his personal manner, strong intellect, and frequent promotions, and increasing responsibilities. What they missed was the fundamental value system that motivated L.O.: power and control.

L.O. would often speak of his preference for decision making and delegation—but he always made important decisions without consulting those who would be most affected by them. L.O.'s concern about losing control was partly evidenced by his unwillingness to let the operating executives reporting to him make important decisions about their own businesses. L.O. not only insisted on approving all key operating decisions, but he also anticipated the need for a decision by analyzing the issues himself and presenting the responsible executive with his plan and recommendations. L.O.'s judgment was usually correct until he was moved into the position of president. This promotion separated him from fully understanding important changes in his industry but did not stop him from exercising his authority and opinions about them.

The board also assumed that L.O.'s frequent promotions were signs of accomplishment. They were not. Rapid movement should not have been confused with accomplishments. While L.O. moved in and out of each position smoothly, he accomplished little in each position. He spent most of his time vocally endorsing his opinions and giving them to subordinates for direction. Many of these opinions subtly communicated his own expectation of becoming president one day, and most of his subordinates were unwilling to confront such a likely candidate. Besides, his personal manner contained enough warmth not to offend them.

The Result.   Within 15 months after L.O. became president the chief operating officer who replaced him and the most effective general manager resigned. They did not want to cope with L.O.'s interference in the way they ran their businesses. They had no quarrel with the quality of L.O.'s thinking, which they welcomed, but they and their staffs deeply resented L.O.'s unsolicited recommendations on issues with which they were both more familiar and competent to address.

L.O., in turn, sought support for his need to get even more deeply involved in the company due to the departure of these two senior executives. L.O. asked the chief financial executive to set up a formal management control process which would assure that L.O. would be directly involved in approving all major operating decisions, even those which customarily went down to middle management. The financial executive refused to become the target of hostile operating executives for designing such a plan, and he also resigned.

Two years after assuming the presidency, L.O.'s company was not competing as well as it did because of the departure of the senior executives as well as several other promising operating executives who did not enjoy L.O.'s exercise of power. The company stopped expanding its lines to concentrate on their core business. Earnings were down and the stock price was depressed. The chairman was puzzled because L.O. had a cutting-edge intellect, a marvelous personal manner, and apparently great knowledge about virtually all aspects of the business.

The actions of L.O. and the results he encountered should have been anticipated. If better questions were asked—about his personal values, his way of managing and delegating, his confidence in subordinates, his ability to build a team—predicting L.O.'s behavior and results would have been fairly easy. A better guide for succession planning was needed. The principles for guiding a management succession process are described at the end of this chapter and will be elaborated on and demonstrated throughout the book.

Second Case

The Background.   A second example of a poor selection process and its consequences shows how often mistakes are made. P.M. was an extremely intelligent, fast-thinking, action-oriented individual. He had a strong educational background in the physical sciences and was a senior executive for a large company. He had been with his company for 24 years in a variety of assignments, starting with two years in research and development and followed by successive managerial responsibility for business units.

Most of all, P.M. wanted to be known for his accomplishments. Personal achievement was his central value. P.M. had a reputation for being a demanding, tough executive who got results under difficult conditions. When, after several years of corporate lethargy, the CEO of the company was retiring, the board wanted somebody who would put a new spark into the company and push it into new areas of activity. P.M. thought of himself as a strong leader. After three meetings with P.M., the board agreed. P.M. was a marvelous communicator and expressed his agreement with their objectives with forceful eloquence. He was chosen over two other candidates because they were less aggressive although equally competent technically.

The Decision.   The board raised several questions, including "Will he be strong enough to get people to think and act differently?," "Will he take direction from the board?," and "Can he develop a set of innovative corporate objectives?" After some discussion they agreed he was a strong leader and that he had the technical depth to assess and manage new opportunities.

When the CEO retired and P.M. was named to succeed him, most other executives—both senior and junior—wondered if the board had lost its collective mind. P.M. was known to be demanding, but most of his subordinates and the people who had worked for him knew him as petty and mean. Within his business, P.M. would push and taunt until he got the results he wanted. The technique was often successful because P.M. knew what was technically possible and his staff members were anxious about their job security during a decade of plateauing in their industry. Nevertheless, there was always fairly fast turnover among the best middle-level executives in P.M.'s business. They saw how their organizational superiors were treated by P.M. and they had no intention of remaining in that environment.

Analyzing the Decision.   The board may have been overly optimistic, but more likely they were nearsighted. Ostrich-like, they stuck their heads in the sand despite clear signals of possible authoritarianism on the part of the prime candidate, that is, somebody who is very solicitous of superiors' concerns but thoroughly autocratic with subordinates. They also ignored his very apparent value system, that is, a "driven" emphasis on personal achievement. The board should also have explored P.M.'s managerial impact on his staff and organization. If they had done so, predicting P.M.'s impact as CEO would have been more accurate. A few carefully defined questions could have resolved this.

Regrettably, P.M. was unaware of how negatively he was perceived by subordinates and, in fact, assumed that his appointment as CEO actually confirmed his managerial philosophy and behavior. Most of his subordinates felt that P.M.'s drive for personal achievement left them out in the cold.

The Result.   When P.M. assumed the CEO position, he immediately replaced a large number of corporate staff executives whom he expected to oppose his leadership. These changes, which were viewed with dismay by most remaining staff executives, resulted in considerable dilution of corporate staff. One consequence was that the operating businesses were deprived of expert advice and the benefit of alternate points of view from corporate staff.

At present, the climate throughout P.M.'s organization is poor. Bright, new university graduates have heard about it from classes that preceded them. P.M. is a strong leader and his presence is felt by most employees more strongly than that of any of the company's former CEOS. Most of all, however, the spirit of innovation and new frontiers is dead. Nobody is willing to risk P.M.'s ire—and innovation does not flourish under a taunting, demeaning, managerial presence.

As senior executives stiffened in defense against anticipated attack by P.M., their staffs sensed the climate. P.M.'s drive for innovation has crashed into a rigid organization whose sense of technical creativity is in *rigor mortis*. Creativity and risk go together. P.M. does not encourage risk because he does not tolerate minority opinions (or any opinions which differ from his own).

The board is very disturbed by P.M.'s impact and would like to replace P.M. But they are concerned about repeating a selection error. Without a better selection process, they have reason to be concerned. Better questions, better information, and better criteria are needed to identify a better chief.

Third Case

The Background.   In a third example, the president thought he had identified just the right person for an executive vice president slot in a new business component. The candidate, S.G., had 20 years experience in the company. He was a responsible executive, ran things smoothly, completed programs and projects on time, and was exceedingly well-liked. S.G. was an "old shoe," and everyone from the president to the most junior person in S.G.'s group felt comfortable with him. He always had time to listen, to talk, to reflect. One of the joys of going to S.G. with problems was that he would help subordinates to explore, poke, turn over all the issues, and then encourage them to consider carefully before committing to a plan of action. Further, in S.G.'s group, everything was done well. He delegated fully to his staff and, as a result, they developed skills and credibility very fast.

The Decision. The new component was intended to enable the company to meet an entirely new business opportunity. It would be staffed 50% from other groups within the company and 50% from outside the company. The executive vice president's task would be to put together a team to act quickly on organizational needs and business opportunities. Who better than S.G. to mold a group of strangers into an effective team? With optimism, S.G. was made the chief.

Analyzing the Decision. Bad things can happen to nice people. S.G. was a marvelous administrator who knew how to delegate responsibility to a staff. He also had the gift of time. He used it to listen and reflect. Unfortunately, S.G. had no sense of urgency. Therefore, S.G.'s abilities were not a match for the challenge of quickly getting a new organization in work formation.

The people in the new organization were strangers. They needed leadership. They needed to be connected as teams, wound up, faced in the right direction, and marched off to the rhythm of the band. S.G. could not do that. He needed time to get to know his people, to talk, to touch.

The Result. In a short time, the people in S.G's division became confused. Then they became frustrated since nothing was happening. Finally, their frustration turned to hostility and they sneered at S.G. In no time, S.G. lost credibility and the job.

The company lost an opportunity to its competitors. All of this could have been anticipated and prevented by a better selection process. The president asked himself the wrong questions and came up with irrelevant answers.

CHANGING THE APPROACH TO SELECTION

In the past, an executive would be certain of a successful career if he was intelligent, articulate, and energetic. No longer. Virtually all senior executives are exceptionally bright people who can do anything they really want to. They have the intellect and the drive to do it. It takes an enormous amount of energy and self-discipline to be a chief. They are all unusual people but they are not always successful at their work. Nowadays it takes more to be an effective chief. Organizational life has become much more complicated and both subordinates and boards are far more demanding of their chiefs.

The approach to the selection of chiefs needs to be changed. For a chief to be effective, his or her personal values and individual behavior must be synchronized. When a chief's behavior departs from principle, or value, an organization will shudder. At one time, values were considered private. They were not even considered as important criteria in selecting a chief.

It is no longer possible to be comfortable with the way succession decisions were handled in the past. There must be the right chief for the right time—and both times and people change. To perpetuate past practices for executive succession may no longer work. The evidence of disappointment is too strong. The old rules for selection cannot be depended upon.

Side Effects of Selection Decisions

Perhaps the least-considered aspects of selecting chiefs are the side-effects of the appointment. Just as every medicine has a side effect, so does the appointment of a chief. There are many variables of side effects: Will the new chief retain or change a staff? What messages are conveyed by his decision? How differently is the organization positioned as a consequence? Will the new chief and his philosophy encourage mediocrity to flourish? Often a strong chief has an un-planned impact because he does not know how to delegate due to a career hands-on managing.

Loyalty

Loyalty is a characteristic often sought in executives. Loyal chiefs are more likely to run things the way their superior or board wants them to run them. Times have changed and loyalty is not something that can be assumed. The opposite of loyalty is not necessarily disloyalty—it is often closer to individualism, innovation, better ideas. Chiefs who are not "loyal" may be the very best people to lead an organization. They frequently communicate progress and encourage innovation on the part of subordinates. This is a marvelous side-effect if one can put up with a lack of traditional loyalty.

Another side effect of selecting a strong leader is that many strong leaders do not know how to build teams. As one consequence, the organization often erodes from within. These managers may lead by strength of knowledge, by force of will, by capturing imaginations, and with personal charm. They often depend upon their one-to-one ability to motivate individuals rather than on their skill in building cohesive teams. While the motivation of individuals is surely important, most organizations require cohesive and self-starting teams. Otherwise, the organization is too dependent on its chief for direction and initiative. The resulting quality of teamwork is a side-effect that should not be overlooked.

DEVELOPING A SELECTION PROCESS

The selection process for chiefs should minimize assumptions, avoid inference, and—most of all—be guided by principle. There are four principles that will increase the accuracy of prediction. This book stands on these principles. They comprise a dependable selection process. They are derived from the best research in the behavioral sciences and combined in a way that adds depth and balance to the important business of prediction.

The four principles are:

1. *A continuous process (rolling) from early identification to imminent appointment.* Potential candidates for chief positions

should be identified fairly early in their careers and reevaluated each year. Individuals initially excluded from early identification should have continuous opportunities to be added to the potential candidacy ranks if their performance so indicates. A continuing, or rolling, process not only assures a longitudinal record of the accomplishments and abilities of each candidate but makes it unlikely that other qualified candidates will be overlooked.

2. *A multi-dimensional process for evaluating abilities and accomplishments must include tangible criteria.* Using several dimensions to evaluate potential based on past performance and measuring against tangible criteria will add perspective, balance, and validity to management succession decisions. Using several dimensions to predict the performance of potential chiefs will reduce considerably the dissonance generated by the task itself. Involving a number of dimensions in the succession decision process is more likely to assure a look at the "whole" man—or woman. In all cases of potential chiefs, the whole is certainly more than the sum of the parts.

3. *Situational predictions are required to improve the odds of future success.* Individuals involved in the selection process should be prepared with questions that anticipate as many of the situations and circumstances in which they expect chiefs to find themselves. Based on their knowledge of the candidates' intellects, abilities, experiences, personalities, and interests, a selection committee armed with a carefully prepared set of questions and identifying what they "need to know" will reach a more satisfactory decision.

4. *A succession process for the selection of chiefs should be led by an individual who has no vested interest in the outcome.* This principle adds immeasurably to objectivity and balance in the evaluation of information. It will also minimize the likelihood of decisions that are based on assumption and questions that do not adequately probe flaws and Achilles' heels.

Those who pick chiefs will find value in applying these rules. Individuals who want to be chiefs should use these principles to understand how selection decisions should be made. At the least, it will help aspiring chiefs to identify their own values and to ensure that their behavior is more consistent with their values. Prospective chiefs who want to be successful ones must also bring their courage and intellect to the task.

— 2 —

Responsibility for Selection

THE SELECTORS

Summarizing the information exchanges at a 1984 conference of corporate chairmen and presidents, Dr. Kenneth Clark, Executive Director of the Center for Creative Leadership in Greensboro, North Carolina, who chaired the sessions, observed, "There is enormous effort going into the identification of a CEO—a lot of concern—and little sharing. There is no literature to help an organization do that."

Only a few people associated with each major corporation actually have the responsibility of selecting the senior executives who will manage the enterprise. While many corporations have individuals or staffs that identify candidates for senior positions, it is usually the board of directors and the chairman (often with major influence exercised by the chairman) who select the next chairman, president, CEO, or chief operating officer. For senior or executive vice presidents, the president or CEO typically recommends a decision for which he seeks approval from the chairman or the board. This level of approval is typical because senior executives often are candidates for CEO or president positions and many are being groomed for these positions.

Those who make the actual selections, however, do not often have a clear choice. Candidates for chief are not without flaw or fault. But once a decision is made, a rationale is built for it that could not be pierced by a salvo of anti-tank rockets—despite any previous ambivalence about the candidates!

BESTOWING—AND HANDLING—POWER

One of the most sensitive aspects of selecting a senior executive is the potential loss of power for his or her organizational superiors, for example, a chairman or president. A board's or chairman's desire to provide for strong leadership to a corporation is often tempered by a fear of losing power or giving a part of it to someone else. John Kotter[1] succinctly nailed the issue:

> Americans, as a rule, are not very comfortable with power or with its dynamics. We often mistrust and question the motives of people who we think actively seek power. We have a certain fear of being manipulated. Even those people who think the dynamics of power are inevitable and needed often feel somewhat guilty when they themselves mobilize and use power. Simply put, the overall attitude and feeling toward power, which can be easily traced to the nation's very birth, is negative.

Power is not passed along to new chiefs without anxiety. Rarely are chiefs given a blank check to exercise power. Sometimes, however, chiefs forget that they do not have unlimited power and they may overdraw their accounts. This is dangerous and can result in the chief's finish.

One example of this was reported in *Business Week*[2] which described how T.A. Vanderslice, president of GTE, the second largest telephone company in the United States, resigned after a tug-of-war for control of the company with T.F. Brophy, the Chairman of the Board:

[1]John Kotter, "Power, Dependence, and Effective Management," in Harvard Business Review (Executive Book Series), *Executive Success*, p. 306. New York: John Wiley & Sons, 1983.
[2]*Business Week*, December 19, 1983.

When Vanderslice was hired in 1979, Brophy reportedly promised him that he would succeed as chief executive no later than the end of the five-year contract, when Brophy would be 61. But company observers believed that Brophy may have been irked because Vanderslice was receiving most of the credit for GTE's resurgence. Further irritating Brophy was Vanderslice's thinly veiled ambition to take over as CEO. "Tom was not very guarded about his desire to take over Ted's duties—and the sooner the better," says a former GTE executive.

Selectors of chiefs understandably try to walk the fine line between picking someone who has the ability and self-confidence to run things without a lot of direction versus someone who has the ability and self-confidence to ignore direction. As one CEO says, "Self-assurance is a most important quality."

WHAT SELECTORS MUST DO

Maintaining Secrecy

Most chairmen and presidents agree that their role in selecting a successor must start early. Thomas I. Storrs, former chairman and CEO of NCNB said:

> Our board's role in CEO selection is to assure the continuity of the business, which needs continuity of management. Since our board has over 20 members, a six-person executive committee of the board is responsible for this. This committee started to identify my successor five years before I retired. Tentative decisions were reached after the first year and they were reviewed annually. The fact that a review was going on sharpened up observations. About 18 months before I retired, the board recommended actions to signal change. Then about six months before my retirement, the board made the final decision. Secrecy was an important issue till just before I stepped down.

Regarding secrecy, the former chairman of a beverage company notes that

> There are some people who can't keep quiet (about succession decisions). So we involved an executive committee of four people in the

decision. But there was one talker so we only included three in the actual decision. Secrecy is very important.

The Role of Advisors

It is uncomfortable for most chairmen or presidents to select a chief without asking for opinions from others. Many large companies have an internal staff, usually in a corporate resource function, who are responsible for assembling candidate inventories and slates of candidates for senior positions. One or two of the most senior people in these corporate staff groups often serve as advisors to the senior executives who must make the selection decision. Their roles are generally known by most middle and senior managers in their company. Not surprisingly, these advisors are very discrete. Since their own effectiveness depends upon their perceptions and their judgment, as well as their integrity, they must add information and insights to knowledge available about the candidates for a chief position.

Typically, these advisors have had extensive experience, with at least several years in their company. They have learned to look at alternatives or "what ifs" with the suspiciousness and thoroughness of a good detective investigating a murder! They probe for specificity and information to test observations and to fill gaps in knowledge. Because of their generally high level of skill and because they usually are not candidates for positions of chief, presidents and other senior executives feel more comfortable talking with them about key candidates than with other corporate executives.

Over-dependence on the advisors may occur, however, if they are asked to go beyond evaluating and comparing candidates. If the advisors are asked to decide which of the candidates should be selected, the selection decision is implicitly delegated to them. The result might be that the selector may not be as strong an advocate for the new chief as is necessary.

In advance of screening or evaluating candidates, advisors should be asked to describe what behavior, personal characteristics, experience, and other qualities they will consider in their assessment of candidates. In addition, the criteria for evaluating candidates in these areas should be clear. There is little need for inference or assumption when there is plenty of evidence based on direct observation and the nature of a candidate's accomplishments.

The CEO as Advisor.   Often, a CEO is the main source of advice for key selection decisions. Nevertheless, a current CEO or president who is asked to name his or her successor can inadvertently cause a problem: The CEO might choose a candidate that will continue existing policies and practices when changes are needed. A chairman who has served on the boards of several companies warns:

> There is a need of a third party to help them with CEO selection—either the chairman of a board's executive committee or outside counsel. Current CEOs do need help. In many instances they have strong egos and won't admit it. They've been in a dictatorial role for many years and it's hard to say you need help with this. . . .
>
> Internal counsel is at risk to some degree—he is put under a lot of strain. I wouldn't recommend the human resources vice-president for that reason.

Psychologists as Advisors.   Psychologists are often used as advisors in the chief selection process. For example in one public energy company a consulting psychologist evaluates candidates on a point system against position requirements. The psychologist also uses several psychological tests and interviews with the candidates to provide an evaluation of the individual's psychological characteristics.

After the psychologist completes his evaluations, he leads top management in a discussion of the strengths, shortcomings and personal characteristics of each candidate. Next, the management staff, with the help of the psychologist, project the candidate's maximum promotability over the next three to five years and determines the personal development plan needed to reach growth potential. The company's CEO reports that the psychologist's predictions are "95 percent right."

Psychological testing is also used occasionally to evaluate candidates at Rubbermaid Inc. Robert E. Fowler, Jr., President and Chief Operating Officer observes:

While I am not totally comfortable with this process, I have to admit that the results have tended to be confirmed by later performance, both on the good side and the bad side.

Not all consulting psychologists use written tests. Tests can be threatening to many managers and, at the least, they are often viewed as demeaning. Most executives prefer to be judged on their accomplishments and, in most companies, there has been sufficient opportunity to demonstrate performance. Despite the generally dependable advice that can be derived from tests, good advice is not dependent on them.

WHEN DOES THE SELECTION PROCESS BEGIN?

It is important that selectors thoughtfully—and in great detail—develop and define the nature of their selection role before they enter into the process itself. It is a good practice for all chiefs to define this aspect of the leadership role as soon as they assume their position because they will be immersed in the planning of management succession almost from the first day on the job. Chiefs will find the selection process difficult and frustrating to manage. In addition, they might risk placing the company's future in jeopardy.

One CEO of a large container company said, however, that succession planning was low on his priority list when he moved into his job. The company was less than $250 million in sales and he had more pressing manpower problems as he built the company to almost $2 billion in sales. In retrospect, the executive feels that he should have started looking for a successor earlier because he no longer has enough time to adequately test candidates.

In contrast, the president of a prominent bank said that CEO succession was "very high on my list as I went in as CEO. I had three top people but was extremely thin below. Unfortunately, I always looked at the weakest person and tried to replace him. This didn't work because it added to organizational instability." This CEO understood his role in succession planning but did not know how to implement it as well as he wanted.

Robert E. Fowler, Jr., President and Chief Operating Officer,

Rubbermaid Inc., emphasizes the importance of involving the board in senior selections. He says:

> We go to some lengths to keep our board informed of our manpower plans and have them acquainted with our key managers. Examples of this are a formal presentation to the board on manpower at our March board meeting and a procedure which gets our key managers at the operating division level together with the board in informal circumstances once or twice a year. In this way, the board becomes more knowledgeable of individuals who are potential candidates for promotion to senior executive positions.
>
> We have also used board members to interview potential candidates for senior positions and we talk with the chairmen of board committees when selecting individuals from outside the company. It's my belief that a close, open relationship with the board greatly contributes to a smooth working relationship as far as staffing key positions is concerned.

The role that chairmen, CEOs, and other selectors should focus on must include:

1. *Quality Control.* Assuring that individuals identified as candidates possess the required characteristics and experience.
2. *Supply.* Assuring that mechanisms or processes develop sufficient candidates so that the selection decision is made *for* an individual and is not the result of voting *against* the others.
3. *Depth.* Unless quality among executives exists in lower organizational levels, the supply of candidates for chief positions will be thinned by mediocrity.
4. *Promotion from within.* The advantages of cultural fit and long familiarity with the candidate for chief will generally outweigh the different perspective offered by a competent outsider. However, there are times when the selection of an outsider is the best way to signal change to an organization and its business community.
5. *Advisors.* Few people prefer to make important decisions without getting opinions from others. The selection of a chief

should be explored with others, but these advisors must be wise and trusted for their discretion.

6. *Holding a minority opinion.*   Even people who select chiefs find that they are not always in agreement with those who advise them.

The senior executive responsibility of boards is summarized by Robert E. Frazer, Chairman and CEO of Dayton Power and Light Company: "Each board I'm on focuses on succession planning for CEO. How can it be otherwise?"

QUALITY CONTROL

Matching Needs with People

Managing the succession planning process is made easier if the quality of candidates for senior executive positions is equal to perceived needs. Chairmen, presidents, and other senior executives who select chiefs usually pay more attention to quality control when they have concerns about the fitness of available candidates. When the quality of candidates is high, an organization eases off a bit on its scrutiny of personal characteristics and experience. The organization assumes that quality candidates will always be there.

In such a setting, quality control of candidates may begin to suffer from benign neglect. It is not easy to continually review and reevaluate the background, experience, personal characteristics, and accomplishments of the same candidates for chief. This chore becomes even more time-consuming as new people are reviewed and evaluated. It is easier to skip a year, or skip a number of people who were reviewed last year.

Symptoms of Poor Quality Control

Symptoms of poor quality control include casual reviews of candidates's qualifications and abilities, a very high or very low estimate of the abilities of potential chiefs, back-up lists showing a paucity of able candidates, an internal management development process that has low credibility for middle-level executives, over-dependence on internal staff or external consultants to make selection recommendations, over-reliance on operating executives and divisions to identify and develop potential chiefs, and selection criteria that are constantly changing and not clearly understood by either selectors or candidates.

The chairman and CEO of an international manufacturing company maintains quality control in this way:

> The way I handle it in my own company is to meet once a month with the CEO candidates and tell them what I'm thinking and find out what they're thinking. I try to get agreement from the board as to criteria for the candidates—"musts and wants." Each year, I go through these criteria with them, one at a time and we rate the candidates. I also want to find out how they think and tell them what I know because it is very difficult for a board member to know these people.

The chairman and CEO of a utility company (Robert E. Frazer, Dayton Power and Light) also says:

> We maintain quality management by annually rating top managers, including CEO candidates against several criteria, such as problem solving, technical and human relations abilities. Periodically, we use the help of a consulting psychologist in these evaluations. We keep our board informed each year on potential CEO candidates and our plans for their development. In our public utility industry, I feel the public limelight wears a CEO down after awhile and we need to turn the job over to new talent at an early age. I plan to step down as CEO next year at age 56 and the board is unanimous in its choice of our president, age 42, as my successor. . . .

Back-up Lists

There is a fairly simple way to monitor the quality of chief candidates—and candidates at other levels as well. Back-up charts or lists should be prepared for every middle and senior management position. This back-up list should show the name of the incumbent and the names of no more than two other individuals who are strong candidates for that position. Next to each candidate's name, two pieces of information should be entered: potential for growth and readiness of the candidate for promotion. For simplicity and brevity, the information can be coded with numbers or letters as follows:

Potential for Growth: 1. No apparent limits

2. One organizational level

Ready for Promotion: A. Ready now

B. Ready within one year

An indication of quality is immediately apparent upon looking at the charts, and necessary actions can be put into motion with appropriate urgency. The chairman and president looking at the chart should not simply assume that quality exists because the chart says it does. They must ask themselves the following question regarding each candidate's quality: If the incumbent resigned, died, or was no longer able to continue in that position, would you immediately give it to the back-up candidate with confidence in his or her ability to do the job? If there is any hesitation or reluctance, the reliability of these back-up charts as well as the quality of the candidates must be challenged.

It is evident that the organization in Figure 2-1 seems to have candidates of high quality. While their qualifications and accomplishments should be probed to maintain confidence in their quality, there is less urgency than in the case illustrated in Figure 2-2. In the latter organization, the number and quality of candidates for chief is poor (as indicated by the coding) and there is considerable urgency about the actions needed to beef up the back-up list.

Over-delegation of Development Responsibility

Perhaps the greatest threat to quality control is an over-reliance on operating divisions and operating executives to identify potential chiefs and to give them the experience needed to test and develop them further. Operating divisions will eagerly assume this responsibility—but, often, their intentions are not equal to their abilities, the resources available to them, or to their priorities. There are two reasons for this: (1) operating divisions must focus on profitability,

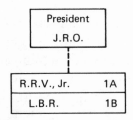

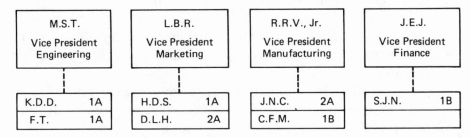

Figure 2-1

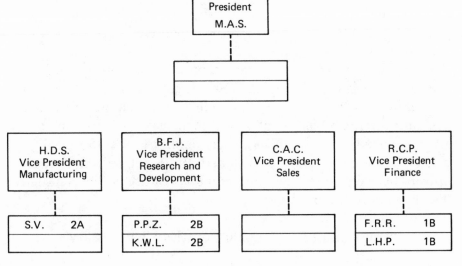

Figure 2-2

not individual development, because that is how they are measured; and (2) operating divisions probably will not use the quality control criteria because they are not aware of them and/or because this activity is not a primary responsibility for them.

Operating divisions need help to perform this function. The help should come from corporate staff people who are directly responsible to the chairman or president. Quality control must be assured by a corporate presence or it is not likely to be maintained. Nevertheless, the chairman or other selector should rely on his or her staff only for monitoring standards and gathering information, not for making the selection decision.

In one multi-division company, the president directed the human resources vice-president of each division to assure the quality of back-up candidates for senior positions within their division. The president inquired about the quality of back-up candidates at the company's annual organization planning and human resources review. For six straight years, he was assured that quality was strong. When three of the six potential chiefs from two divisions resigned to join another company, the president anxiously inquired about the quality of the remaining potential chiefs. To his surprise, he was told that the three people who left were outstanding but that the remaining executives who had been identified as potential chiefs were not up to the highest quality. A halo effect for this management level had been operating. When the three executives left, the halo disappeared. Closer ties to quality control would have prevented this.

In almost direct contrast to this situation, another threat to quality control is the selector who assumes full responsibility for assuring the quality of candidates for chief. One person cannot do this in a company or organization of any size because of the amount of attention needed. As a consequence, quality will suffer because it will be neglected—and the responsibility for it will be delegated upward by everyone who assumes quality control will be handled at the level above them.

Understanding the Expectations for Quality

Another aspect of quality control can probably be managed by chief candidates and chief-aspirants themselves. It is to their advantage, and the company's advantage, for the experience and ability requirements to be as tangible as possible and communicated as clearly as possible. This information must be understood by selectors and candidates or quality will vary too widely among candidates and over time. Continually changing criteria will also dilute quality control because this kind of vacillation will cause selectors to focus more on the personalities of candidates than on the nature of their accomplishments and abilities.

ASSURING A CONTINUING SUPPLY OF CANDIDATES

A continuing supply of candidates for the various chief positions in a company requires a processive mechanism that can be maintained with a minimum of attention. The information that drives the mechanism is the ages of the potential chiefs. Age and experience are highly related. While an executive learns from experience, age cannot be disregarded.

Distinction should be made between *potential* candidates and *key* candidates for chief. Potential candidates have not yet demonstrated their ability to assume a position of chief—they are simply positioned organizationally so that they have the opportunity to demonstrate superior competence. Key candidates are those who have demonstrated superior competence and are leading candidates for chief positions. Succession planning should assure that the supply of potential candidates is fully exposed to opportunities that will facilitate the identification of key candidates for succession.

Assuming that quality control is good, the number of candidates will probably be sufficient at any given point in time. However, unless the candidates' ages are carefully noted, there may not be a sufficient supply of candidates for more than one or two points in time. For example, if a senior executive below the president resigns or retires, there are likely to be several candidates of about the same age and experience behind him. If one is selected, it is not unusual for some or all of the others to resign for positions in other companies, since they may feel that their aspirations are blocked if they remain where they are. If this happens, it will thin out the supply of good candidates below the presidency, thus leaving a company vulnerable in the event of other departures or death.

A Rolling Process

A good supply of candidates depends on a rolling process. Waves of potential chiefs should be arranged by age categories of about five to six years. In no way should age by itself enhance or detract from the candidacy of individuals. It does, however, connote the acquisition of experience required for specific chief positions. With candidates grouped by age, and with retirement (or reassignment) dates of the current chiefs noted, it is easy to know whether there will be an adequate supply of qualified candidates for chief on the dates they will be needed.Any gaps in the availability of candidates for chief positions that will become vacant can be addressed far in advance.

A "gap chart" should be maintained by every chairman or president to monitor the supply of chief candidates. A similar chart should be kept by other senior executives to monitor management succession in their own organizations. Without a convenient way to monitor the supply of potential chiefs down to middle levels of management, supply and quality control of candidates for chief will be diminished. Chase Manhattan's former Executive Vice-President for Human Resources, Alan F. Lafley, says, "You've got to start five to ten years ahead of time to have the kind of people you need when you need them."

Catching a Wave

Aspirants for chief positions should also try to ascertain their "wave," or age category, starting with the current ages of corporate chiefs and identifying the most likely candidates for those positions and their ages. Doing the same for the most likely replacements for the chief-candidate positions will enable a chief-aspirant to identify his or her wave. Of course, there is no certainty to this process but it serves as a guide to progress and it helps to compare one's abilities and experience against the competition. Better insight can lead to better preparation and development. It is in everyone's best interest to develop and demonstrate ability.

If a chief-aspirant finds that a wave has passed by without his inclusion, honest introspection and clear action are more likely to result in catch-up than surliness or vocal complaints. For example, in one company that has large U.S. and international operations a very ambitious middle-level executive was not highly regarded by the corporate chiefs. Although he was as competent as any of his organizational peers, he had no strong sponsor in operating management. His division was reorganized, leaving him without a job. At the urging of a human resources executive who saw more potential in him than did the corporate chiefs, he was given a choice: assume a second-in-charge role of the company's business in a mid-sized Latin American country. After a lot of reflection, he took the chance.

This executive worked hard to build the strengths in the areas where he needed to demonstrate accomplishments. Within two years, the executive had proven his abilities to be a potential chief. Within three years, he was promoted to head the business in that country. Two years later he was promoted to run the company's business in a large European country. Subsequently, he was identified as a potential candidate for CEO of the entire corporation.

This is not a rare incident. However, it would happen more often if aspiring chiefs would focus on acquiring the right experience and demonstrating their abilities instead of reacting defensively to missing their wave.

DEPTH OF QUALITY IN AN ORGANIZATION

No matter how promising executives look when they are hired, most of them will reveal behavior or personality characteristics by mid-career that will put them off the track for chief. While most senior executives cannot become closely involved with the recruiting, selection, and training of new executives for entry level positions, they can and should set the standards and monitor the process.

Standards should be straightforward, as directly observable as possible, tangible (i.e., measurable at least on a comparative basis against either expectations or other candidates) and relatively easy for middle and lower-level managers to apply. These standards must be based on what an individual is expected to do in his or her current role.

As some executives in middle levels become increasingly proficient, others level off and still others are unable to satisfy organizational needs. The most promising middle-level executives are generally well-rewarded and recognized in their own company. However, some of them are less patient about the uncertainty of promotional timing. These dissatisfied executives will be attracted to other companies that represent accelerated career progress. As a result, executives with the required level experience, ability and reputation are often not available within the company. Companies in such circumstances frequently turn to management search firms to actively seek outside talent whose individual aspirations and interests mesh with the corporation's needs.

When recruiting from outside the company, the selectors of chiefs should keep in mind that too much hiring from the outside for middle levels will probably cause a loss of confidence in the succession planning system among the lower levels of management. This will certainly not encourage the best of the people to remain when unavoidable frustrations come up or when other opportunities in other companies are presented.

Inattention to the identification of back-up candidates for middle-management positions can virtually wipe out an organization's management strengths for several years. For example, the company president of a multi-national manufacturing enterprise ignored the process of back-up planning at middle levels, preferring to concentrate on senior management succession and assuming he could always bring in more junior management talent if it was needed. At the same time, the company spent a great deal of energy and time on recruiting new middle-level executives from the best MBA programs in the country.

The company attracted extremely promising and able young men and women. Unfortunately, the best of them left after about four years because they were given no feedback about the availability or timing of promotional opportunity. When middle-management positions opened, therefore, the division general manager was forced to recommend the promotion of individuals with no clear strengths or accomplishments.

When the company president asked the human resources vice president why the openings were not filled by middle-managers from the outside, he was told that it would harm the morale of junior people who were led to believe in promotion from within. Ignoring the human resource vice president's logic, the president directed three open middle-management positions be filled by qualified outside hires. The new hires were sufficiently experienced to do the middle-management jobs, but they did not have the scope or experience of those who left.

Within six months after the third position was filled, the remainder of the MBA's recruited within the last two years resigned for positions in other companies. For this organization, management depth no longer existed.

PROMOTION FROM WITHIN—OR FROM OUTSIDE

Opinion varies among chiefs, but their preference is clear:

> Our company tries to destroy outsiders. [A clothing company president.]

> It is possible to bring in high level outsiders, but bring them in when they are older and when there is a gap or need. [A beverage and food company president.]

> Outsiders don't understand the company's culture and it takes too long. [A personnel vice-president.]

> People from outside sometimes do better in our company because we transfer so many people internally—and everybody is a stranger anyway. [A senior corporate officer of a conglomerate.]

Most senior executives are drawn from within a company. The advantages of selecting a chief from within include (1) a better understanding of the candidate's abilities, (2) better knowledge of the company and the people, and (3) perhaps a faster start. There are times, however, when a chairman or president wants to change the direction of an organization or alter the ways of working within it. Pronouncements and exhortations often do little to bring about change. When there is a need to signal change, it may be desirable to ignore a promotion-from-within tradition and bring in a chief from outside the organization. This requires courage on the selector's part, since he must assure advocacy for the new chief from within the company. Special attention to the compatability of staff who will be assigned to the new chief will help in this regard.

Without solid internal staff support, a chief brought in from the outside is not likely to meet the selector's expectations. In any case, outside selection is usually guaranteed to signal change—and change can cause vibrations throughout a company.

The Benefits of Promotion from Within

There are many good reasons for finding candidates for chief from within a company that going outside should be considered as a poor alternative. The latter course is chancy at best. If there is enough attention to quality control and if processes for assuring the supply and organizational depth of chief candidates are in place, it should be relatively easy to avoid straying from a promotion-from-within policy for senior executive positions.

An example of unexpected results for not promoting from within occurred in a U.S. corporation that had a culture based on years of traditional promotion-from-within. The CEO was planning to retire and it was common knowledge that the board was trying to identify a successor. Rather than simply selecting one of the most senior executives to replace him, the board decided that dramatic changes within the company's strategic goals and structure were needed. They selected a CEO from outside.

Almost immediately, all of the next tier of senior executives took positions in other companies. The new CEO created chaos in the organization with new goals and new structures. The CEO was not replaced for fear of further damage to the operation and reputation of the enterprise. The board who selected the CEO found itself captive to the new chief, despite their dismay about the way the business was being run.

A CLASSICAL CANDIDATE

Ideally, chiefs should be selected from among an outstanding group of inside candidates. Therefore, chairmen and presidents who select chiefs should encourage the "mechanisms" or processes of supply to find people to "wear well." Chiefs must wear well or they may not last long; they certainly will be less effective.

A chief-candidate of classical caliber can be compared to a book that is a classic. Candidates for senior executive positions should

1. Demonstrate an ability to make things happen;
2. Have an impact on both the opinions and actions of others—an impact which may be so subtle that the power of his influence may not even be noticed;
3. Have a record of living up to their commitments;
4. Have a sense of organizational history;
5. Be able to recognize their mistakes;
6. Be able to express their perspectives and ideas in a unique way;
7. Show evidence of insights that engage the character of the organization or industry; and
8. Have concrete ideas about change or improvement and have successfully acted on their philosophy.

It is not likely that classic qualities will be found in candidates outside the organization because an outsider's qualities can rarely be thoroughly ascertained during the short time span involving the search for a chief.

While executive search firms try to learn as much information as possible about an outside candidate, there is no substitute for service time and in-company experience.

HOLDING A MINORITY OPINION

If a succession planning system is working well, the best qualified candidate for a senior executive position will be generally agreed upon. There are times, however, when a selector, for example a chairman or president, feels strongly about the fit and quality of a candidate who is unusual enough—because of age, experience, or personality—to be a controversial choice. When the selector's views are expressed to other senior executives, they are likely to be met with arguments, dismay, or disdain. It is important for the selector not to cave in prematurely. In fact, the selector must act on his or her initial judgment by asking the opposition questions that surface and crystallize the key issues. As a result, the selector will either be reassured about the validity of his or her minority opinion or willing to change his or her mind.

In one large North American company, the board and its chairman was actively considering two candidates as a successor to the president. The president had been in office for five years and the board was not pleased with corporate growth. In particular, they were displeased with the lack of new products or product improvements.

The board put enormous pressure on the president to achieve better business results for two years. Ultimately, he decided to resign as soon as the board could find a successor.

The board, exclusive of its chairman, actively supported the candidacy of a 43-year-old executive who joined the company after receiving an MBA from a top business school. The candidate, who was universally liked, had a record of promotions and was associated with highly profitable business units. He also had a reputation for creativity. In addition, the candidate was a vocally appreciative supporter of all the ideas and work of his peers and subordinates. Except for the chairman, the board agreed that this executive would know how to put enthusiasm, energy, and creativity back into the entire work force. This candidate, they reasoned, would provide a "shotgun effect" on new products with a virtual blast of creativity.

The chairman, however, was uncomfortable with this candidate. He felt that creativity was needed, but that it should only be focused in two or three areas. The chairman was concerned that the board's preferred candidate did not have the personal discipline to confine the creative effort to the two or three most promising areas—and that the result would be the dilution of business energies. The chairman pointed to the candidate's history: association with profitable products in his business group along with responsibility for active endorsement or pursuit of a line of expensive dead-ends and inadequately planned projects. It seemed that the candidate would try almost anything and hope for enough success to offset the costs of his failures. In fact, the chairman's major question about the candidate was whether he would know when to walk away from an idea.

Upon reflection, the chairman thought that perhaps his concern was due to the risk involved in a change of leadership. On the other hand, he also felt that his opinion about the candidate was correct. Therefore, he asked for a board meeting on this subject. The conversation went like this:

Chairman:	It's not easy to maintain a position when everybody you know thinks your wrong. But I'm not sure I am. I'm concerned about (the candidate's) judgment when it comes to business focus. He's creative, I'll agree, but it may be too much trial and error. He's not a disciplined thinker.
Board Member:	This business needs a president who is flexible, who is willing to try new things. That's been our problem for at least five years and that's why we're in a ditch now.
Board Member:	[The candidate] knows how to push ideas into products and product improvements. He's a great listener and people who work for him say he is a great motivator. And he has been involved with a bunch of our best products.
Chairman:	Look, I agree he's everything you say he is. I also think he doesn't know the difference between walking away from an idea—or tentatively exploring it— and putting all his energy behind it. The trouble is that he puts all of himself behind everything. He doesn't have a good sense of priorities about what idea is worth pursuing and what he ought to be scared blue about.
Board Member:	Come one, he hasn't been successful because he doesn't know good from bad. He's made good things happen.
Chairman:	Yes, he has. But he hasn't done it alone. He's done it with others. I can't tell which have been his ideas, or how much of his undisciplined thinking was screened out by the judgment of others he's worked with. You can bet that the other people in his business served as a good balance on him.

Board Member:	Who do you think is better qualified to drive this company where it should go?
Chairman:	[Chairman names another candidate.] He has all the interpersonal qualities of the first candidate but he has enormous analytical strength as well.
Board Member:	O.K., but [the second candidate] doesn't have the innate creativity of [the first candidate]. We need creativity.
Chairman:	He may not be as personally creative but he knows how to evaluate ideas and he is not a push-over for everything. He knows how to put focus on an effort. And he knows how to motivate. He is well-respected and people like to work with him.
Board Member:	He'll be the same as what we've got now.
Chairman:	No, he'll be different. He knows how to set up a climate for creativity and he knows how to test ideas. Most of all, he knows how to mobilize force behind an idea to make it work. [The first candidate] has a reputation for creativity—and it is probably deserved—but he has never proven that he can treat ideas differently. They're not all the same. This Board has to recognize that. If you're wrong and I go along with you, we'll have a problem.

This portion of the board meeting concluded with the board members agreeing to consider the second candidate as a potential president. The chairman scheduled a meeting one month later to continue this selection discussion. At the second meeting, the board reconciled their desire for developing new ideas with the need to put order into the focus on creativity—and they voted for the chairman's candidate.

An interesting way to summarize and to remember how to handle a minority opinion is in the words of a tune sung by Kenny Rogers. The name of the song is "The Gambler" and it tells about a lonely young man who is down on his luck and who meets a gambler on a night train. For a share of the young man's whiskey, the gambler gives him advice on how to approach some of the tough decisions in life:

> If you're gonna play the game, boy, you got to play it right.
> You got to know when to hold'em, know when to fold'em,
> Know when to walk away and know when to run . . .
> . . . Every gambler knows that the secret to surviving is knowin' what to throw away and knowin' what to keep . . .[3]

[3]"The Gambler," written by Don Schlitz, Copyright© 1977, Writers Night Music.

— 3 —

Early Identification

SUBSTANCE VS. PRESUMPTION

The early identification of potential chiefs is difficult, not only because of the fragile information on which it is based but also because the identification process should not bog down in the security of the past and perpetuate the kind of executive leadership that may not work any more. Leadership in the near future may require a combination of values and behaviors quite different than many current chiefs manifest.

Early identification is sometimes torn between finding people who will meet the immediate and obvious needs of a business and encouraging the diversity of executive who will enable a flexible management response to unanticipated events. While it is difficult to know for certain what challenges will face a company, it is vital that early identification is based on substance and not on presumption.

LONG SHOTS AND BAD SHOTS

Of all the long shot bets in the world, surely one of the most presumptuous is predicting which young person will become a chief. Such predictions are not made only by naive or over-confident senior executives; they are also made by a great proportion of each year's business school graduates. Fortunately, according to a study conducted at AT&T,[1] this expectation fades relatively early in a career (at about the fifth year). It would be a terrible burden to carry this hope for too many years.

Not long ago, a chemical company organized a meeting in Europe for most of its marketing and sales managers from around the world. The meeting, which was hosted by the company's senior operating executive, took place in a grand hotel in a Western European capital. This executive was an exceptionally intelligent, urbane, and experienced businessperson. He had worked in several countries and spoke six languages fluently. As he sipped wine at an evening reception session for his 100 or so executives, he talked with his personnel vice president. "Which is that new man," he asked, "the one just hired into the junior marketing position in London?" The personnel vice president pointed to a young man across the room who was chatting with a group. "Him?" said the urbane senior executive, "He'll never make it." When asked how he knew this, the executive said he could tell just by looking at him.

The same executive took pride in his ability to tell whether an employee was any good, judging by their handshake, a steady gaze, or attractive appearance. This "talent" of early identification had considerable impact on the opportunities and careers of many young people in this company.

It is not a surprise, therefore, that the senior executive was so often wrong. In fact, most of the young people he disdained because of their early impression on him have made excellent career progress—in other companies. Conversely, almost all of the young people who made a positive early impression were encouraged to leave within three years of their employment because of their inability to perform effectively.

Unfortunately, too many careers are adversely influenced by superficial judgments. If senior executives are aware of the personal appearance characteristics that influence them, they might prevent some bad selection decisions.

[1]A. Howard and D.W. Bray, *Career Motivation in Mid-Life Managers.* Paper delivered at American Psychological Association Convention, Montreal, 1980.

TYPICAL IDENTIFICATION SYSTEMS

Typical and systematic examples of corporate activity for the early identification of management talent are in place at Goodyear Tire and Rubber Company (Goodyear) and at Eastman Kodak. At Goodyear, which reports 95% promotion from within, 600 young managers are identified as "high potential" each year on the basis of performance and individual characteristics. The list is updated and revised annually from the total manager inventory of 10,000. The average age of the designated "high potential" (hp) is 35. High potentials have an average of 10 years of service with the company before they are identified as such.

At the lowest management levels of this group, the hp label is based on the tentative judgments of supervisors who compare individual performance against peer performance and managerial expectations. For middle-manager levels, the division group executive vice-presidents, the president, and the CEO meet quarterly to discuss the hp inventory, individuals, and succession plans. These discussions also determine what must be done at the level of college recruiting. Richard Martin, corporate director of management development for the Goodyear Tire and Rubber Company, says that he is constantly monitoring the early identification system because he feels it must be reflective of their corporate culture for it to be workable. Of course, there are always occasional problems of fizzled hps or inadequate supply to meet unexpected needs.

At Eastman Kodak, the identification of potential managers is also made by the supervisors. According to James S. Bruce, former Senior Vice President, the company strives to have a uniform identification system with everyone using the same criteria. Since every selection process involves subjective evaluations, more than one evaluator must evaluate management potential in more than one assignment.

An equally concerned attempt to assure that hp designates are not overlooked is maintained in an automobile parts manufacturing company. This company keeps a running list of the 100 best people (as judged by their performance appraisal and supervisor's recommendation) who are not in top positions. The company feels that it can only operate successfully through the most capable people and it wants to assure their availability when they are needed.

These experiences are typical among large companies who have early identification systems. Aspiring chiefs should find out as quickly as possible the criteria that are used to judge their potential. They should also inquire about the nature of the early identification system, with reference to both formal and informal aspects. Discussing this with one's supervisor increases the awareness that early identification has a lot to do with career progress. Early identification is important to an aspiring chief because there is good research in more than one company showing that senior managers are promoted significantly earlier in their career than managers who top out at lower and middle levels. Also, the criteria for obtaining the hp designation are less likely to be left to personal chemistry without properly accounting for ability.

A Comparable System

Senior executives should work closely with the human resource or management development staffs and their key operating executives to assure that the criteria used for early identification are uniform within their company, with specific differences agreed upon for functions or divisions with different needs. Inter-divisional transfers at any level are more successful when cultural expectations are both familiar and similar. To the degree that this is the case, the number and quality of potential chiefs will be greater. Executive flexibility is rare but it is very valuable. Chiefs should insist on it.

SELF-FULFILLING PROPHECY

In their eagerness to develop an adequate supply of candidates for middle and senior levels, many companies invest heavily in college recruiting, from both undergraduate and MBA programs. After campus interviews, students who appear to be best fitted for an organization's needs will be invited to further interviews at the company location. As a result, a few are hired and often immediately dubbed as high potentials. For too many of these new employees, their potential will be judged less on their performance or accomplishments but more on their image as an hp. Since a manager's expectations of employee performance often drive his or her behavior and beliefs, an employee's responsibilities are frequently increased with little evidence of how well the job is really being done. For example, it is expected that an hp will be good—and many are perceived that way for a longer time than the evidence would support. Frequently, however, the hp's fall off the "most wanted" list and they receive implicit or explicit clues that they are no longer on the fast track.

The overestimation of what can be learned about the future from several hours of interviewing college applicants, in addition to reviewing academic records and work history, is what makes predictions by executives and recruiters inaccurate. An interesting experiment would be to randomly identify one-half of a year's college and MBA recruits as hp's and then to watch their career over a 10 to 15 year period. A reasonable hypothesis is that those individuals randomly designated as hp's will make better career progress than a randomly selected control group who are not designated as hp's— simply because their managers have been told they are hp's.

WHERE DOES EARLY IDENTIFICATION BEGIN?

Most corporate recruiting and selection from college campuses operates from the theory that early identification begins with a young person's first interview. By intention, this is probably true. Each of the following five methods of early identification are active in every corporation:

1. College recruiting and selection interviews
2. Assessment centers
3. Sponsorship
4. Supervisor recommendations
5. Performance appraisal

When individuals are described as having unusual potential for growth based on more than one method, the probability that early identification of a potential chief has been made is increased. In some corporations, a potential hp list is developed and reviewed annually. In most companies, however, the label is informal—but hp designates are treated differently and most know it. So do their peers. Psychologically, this is a giant step in a young person's career.

Most young people are not assigned an hp designation, however, because no opinion has been reached about them. Individuals who aspire to be a chief, therefore, should do everything possible to obtain advocacy for their early identification through as many of the five methods as possible.

Citicorp's Policy Committee members describe the qualities they look for in potential chiefs with exceptional clarity. For example, one senior executive says:

> Imagination starts with inquisitiveness, and I think you'll find it will serve you well throughout your career. I define imagination as the ability to look at something—a job, a routine, an idea—totally differently than anyone has looked at it before. By looking at it differently, it may suddenly become apparent to you that the idea is bad, or it's brilliantly good, or it is something in between.
>
> Next, and related, you should be kind of omnivorous and universal in your willingness to learn. And finally, you should be able to communicate what you've learned or discovered to your colleagues, superiors or subordinates in such a way that they catch your enthusiasm.

These statements are complemented by another senior executive who has this personal observation:

> Thinking of traits that will serve a person throughout a career, my first choice would be integrity. You have to be viewed as someone who stands by his or her commitments and that is by far the most important trait in this company.
>
> Next would be fairness—that you are someone who is viewed as being straightforward with people and you tell them in advance what you expect of them and you don't switch signals on them all the time.
>
> Third, I think you have to be viewed as someone who is a producer—that you come in here to do your work, you get your work done, and you can be counted on to achieve something for the company and for the people you work with.

Walter Wriston, Citicorp's Chairman, succinctly combines wisdom, reality, and practicality in his advice to aspiring chiefs:

> The most important advice I can give would be don't worry too much about what you are going to do next, but do what you are doing as well as you know how. If you do, tomorrow always takes care of itself.
>
> Learn as much as you can about what you are doing and then reach out across the organization and learn what other men and women are doing and how they do it, and in that way you begin to broaden your experience.
>
> Over time, your track record gets noticed and as opportunities rise, which they do every day in this organization, people will reach for you for a different job.

Citicorp's statements about career growth toward senior positions are especially well-articulated because they emphasize the organization's values of hard work, broad knowledge, and the importance of learning. The comments are also straightforward and tell a lot about the senior executives who run the company.

COLLEGE RECRUITING INTERVIEWS

College recruiting interviews are the first method of early identification. Companies who recruit at universities often send someone from a corporate or division personnel staff to interview students on campus. It has become more prevalent, however, to include or substitute an executive from one of the business functions, for example, marketing or finance, to interview students. Universities or colleges arrange these visits through their placement office. Some placement offices represent the entire university and others only the business college or just the MBA program. In virtually all cases, interviews are limited to 30 minutes and interviewers often talk with 12 to 14 students a day on each day of a one- to two-day recruiting trip. The recruiters are expected to spot potential talent in the brief interview and invite the most apparently qualified students to the company location for further interviews. Senior executive management, however, is usually unaware of the handicap that the pace of campus interviewing places on early identification.

Corporate optimism is behind the campus interview. This is partly because recruiters typically return to their company pleased with the bright young people they have met. However, in view of the small proportion of college-recruited executives who even become candidates for chief and the large proportion of college-recruited people who do not meet the high expectations for them during their first two or three years of employment, some changes in the campus interview are required. This would be to the advantage of both the company and the applicant.

Failure to prepare campus interviewers is inexcusable. Nevertheless, most corporations send campus representatives who are not prepared to ask the right questions or evaluate what they hear. Without thorough training in the interviewing of university students, it is unlikely that they will learn anything useful about them in less than 30 minutes. These screening interviews, therefore, often result in nothing better than random selection. Even with training, interviewers often miss important information. Often, students are invited back for further interviews based almost entirely on the interpersonal and conversational skill of the student.

What to Probe

If the right questions are asked, it is possible to screen a candidate effectively during a 30-minute interview. Questions should probe the student's accomplishments, analytical ability, innovativeness, and initiative, that is, the student's capacity for self-starting. Interviewers should have reviewed each student's resume so that a few questions can be prepared in advance. These questions should address areas that are important to the interviewer as well as questions about the content of the resume.

Thirty minutes is sufficient to ascertain whether it is worthwhile to invite the student for further interviews. The following conversation was recorded during the campus interview of an MBA student. It illustrates how the process of early identification is off to a poor start because it rambled instead of exploring a student's accomplishments, analytical skills, innovativeness, and initiative:

Interviewer: Hi, Carol, my name is _____ . I'm a manager of marketing with [company name]. I've looked at your resume and you've done some interesting stuff here.

Student: Glad to meet you. Thanks.

Interviewer: [In an attempt to put the student at ease] I see you're quite an athlete—tennis champ, golf, track, field hockey. What made you interested in amateur competition? Most people feel lucky if they can get out on a Sunday morning for a couple of hours but you've been serious about sports.

Student: Well, I've always enjoyed competition—and I really like intense physical activity.

Interviewer: It sure seems that way. Tell me about your interests in marketing. What are you looking for? [Interviewer wants to learn about student's reason for career choice.]

Student: I want a position in consumer marketing—there is so much competition in most consumer product lines that only the best marketing plans and advertising can make a business profitable. For me it's the challenge of competing in a tough business and being part of the team.

Interviewer: What do you know about consumer marketing? Have you ever held a sales job? [There was no need to ask the second question since it distracts from the first one and the student's resume had no listing of a sales job under her listing of work experience.]

Student: I've had several marketing courses and I had a summer job as marketing intern with [company name]. I learned a lot about marketing there and it convinced me that's what I wanted. I also just finished a senior project—with three other students— where we had to identify a new product, plan the market research to see if we could break into the market with our idea, and then do a marketing plan and the advertising strategy. That was great and I learned a lot from it. [The student did not answer the interviewer's question and the interviewer failed to probe what the student knew about marketing.]

Interviewer: Tell me about any new ideas you've had—anything you've done on your own. I'm interested in your innovativeness. [With a question like this, the answer is predictable and worthless.]

Student: New ideas . . . [pause for a few seconds]. For one thing, my senior project had some great ideas. One product was a new cereal especially for people who are active outdoors daily in the winter. It was fortified with special nutritional supplements for these people. Our plan was to sell it only through health food stores and to advertise it on TV. I think that if you limit the sales sources for a product, it makes it seem more desirable. [Student laughs]. Maybe that's why I buy half my food at health food stores. I love going there.

Interviewer: Half your food? I guess you're sold on the product claims.

Student: I suppose I am. I read a lot about nutrition and I'm interested in a business that is related to it.

Interviewer: Any other examples of your ideas and how you put them to work?

Student: [Thinks for about twenty seconds]. Yes, I started a business when I was in my sophomore year in college. I arranged for all the party things, plastic glasses, paper plates, plastic utensils, even food and beer, and decorations for campus parties. We had very big dorms at our school—high rises— and there were a lot of kids in them with parties going on all the time. I advertised on the bulletin board and made it easy for them by bringing those supplies to the dorm or student apartments and then even cleaning up the next day—for more money, of course! I did it cheaper than they could buy the same supplies and food for and I made it easy for them.

Interviewer: Well, that's sure creative. Did you make money?

Student: And how! We made about $2,000 profit for each of my three last years in college.

Interviewer: Who else did you do it with?

Student: One other girl. She was interested in hotel management and figured this would give her a taste of it. But I can't say our parties were all in good taste!

Interviewer: I guess not—not at dorms, anyway. I bet your energy and enthusiasm helped to make that a profitable business. I would also be interested in what you feel are your major weaknesses.

The student answered and the conversation continued for a total of 25 minutes. At the end of the recruiting visit, the interviewer selected the student as one of five to be interviewed at his company headquarters. Nineteen other students who were interviewed were not invited. The interviewer's note for this student contained this recommendation:

> Carol has an immense amount of energy which she has disciplined through active participation in several competitive sports throughout high school, college and graduate school. This energy and enthusiasm and her excellent interpersonal manner should give her unlimited potential in [Company's name].

The observer who recorded the interview noted that the student's ability to speak naturally and with humor were the major components of her oral communications skills. In contrast, an ability to describe her accomplishments with clarity was lacking, as was evidence of her analytical strengths. While this evidence might have emerged during a skillful interview, it did not emerge in this case. Still, the student was tentatively identified as having unlimited potential. It is important to note that an over-optimistic expectation is not to the advantage of a student. If the student does not do well in a position, the right kind of experience will not be gained.

Self-Defense for the Qualified Student Candidate

Another kind of interviewing error is equally costly to the corporation and the student. In this case, the interviewer's inability to identify unusual levels of accomplishment, analytical ability, innovativeness, and initiative may defeat even a strong candidate.

Since it is difficult to predict when an interviewer will be inept—or even for a student to know it—students should assume that all interviewers are inept. It is vital for students to decide what they want an interviewer to know—and then to make sure that they tell him. If the interviewer is competent, the student will make an even stronger impression if he or she can describe personal accomplishments, give examples of analytical ability and innovativeness, and illustrate how personal initiative brought about good results. The student must be prepared to do this. Preparation requires the organization of what he or she wants to say and some practice in doing it. The most important things a student should do when preparing to meet with potential employers is to organize one's ideas, and to practice communicating them to an interviewer. Aspiring chiefs can considerably improve the chances of their early identification if they prepare and practice. If they do not, aspirations may be delayed or side-tracked.

Accomplishments. The student should decide his or her two or three most significant accomplishments and why they are important. These may include academic achievement, unusual projects, or activities which he or she has initiated and/or completed at school or any other place, responsibilities that he or she has assumed, work that he or she has accomplished, and personal efforts that have had special significance for himself or herself or others. For each accomplishment, consider why it is significant for the interviewer to know about it. That is, what should the interviewer learn about the student? For example, it might be important for the interviewer to know about strong leadership characteristics or outstanding organizing abilities or tremendous persistence in the face of obstacles.

The accomplishments the student describes can reflect either a clear pattern of ability or a broad scope. The important thing is to decide on a presentation in advance of the interview.

Innovativeness. The student should carefully think about both the level and characteristics of his or her innovativeness and how they are usually manifested. Only a few people possess both the ability to conceive an entirely new idea or method and the drive or organizing skills to bring the innovation to practical use. Some people are especially good at conceptualizing and connecting previously unrelated information to form a new method or idea, but do not have the inclination or ability to develop it for practical or widespread use. Other people are good at picking up on a small idea that they have heard or read about and then expanding and developing it for practical and widespread application.

Aspiring chiefs should reflect thoroughly on the nature of their own innovative ability and then prepare to describe two or three examples, from start to result, for an interviewer. These examples should accurately describe one's own role and ability. Examples of strong conceptual skill include the circumstances that spark the original idea, how the idea was formed and tested, and why the idea is unique. Examples of strong development ability include a description of how an idea was obtained, why it was judged by the aspiring chief to have potential for development, obstacles to development that were overcome, and the results and their benefits. Focusing on the nature of personal innovativeness with specificity will communicate that a student not only understands the importance of the process but has apparent proficiency with it.

Analytical Ability. The student should carefully describe the depth and dimensions of his or her analytical ability. Analytical ability varies widely among individuals. Some are strong deductive analysts, thinking more like a detective or accountant. Others have stronger inductive ability, reasoning more as a lawyer who forms a position to support a client's allegation or an inventor who starts with an original idea and then figures out how to make it happen.

Analytical ability also varies along quantitative and subjective dimensions. For example, some individuals can analyze a company's financial statement so well that they not only learn about the health of an organization but they also draw inferences about nonstated circumstances which would be supported by reality if further information was available. Other individuals exercise superb judgment when faced with the need to make a decision or act under circumstances which are characterized by ambiguity or lack of information; these individuals may analyze on the basis of analogies with past experience and then extrapolate general probabilities.

Prior to an interview, therefore, two or three examples of how an issue or problem was analyzed should be prepared. Description of analytical skill should include the kind of information available at the start of the analysis, the method of analysis (e.g., how facts, probabilities, ambiguities, and lack of information were assessed), one's own role in the analysis and the results. Aspiring chiefs should begin to understand the nature of their analytical strengths as early in a career as possible so they can use it to their advantage as soon as possible.

Initiative.   Aspiring chiefs must be self-starters if they are to reach their career objective. It is important to give examples of one's initiative. Not every otherwise competent aspiring chief has the ability to initiate action for oneself and/or others without direction. Aspiring chiefs should carefully consider those events that may have caused them to act on an issue or problem without waiting for direction or suggestion or agreement from someone else. More than one example illustrating the student's willingness to act independently even when there may have been some apparent (although not necessarily actual) risk in the decision or action should be described to an interviewer.

The First Evidence of a Potential Chief

Unfortunately, the earliest identification of potential as a chief is often based on a campus or office interview. As indicated previously, this kind of early identification is generally both premature and inaccurate. An aspiring chief who is able to sustain performance in concert with predictions will be off to a better start. Other things being equal, faster starts enhance the chances of reaching one's career objective.

The interview is the initial determinant of how good is the match between candidate and company. The following excerpts from an actual campus interview demonstrate how training and practice on the part of the candidate will result in a more positive perception of abilities by an interviewer. The interviewer was the same one who interviewed Carol (above). This interview took place on the same day. In this case, the candidate had received four hours of training and practice in organizing and describing his accomplishments, innovativeness, analytical ability, and initiative.

Interviewer: Good morning, Mark. My name is _____ . I'm espe-
                cially glad to meet you after reading your resume. I'm
                going to ask you a few questions and then I'd like you
                to ask me anything you want.

Student: Glad to meet you. I've been looking forward to this
                interview.

Interviewer: Is this your first?

Student: Oh, no. I've had two others.

Interviewer: Well, you're used to the routine by now.

Student: I don't think I'll get used to it but it's a challenge each
                time.

Interviewer: What do you mean?

Student: Well, these interviews are so short that I wonder
                how much I can learn about the company and how
                much they can learn about me.

Interviewer: Yes, I understand. Tell me about yourself. What do
                you want to do and why did you decide to go to
                business school?

As a reply to virtually any question the interviewer asks, the
candidate should reply with an outline of accomplishments that
suggest analytical ability, innovativeness and initiative. For example, in reply to "Tell me about yourself," "What have you been
doing in college?," "What are you interested in?," "What are your
career goals?"

Student: Well, I think I've got analytical skills. I'm reasonably
                innovative and I'm a self-starter. One accomplish-
                ment I feel especially good about was teaching high
                school kids to use a computer and how to program it,
                using BASIC language. These kids were from a run-
                down neighborhood and I was beginning my senior
                year in high school. I organized several other students
                in my high school fraternity and we spent two after-
                noons a week all year with them. By the end of the
                year. . . . [Student briefly explained result of his effort
                and then briefly described why and how he decided
                to initiate the project, the obstacles he overcame, how

he arranged to get some financial support from several local merchants, and how he exercised resourcefulness in coping with the students' and teachers' suspicion of them. His explanation took about four minutes but touched on each point he wanted the interviewer to know. He was also prepared for questions which might probe his remarks]. . . and when I looked back on the project, I realized that maybe I did have the organizing and anlaytical and interpersonal skills that are needed in business.

Interviewer: Well, that's a very impressive story. That must have given you great satisfaction and a real feeling of accomplishment.

Student: It did. I got the same feeling of accomplishment when I worked in a small department store last summer in my home town. The store is located downtown and most people will go into the suburban shopping centers for things like clothes, appliances, lamps, kitchen stuff. The assistant manager asked some of us—the summer help—to think about how we could attract more people to the store. With two other kids, we worked out a plan to run special events every day in the main lobby of the store. We had a crafts show, cooking demonstrations, special food events like Italian week or Mexican week. We had clowns for kids, animal shows where kids could see all kinds of small animals, birds, fish. I even went to three hi-tech companies in the area and asked them to set up a display of their products. They were glad to do it and with all this action, it brought more people to the store. Each event ran for one week. I think the extra business has helped that store to survive. Without it, a lot of jobs would have been lost and I feel good about that.

Interviewer: Interesting idea. It shows what a little ingenuity can do. But I would also like to know what you consider to be your greatest strengths.

Student: Oh, I'm good analytically—at sizing up a situation

and coming up to the right decision about what to do next. I'm a self-starter and I'm fairly innovative. At least I know a good idea when I hear one and I can make something work. [For example, the student described two ideas and how he made them work.]

Interviewer: What about your weaknesses?

Student: [The student had prepared for this question and he described his tendency to have too much confidence in people, resulting in occasional disappointments.]

The interview continued for 30 minutes. The interviewer's post-conversation notes included this statement:

Mark is a most impressive and hard-hitting young man. He knows what he wants to do and then goes out and does it well. He likes to take on tough challenges and he has a record of success over his high school and college years. He knows how to analyze situations and he has innovative ideas. Mark is also able to work independently without close managing. By all standards, he is exactly what we need in this company—somebody with ideas who knows how to put them to work. I recommend we do whatever is necessary to recruit him.

During the interview, Mark did nothing more than outline what he wanted the interviewer to know. To do less, an aspiring chief works against himself or herself. Mark was in full control of the interview and would not have easily fallen victim to an inept interviewer. The results of the pre-interview preparation and subsequent practice are apparent. They should result in better career opportunities because there are likely to be fewer disappointments about the match between individual abilities and organizational needs. Together with interviewer training for college recruiters, it should also result eventually in a more solid supply of candidates for senior executive positions.

Board chairmen, CEOs, and other senior executives should add to the quality control of chief candidates by insisting on thorough interviewer training for executives who recruit at universities. Part of this training should include practice interviews with college seniors and MBA students under the guidance of a skilled interviewer. Internal corporate training resources should be tapped for such instruction.

Since so many companies prefer to promote from within, college recruiting is a critical source of eventual candidates and early identification must stand up over the long run for an adequate number of them. It might also be a good idea for senior executives to provide some interviewing training resources to students on those campuses where they recruit frequently. This would help students present themselves more effectively and help companies understand candidates better.

ASSESSMENT CENTERS

Simulation of Tasks

Assessment centers are a second method of early identification. So much information is available about this process that there is no need to do much more than briefly describe their purpose and function. The assessment center is not a substitute for performance appraisal. Instead, it is a process comprised of exercises that simulate actual management tasks that the aspiring chief might encounter in the future. Performance appraisals focus on past performance; assessment centers try to predict future performance.

Requiring an aspiring chief to respond to a variety of simulated interpersonal and problematic circumstances which an executive is expected to cope with and manage, allows an aspiring chief to demonstrate a range of abilities and skills. The simulation takes the form of written and/or interpersonal exercises which last from about 30 minutes to two or three hours. Typically, oral and written communication skills, analytical ability, organizing skill, and interpersonal effectiveness, are demonstrated. The level of these abilities and skills are observed by an independent staff, usually comprised of three or four more executives who are at least two organizational levels above the individuals assessed.

Make-up and Advantages of Assessment Centers

Some assessment centers include psychological tests that measure aspects of intellect such as verbal reasoning and conceptual fluency or dimensions of personality such as introversion-extroversion, hostility, or self-confidence. Most assessment centers take place at a location where about 6-to-12 assessees, three or four staff members and an assessment center director gather for two-to-five days.

The advantages of an assessment center include the evaluation of skills and abilities by several raters who focus only on the observable. Inferences are not acceptable, since they are not directly observed and, therefore, can only be assumed. This tends to minimize personal bias, which can arise from only one point of view. Perhaps the main advantage of the assessment center process is that it facilitates prediction because the exercises are based on the requirements of positions at least one or two levels above the assessee. Short of putting the candidate into a new job to try him or her out on a trial and error arrangement, simulation of situations allows a look at how well a potential candidate handles them and which abilities or skills require development. Another advantage is that an individual can be promoted or not on the basis of more reliably predictive information than hearsay or assumption.

Evaluating Future Potential

One frustration expressed by many assessees, and their managers as well, is that the assessee's performance in the assessment center process does not come close to the individual's actual job performance. The fact is that individuals can be outstanding at their current role but not possess the abilities or skills required in more senior positions.

While most assessment centers are designed to evaluate and predict ability for lower and middle management levels, the immense advantages for a senior executive assessment center should not be overlooked. Certainly, assessment centers for any organizational level are not a substitute for good observation in actual situations, but it may be possible to avoid a number of disappointing chief selections if candidates for those positions demonstrated their abilities and skills to handle those positions in advance of the selection decision. In practical terms, however, it is unlikely that any one will suggest to CEOs and senior executive candidates that they participate in an assessment center to determine the level of their candidacy. In all cases, there has been plenty of opportunity to observe them. The problem is, however, that observers have not properly framed the issues, questions, or behaviors they should address. If they did, they would have a good alternative to an assessment center at senior levels. This approach will be covered in Chapter 6.

A Senior Manager Assessment Center

A good approximation of an assessment center for chiefs is the process developed and begun in 1984 by Richardson-Vicks, Inc. primarily a consumer products company with locations all over the world. An issue faced by one division of this company is the need for outstanding and reliable executives to manage the businesses in countries that are relatively remote by distance and not as accessible as countries in Western Europe. For example, countries such as Indonesia and Thailand require managing directors who can assure the profitable conduct of business under the policies and principles of the corporate organization.

The Richardson-Vicks assessment center is a combination of a day of exercises designed to combine simulated country management problems with participation in a five-day leadership development program conducted by the Center for Creative Leadership in Greensboro, North Carolina. Because of its focus and the combination of observations from two separate perspectives, this unique process is expected to contribute to more incisive individual development recommendations for country manager candidates. Recommendations to improve managerial skills can also be made with more specificity. As one consequence, even better selections are expected in appointing managing directors in these distant countries because recommendations based on this assessment procedure should improve managerial performance. Further, managing directors will be among the candidates for more senior positions in the future.

From an Assessee's Point of View

Since many companies invite junior- and middle-level managers to participate in assessment centers, they should know how to behave during the process and how to react after it. Despite the understandable anxiety experienced by participants, it is probably the only time in their lives that they will hear such wide-ranging, tangible, and constructive comments about themselves. It is an opportunity that should be squeezed dry of every drop of useful information. Many participants, however, cringe if they hear they are merely "outstanding" and not clearly "superb." Too many participants listen carefully for their strengths but ignore or do not sufficiently explore how to improve their shortcomings or develop further in some areas. This is a mistake, since the observations of the assessment center staff are likely to be paralleled later by senior executives having control over the career progress of an aspiring chief. At that point, it will probably be too late to act on the needs for improvement in sufficient time to stay on the track for chief.

Almost all assessment centers conclude with an oral summary to a participant of the staff's observations about the participant's personal characteristics, strengths, weaknesses, and improvement needs in specific areas. Typically, the emphasis is on skill and behavioral areas which can be improved or changed with practice. Other areas, such as personality characteristics or intelligence, which are unlikely to be improved or changed by practice, are sometimes reviewed to help a participant work from his or her strengths and minimize the potential negative impact of shortcomings. Since even the most promising people show evidence of improvement needs in some areas, most participants do not like everything they hear.

Most participants accept the validity of these observations, even if they disagree with them, in view of the manner they were obtained and the constructive intent behind the feedback. Some participants recoil defensively, however, and argue about the information they hear. They—and sometimes their manager—will claim that the observations are incorrect, since they do not behave that way at their work. They forget that the assessment center is not a performance appraisal, that is, an evaluation of how well they do their current job. It is instead a forecast—a look ahead—at how they will perform in activities and situations different from their current role.

Participant's Reactions to an Assessment Process. A participant's response to assessment center feedback is often as revealing about them as their performance on the exercises. Participants should prepare themselves to respond positively to all kinds of information. Positive responses do not necessarily include agreeing with what is heard, but they do include asking good questions to explore and probe how observations were obtained, formed, and shaped. A line of questioning that shows curiosity, a desire to learn and improve, and perceptive probing will go a long way to impress a staff about a participant's chief potential. For example, in response to a staff's observations that a participant is not as thorough as possible in analyzing information, a participant should test the limits or boundaries of this observation (which could be very damaging to a career) with questions such as, "Can you give me some (other) examples of where I did not analyze thoroughly?," "Can you give me some examples of what I should or could have done?," "What would have been some better ways to handle it?," "Were there any situations where I did analyze well?," "Any suggestions on how I could have identified other alternatives?," "What were other questions I could have raised or explored?"

Participants will find that defensiveness on their parts serves no purpose. In addition, they will deprive themselves of opportunities to learn from the observations in a way that they can build on for the future.

Post-assessment Follow up

While the immediate post-assessment center feedback is sometimes followed by a written report, participants should not depend on their own management to follow up and coach them. Although this sometimes happens, post-assessment coaching is generally weak. Individuals must take the initiative to act on everything they have learned about themselves. They should go back to the source of the information, if necessary, for more questions and clarification. If a participant acts deliberately to improve in the indicated areas, it is likely that the changes will indeed be noticed, discussed, and remembered when their potential for chief is reviewed.

Career Impact of an Assessment Center

Some companies use assessment center information to provide most of the information on which a promotional decision will be made.

Other companies use it only to identify areas for development because they are reluctant to base any part of a promotional decision
on observations in anything outside of actual job performance. On
the one hand, this reluctance is understandable. On the other hand,
there are too many disappointments in the performance of executives selected by traditional criteria (i.e., job performance) to have
too much confidence in these criteria. A strong advantage of assessment center observations is that they are the collective opinions of
several people using sound and observable criteria rather than the
opinion of one or two persons using questionable criteria and little
opportunity for direct observation.

For these reasons, senior executives are encouraged to explore
both the advantages and the drawbacks of assessment centers' contribution to selection decisions at all management levels. The process
of early identification and better long-range prediction can be improved with an assessment center process that is a good simulation
of management positions higher up in the organization.

Certainly, these assessment procedures are not a substitute for
what is or has been directly observed from actual work performance.
Instead, they are an important addition. They provide predictive
information and insights for early identification that cannot be obtained in any other way.

Assessment Centers at Colleges

Another opportunity to use an assessment center process for early
identification is when recruiting on university and college campuses.
Although this is rarely done, it may be one of the more productive
methods of early identification. Since college applicants have not
demonstrated their work performance in a company (unless they
have had a summer job, internship, or part-time experience in that
company), decisions to hire them are nothing more than an attempt
to predict their future performance from their resumes and the
interview process. The early turnover of so many of these college-
recruited employees suggests that the match between employee and
company did not work out as originally intended.

To improve predictability by better early identification of individuals with strong development potential, one multi-national con-

sumer products company is experimenting with an assessment center process for potential employees who are recruited on campus. In this case, the company selected a small New England university with a reputation for attracting and educating very able students. To select between eight and ten students to participate in an assessment center at the university, the company met with about 60 seniors for a general presentation on corporate careers. At the end of the presentation, the students were invited to write an essay on what careers they were considering and why a career in business might be of interest to them. Skill in written communication is a good indicator of various aspects of intellect and personal characteristics.

Almost all of the students remained at the meeting for an additional 45 minutes to write the essay. Three company executives read the essays and selected eight students to participate, based only on what they said and how they expressed themselves. Three weeks later, the eight students participated in a half-day on-campus assessment center comprised of two problem solving exercises and one interpersonal skills exercise. Three standardized tests were also administered to provide other information about personal characteristics, intellect, and judgment. Four students were then invited to the company's headquarters for job interviews. Early evidence indicated that the students invited to interview at the company's headquarters were exceptionally able. Time and repetition of this experimental process will enable a determination of the predictive validity of this alternative to early identification.

SPONSORSHIP

Sponsorship is a *sine qua non* of early identification. Without a sponsor, even the best potential chief is not likely to be identified. Somebody with organizational credibility must be willing to make a prediction about the future performance of an individual. When a positive statement is made by a respected executive, however casually, the sponsorship of an individual is usually perceived.

Potential sponsors must be aware that their opinions about people are attended to carefully, especially if the potential sponsor is a senior executive. A phrase, a comment, even an off-hand reaction or remark about a potential chief can have a dramatic career impact— for example, a self-fulfilling prophecy for success or a premature derailment from the track toward chief. In fact, it is difficult for a senior executive to talk about others without telegraphing something of his opinion of them. In most cases, careless statements do not work to the advantage of the senior executive or the aspiring chief.

Corporate chiefs should encourage their senior executives to actively sponsor the candidacy of subordinate executives for positions of greater responsibility. The process of sponsorship is an evident one. Its encouragement will generate an enthusiasm for growth on the part of an organization's most promising executives.

Sponsorship, however, should not be an expression of unlimited optimism. It should reflect operational and situational predictions. For example, senior executives should be urged to say more than "He's an outstanding person," or "She's got unlimited potential," or "She's the brightest person we've hired in three years." Generalizations of this kind should be challenged for specificity by senior executives because they provide no useful information and may be nothing more than overreactions to an individual's personal charm. Senior executives should insist on better descriptions of potential chiefs. These descriptions should suggest how future organizational needs may be met by the specific talents of these potential chiefs.

To the extent possible, sponsorship should be situationally specific. For example, the sponsor should make observations such as "Her analytical skills are growing so fast that she will be able to handle our most complex problems within one year" or "He has become so knowledgeable about key marketing issues that his contribution to product strategies is sought by every manager in the division." Reasons for sponsorship are necessary to convey the quality and dimensions of an individual.

Sponsors need to depend on others to pass on their observations and optimism. This is easier to do when the sponsor's remarks are based on how specific behaviors or personal characteristics are likely to influence organizational performance or outcomes. Chiefs should require such specific information in order to encourage high standards among candidates for senior executive positions.

Seeking Sponsorship

Aspiring chiefs should seek sponsorship from credible executives. However, it is important to keep in mind that sponsors are not necessarily mentors. Many sponsors like it that way. Aspiring chiefs should be cautious about overburdening a sponsor with the task of mentoring.

One good way to attract a sponsor is to find opportunities to acquaint possible sponsors with one's work. This can be done by sharing information, asking for the opinions of a potential sponsor, or becoming involved in an activity or aspect of work with the potential sponsor. Since sponsorship ranges from explicit to implicit, from formal to informal, there are many opportunities to obtain it. Overt politicking is not a good idea.

In addition, aspiring chiefs should remember that good performance is probably not the major reason for being identified early as someone with high potential. Recognition for good performance is not an I.O.U. for management. Instead, early identification is based more on a projection for the future. Aside from good performance, sponsors will look for scope, innovative ideas, and candor. One lesson for aspiring chiefs is to say what they think but to think carefully first.

Premature Judgment Versus Actual Accomplishment

Advantages accrue to executives who are willing to sponsor an individual, especially for the purpose of early identification as a potential chief. Sponsors can assure that certain individuals are not overlooked as candidates for position of chief, particularly when an individual's lack of sponsorship might result in a subsequent loss of executive talent. Also, since sponsorship is often evident, the executive sponsor will probably develop increased loyalty toward himself or herself from the sponsored individual. Increased cohesiveness of this kind improves the quality of teamwork in an organization because mutual confidence is greater.

However, there are risks to sponsors. The greatest danger is probably overestimation or overgeneralization about the positive attributes of an individual. For the most part, these risks are significantly increased by a sponsor's premature judgment. The negative side of sponsoring individuals who do not work out as predicted is a loss of credibility for the sponsor and the loss of organizational support and cooperation from sponsored individuals because they themselves are ineffective.

Premature judgment can be avoided. One ground rule is for a sponsor to thoroughly ascertain an individual's actual accomplishments before actively sponsoring him or her. Many aspiring chiefs have excellent communication skills, and it is often difficult to distinguish their real achievements and contributions to organizational effectiveness. While a potential sponsor should arrive at a tentative opinion about an individual, sponsorship should not begin until the sponsor actually talks with other people who are familiar with the individual's work and impact on the organization.

The potential sponsor should note examples that establish a pattern of accomplishment from which reliable prediction can be made. In addition, a potential sponsor should determine how an individual's accomplishments have been judged and the circumstances in which they occurred. Understanding the criteria used to evaluate the nature of accomplishments will make it easier to describe how an individual is expected to behave. Knowing the circumstances in which an individual has been effective will improve the predictive accuracy of a sponsor's expectations. The following three actual cases illustrate both the advantages and the risks of sponsorship.

In the first case, a corporation exceeding $2 billion in sales was active in acquiring new businesses. Small companies were bought and corporate efforts were put behind this growth. The chief responsible for the acquisition and operation of these new businesses was an operating vice president. He selected a 31-year-old executive from another corporate division to become marketing director of a newly acquired business. The selection was made primarily on the basis of a conversation with another highly respected senior executive (who was the sponsoring executive). The sponsoring executive, who was in another part of the organization, was unequivocal in his endorsement of the candidate. When the hiring executive looked for opinions in the company to confirm the sponsor's views, he found general agreement that the successful candidate was a highly energetic, hard-charging, innovative young executive who would know how to build and motivate a team. The candidate's candor and willingness to depart from traditional ways of doing business was seen as refreshing and desirable. When the sponsor was advised that he had influenced the selection decision, he congratulated the hiring executive on the wisdom of his decision.

During the first year as marketing director of the new business, the chief was full of praise for his new man. "This guy knows all the pieces of marketing—he has six eyes and four ears and doesn't miss a thing," said the chief. "He's going to run this whole company some day if we don't hose down his enthusiasm. He's got the marketing and sales departments on their toes and working 20 hours a day to meet their goals—and they'll make them," continued the chief. Despite the chief's continuous support to the new marketing director and his public endorsement of his actions to expand the product lines and introduce new products, the business did not meet its profit objectives at the end of the first year. During the second year, none of the new products were doing well and the old line of products had leveled off somewhat but did not show any sign of growth. Still, the chief continued to have confidence in the marketing director and predicted success for him.

Then some things happened. The marketing director, in his desire to meet business objectives, fired some of his key staff and replaced them with people from outside the company. He also spent most of his time visiting his key staff and some of their subordinates to pesonally review their activities and results on a day-to-day basis and to direct their work. It is not surprising that this was resented by everyone and presented a threat to most. Under continuing pressure to improve profitability, his frustration caused him to threaten several employees with loss of their jobs. He also verbally intimidated several other employees by loudly questioning their loyalty to him.

At this point, the senior executive to whom the marketing director reported telephoned the sponsoring executive to describe his surprise and disappointment. He also asked if there was anything in the man's background that could have predicted his inappropriate reactions. The sponsor expressed considerable surprise and told the chief, "I'd fire him. You can't have a marketing director who folds under pressure."

The chief was annoyed at this remark, since it was not a very constructive response to a request for help or ideas. It merely represented a fast disassociation with an individual he had previously sponsored without reservation. The senior executive then made two other calls to people who had worked closely with the marketing director. The chief found that the marketing director had acted impulsively under pressure on several occasions and often scapegoated others, such as young product assistants, when things went wrong. While the senior executive was angry with himself for not being more thorough in the preselection decision process, he was especially resentful of the sponsoring executive's "careless and premature judgment." The sponsor's credibility was not helped by the marketing director's failure.

In a second situation, a financial vice-president of a company's chemicals' division frequently praised a young accounting supervisor in his division as "the only other financial executive who understands his business" and as an "ambitious and very smart manager who will probably be chairman of the board one day."

When a promotional opportunity came up for the accounting supervisor in another division, his boss called the other division to volunteer his high opinion of the individual. This endorsement brought a job offer to the accounting supervisor, which he accepted. On the day that the accounting supervisor's promotion and transfer was announced, the financial department buzzed with joy. An anonymous interoffice memo was sent to the financial vice president of the other division, to whom the accounting supervisor would report. The anonymous memo expressed gratitude for taking the executive from them and suggesting that a muzzle and leash would be a prudent investment in keeping him away from the financial staff.

Apparently, the sponsor was unaware of how the aspiring chief was perceived by organizational subordinates; he had assumed that the executive was as responsive downward as he was upward. The sponsoring executive was very embarrassed by the unexpected reaction and was questioned by his chief about how well he was in touch with the climate of his division.

A third case illustrates how sponsorship can work to everyone's advantage. A food company had several regional sales managers located around the United States. One of them, a 29-year-old midwesterner, was quiet and reserved at all social occasions and in business meetings with other sales and headquarters staff. Nevertheless, for the past three years his region always exceeded their sales targets and had almost no turnover of sales persons. The national sales vice president found that he had to constantly assure other sales executives and headquarters staff that despite a withdrawn manner at business meetings and an awkward social manner, the young regional sales manager was extraordinarily effective.

When the national sales vice president was promoted to administrative vice president for the corporation, the sales force was reorganized under two area sales manager positions. He actively sponsored the regional sales manager's candidacy for promotion to area sales manager. He was just as actively opposed by skeptics. He persisted and explained, example by example, how the sales manager acted in a variety of situations and how he had accomplished so much. With specific observations and information to predict future performance, the appointment was made and the sponsor has been receiving appreciative comments since.

A lesson for sponsors: Do your homework and do it carefully; predictive accuracy depends on it. Be specific, do not generalize, and give examples which describe a pattern. Do not assume that outstanding accomplishments at a relatively junior position will accurately predict performance in senior executive positions. The nature of work, environment, and pressure are so different that sponsors should thoroughly understand the environment or work climate in which the younger person has achieved. Environments must be part of the equation in the early identification process.

THE SUPERVISOR'S ROLE IN EARLY IDENTIFICATION

Some supervisors, in their enthusiasm for good performance, overstate the abilities of young people. They often assume that effectiveness in a current role will continue when responsibility is added or the position is changed. Conversely, many supervisors assume that a young person's failure to display managerial or technical talent in a junior role is due to the person rather than the conditions under which the person works. Both assumptions obscure reliable early identification. Performance should be observed and judged from more than one situational perspective. Quality control of potential chiefs requires objectivity and balance in their predictive descriptions. Supervisors who unintentionally do a poor job of early identification can damage the organization, as illustrated by the following four examples from the same company.

In the first instance, a middle-level manager recommended a young MBA to participate in an assessment center offered by a consultant. The assessment center, which was designed to identify aspects of personal behavior, interpersonal skill, and problem-solving abilities that would benefit from improvement and increase the competence of the participant, was only offered to high potential individuals. Prior to the program, the middle-level manager said that he was sending his most outstanding young person and that he would be surprised if his impressions were not confirmed. They were not. In fact, the young man's problem solving skills and inter-personal behavior was strong, but his personal manner was extremely defensive. This unnecessary defensiveness interfered with his ability to reason under these circumstances because he took disagreement as a personal insult. At these times, he would sulk. When given this feedback, the participant claimed he did not behave this way in his position.

The young man's manager was surprised at these observations by the assessment staff. He agreed, however, to go along with the assessment center's recommendations to challenge the young man more aggressively on aspects of his work. If the young man responded inappropriately, the manager could actively counsel him. As it turned out, the young man did react over-defensively when challenged—and this trait did interfere with his ordinarily superb ability to properly address tasks. Fortunately for the young man, his manager was a perceptive and willing coach and the undesirable behavior was stamped out before it interfered with his career process. Without the additional perspective of the assessment staff and the follow-through of a supervisor, early identification in this case would have led to a dead end.

In the second case, an aggressive and hard-working young woman was described by her middle-level supervisor as "smart as a whip, doesn't let anything fall through the cracks, impatient but effective." The supervisor said she had a lot of career potential and he saw no apparent obstacles to growth. The supervisor should have also judged her on aspects of behavior other than the timeliness of her work and the thoroughness of her reports.

When the young woman was recommended for promotion, the company's personnel representative in the manager's department overheard two other people talking about the young woman. Their remarks were so unkind and so emotionally charged that the personnel representative informally explored them with several people. He learned that the young woman was perceived by everyone but her supervisor to be dogmatic, rude, and domineering in most business interactions. The supervisor, advised of these observations, watched the young woman carefully for several months. He finally concluded that the young woman did not have the potential for career growth in the company. He told her why, and she left for another company.

The third situation involves a young woman who was known to be exceptionally bright but was regarded as awkward and somewhat withdrawn. For these reasons, her supervisor was unwilling to say that she had a lot of career potential. One of the company's personnel executives, however, urged operating management to transfer the woman to a department where her great analytical ability was needed.

When she started her new position, the personnel executive met with the young woman's new supervisor. They developed a set of criteria to evaluate her performance. Each criterion reflected high standards and expectations. The young woman not only exceeded every expectation, but became more outgoing as her accomplishments were recognized. The reasons for her early identification as a potential chief were documented by her supervisor to support this prediction. This has resulted in a fast track for a potential chief who is expected to be a future candidate for general manager in her company.

The fourth case involves another tricky situation. An executive with three years work experience had a manager who was unable to describe his performance in anything but vague terms. Because of his manager's inability, the executive found that he was being passed over for promotion in favor of other people who had less experience and, in his opinion, less promise. When he complained about the situation, his manager arranged for him to interview with another group that had a position opening in a distant city. Although the executive did not want to move, he decided he needed to work under somebody who could recognize his abilities and describe them to others. For this reason, he actively sought the other position even though it was more of a lateral transfer than a promotion.

During his job interview he carefully assessed the ability of his prospective new manager to evaluate him accurately. He also initiated a discussion on the criteria against which he would be judged. Fortunately for him, he was offered the job and did exceptionally well at it. Five years later, he had received two significant promotions— mainly because his new supervisor was able to accurately describe the quality of his performance. The executive is now managing one of his company's largest businesses, and he is a strong candidate for senior executive. Nevertheless, this was a near-miss, because of the premature negative judgment implicitly conveyed by inadequate early identification.

PERFORMANCE APPRAISAL

The fifth method of early identification is the performance appraisal. Because it compares an individual's performance against original expectations, a good performance appraisal tests, at the least, the predictive reality of the other methods of early identification. Expectancies about an individual's performance for the next year are generally the basis of a sound appraisal process. These expectancies, which are stated as goals, should be set with the mutual consent of subordinate and manager. In an actual sense, both subordinate and manager predict performance outcomes; they will often anticipate obstacles and plan how to go around them so that their results are achieved as predicted. In another sense, both agree to control defined aspects of the future by achieving the goals. The ability to do this dependably is a necessary characteristic for any senior executive candidate.

Performance appraisals have three purposes. Unless all three are met, the appraisal has not been done well. Appraisals should

1. Review and summarize how performance goals were met;
2. Explain the relationship between an individual's performance and the size of the merit pay increase or extra compensation that an individual will receive; and
3. Serve as a basis for improving performance in indicated areas.

Since so much has been written on performance appraisal, the remainder of the discussion emphasizes the language and the process of performance appraisal as they relate to early identification.

The Appraisal in Writing

The choice of language used to write an appraisal (e.g., vocabulary, inferences, thoroughness of expression) generally reflects the supervisor's stream of consciousness or the supervisor's attempt to be operationally literal. It rarely conveys the subordinate's enthusiasm (or lack of it), the originality (or lack of it), or how an individual made a difference in organizational results. Performance appraisals tend to portray executives as managers of resources and events with almost no attention to how they exercise their imaginations or excite others with ideas or explore new opportunities or take risks. Even companies with performance appraisal training required for all its managers—which are still surprisingly rare in U.S. industry—concentrate on behavior and personality trait descriptions that are linked to objectives. As one result, information from performance appraisals does not distinguish the qualities that signal the emergence of a potential chief.

The effective use of language is illustrated by the following examples of typical (and not sufficiently specific) appraisal language:

Objectives	Results
Increase market share of Brand X by 7% by end of calendar year.	Brand X market share increase by 4%. While he worked hard to get results, two new products introduced by the competition took some of the business that we went after.

Objectives	Results
Revise incentive compensation plan for middle management to be consistent with new salary guidelines; complete by October 1.	Plan completed on time and introduced to managers smoothly.
Complete conversion of automated warehouse by July 1 within original budget.	Conversion completed after several unanticipated problems with the computer. Budget was met despite last minute programming changes.
Build enthusiasm of sales staff to accelerate coal conversions to exceed last year's results by 12%.	Sales staff is more enthusiastic about coal conversion due to the frequent information exchange meetings and Mike's persistence. Conversions exceeded last year by 15%.

None of these statements tells very much about the abilities or behaviors that characterize a potential chief. They are sterile descriptions of what was accomplished. They do not even hint about how things were done. Further, the appraisal seems to be especially dry for a new and younger executive. When senior executives read performance appraisals of this kind at human resources reviews, it is impossible to understand who has the potential to be a chief. Thus, early identification of potential chiefs is blocked—even though the appraisal process can contribute considerably to reliable prediction.

Aspiring chiefs should be aware of the dangers of performance descriptions that do not include how personal resourcefulness helped to overcome obstacles, how ingenuity solved a difficult problem, how careful analysis and examination of alternatives led to a conclusion, how long hours and frustration were handled with coolness and tact, how curiosity led to better ideas, or how independence and personal conviction resulted in winning the support of others. For this reason, performance appraisal training for subordinates would benefit early identification. If subordinates are trained to discuss what they did and how they did it—and if they know what has made their contribution unique or important beyond the description or results—they will be more likely to make sure that their supervisor (1) is aware of this information and (2) will include it in the written performance appraisal. Without fuller written performance descriptions of young executives, senior executives will not be able to learn much about the quality and supply of the executive inventory at this level. Also, some aspiring chiefs will find their progress delayed and others will be identified as a high potential for the wrong reasons.

Senior executives and aspiring chiefs should insist on performance appraisals that provide for fuller understanding of the nature of accomplishments in specific situations. If their expectancies are firmly expressed, they will probably be met. Both chiefs and subordinates can ask that appraisals be properly written. One way to do it is to ask one's supervisor to include their perceptions of how the job was done and what personal characteristics seemed to cause specific results. A better appraisal, such as those in the following list, should result.

Objectives	Results
Increased market share of Brand X by 7% by end of calendar year.	Market share increased by 4% even with unexpected competition from competitors. This result is very strong because of his flexibility in changing campaign strategy when he saw the competition's approach. His fast analysis of what was needed, his willingness to do it, and his leadership in obtaining agreement from all parties concerned, did not permit initial disappointment to take over.

Objectives	Results
Revised incentive compensation plan for middle management to be consistent with new salary guidelines; complete by October 1.	Plan completed on time and introduced to management groups in a way that helped them to understand why the more limited incentive compensation awards would enable competitive salary increases. Her skillful communication on a difficult subject and her poise in fielding questions added to management's confidence in the new plan.
Complete conversion of automated warehouse by July 1 within original budget.	Conversions completed on time even though he did not anticipate several problems which more thorough analysis would have indicated. In his desire to get results, he pushed some people very hard and aroused a lot of anger and bad feelings about the program. The last minute programming changes did not cause budget overrun because Jerry and Alan volunteered to help out since their own schedules would have been delayed somewhat.
Build enthusiasm of sales staff to accelerate coal conversions to exceed last year's results by 12%.	We have a more enthusiastic sales staff mostly because of Mike's frequent personal contacts and "touching of flesh" with them. His ability

Objectives	Results
	to paint the picture of the future, and how accelerated conversions will lead into new areas of business, caught the imaginations of everyone involved. The entire sales staff developed tremendous confidence in Mike.

Any senior executive reading performance appraisals containing these more tangible criteria will feel more confident in his or her understanding of individual abilities—and consequently in his or her ability to predict how the young executive might perform in positions of more responsibility. These improved descriptions are also more memorable and therefore more likely to be repeated. This is another way that sponsorship begins.

The Appraisal Discussion

A written appraisal does not have to be completed prior to the appraisal discussion. The main rule is that neither one contain any surprises. All aspects of performance coverage should have been discussed previously on an on-going basis. The appraisal discussion, however, can be designed to identify those behaviors, characteristics, abilities, and skills that enabled (or prevented) the meeting of goals in a particular way. The superior can use the discussion to generate information that is useful for early identification. After the discussion, the supervisor can write the appraisal and show it to the employee to be sure that mutual understanding—though not necessarily agreement—exists.

In other words, the appraisal discussion should not only focus on what was accomplished and how it was done. It should also be a joint exploration of the employee's strengths. A review of strengths increases the employee's confidence that his or her potential for chief is not being overlooked. A review of performance improvement needs will add assurance for senior executives that quality control is not being overlooked. Both strengths and needs should be discussed in terms of how they affect an individual's potential for promotion and, when desirable, their potential for chief.

Appraisal Policy.   Virtually every large- and mid-sized corporation has a performance appraisal policy and a formal process. In many companies, performance appraisal practices do not comply with the intentions of policy. Still, aspiring chiefs should assume that a performance appraisal is being written for them annually. Aspiring chiefs should also request performance discussions when they are not initiated by one's manager.

Aspiring chiefs should understand their company's appraisal policy and intended process. This may require some conversation with their personnel or employee relations department since it is not unusual for managers to be uncertain about what is required.

Aspiring chiefs should also ask to see what has been written about their performance. It is important for young aspiring chiefs to overcome their understandable reluctance to raise these questions with a supervisor. Awareness of what is being said and written, especially when the written appraisals are reviewed in organizational planning or career planning meetings, is vital. In that way an aspiring chief can retain more control over his or her career progress. Without this awareness, career progress becomes less certain.

Senior executives must also ensure that performance appraisal discussions are actually held with each employee. Otherwise, alternate forms of appraisal—the secret appraisal, the casual appraisal, the fork-tongued appraisal, and the whitewash appraisal—can be expected. The secret appraisal is completed by a supervisor who never tells the employee about it. There may even be tacit agreement that the employee will not see it. In these cases, the manager is usually unwilling or uncomfortable about telling the subordinate what he thinks. Casual appraisal is not much more than an off-hand, perfunctory review of what the manager said about the employee on the written form. The fork-tongued appraisal happens when the manager is negatively critical of a subordinate in writing, but expresses only satisfaction during the discussion. The whitewash appraisal is a verbal glossing over of the subordinate's abilities. It consists of cliches (e.g., "good communicator," "tough-minded," and "good interpersonal skills") and can apply to a wide variety of people.

Training both subordinates and managers to discuss performance issues honestly will assure more accurate descriptions and improve the predictability of early identification. The consequence of no training, or only training managers how to handle their side of appraisal, is an early identification process that cannot be trusted.

IS EARLY IDENTIFICATION WORTH THE TROUBLE?

Recruiting programs at universities are carefully planned. Elaborate descriptive material is prepared to attract candidates. Companies take their best people away from work, where their minds and energies are badly needed, and send them to universities to interview students. And yet, how well can engineers, marketers, accountants, or scientists recognize extraordinary students when the students do not even speak much of the interviewer's language? Assessment centers are developed at great expense in time and expertise to discern participants with unusual potential. Sponsors risk their reputations by predicting that a particular person will make an unusual contribution to a company. Supervisors also take a risk in predicting that an individual has high potential. All this costs a lot of money.

Early identification processes are not perfect. Sometimes the wrong people are identified too early and too much is invested in them before they fall off the track. Sometimes the individuals with the best potential for chief are missed. Alan F. Lafley, Chase Manhattan's former Executive Vice President for Human Resources, feels that trying to identify potential too early results in "too much image and past history" and too little emphasis on performance skills.

What is needed are the very processes that are now used—but they need to be managed more carefully. The company must agree on specific criteria. The training of individuals must explore and apply these criteria. Ignoring accurate early identification will prematurely discourage the drive and curiosity of those persons who are likely to become the most effective chiefs.

— 4 —

Career Sense

CAREERS SHOULD BE PLANNED

In his book on career and life planning, Campbell[1] refers to an old saying:

> You have to take life as it happens, but you should try to make it happen the way you want to take it.

Career guidance is something that senior executives should demand for their middle managers. Potential chiefs are drawn from the ranks of middle management. The accuracy of predicting the performance of senior executives depends in large part on the quality of career advice they have followed to become a chief. Without good career advice, otherwise strong potential senior executives may fall out of the running. A lack of guidance or direction may cause an executive to take a career turn or behave in a way that will cause others to think less of his potential—despite earlier predictions. Planning is vital and its absence can be damaging.

[1]David Campbell, *If You Don't Know Where You're Going, You'll Probably End Up Somewhere Else.* Allen, Texas: Argus, 1974.

David Campbell struck at the heart of this issue in his book. He also said:

> If you are reading this book at age 37, in the next ten years you will probably reach your peak in your occupational life, your income will probably reach a maximum and level off, your children will probably be reaching college age and leaving home, your body will be aging more rapidly, and you will probably have less energy and endurance than you have now. You may well be on your way to middle age. Distressing, perhaps, but a fact, and one that you should plan for.[2]

The stages of a career can be defined in different ways. The most straightforward of them is described by a five-stage process, from entry to CEO. Unless the questions and issues associated with each career stage are resolved, they may be more harmful to career progress than if they were openly confronted when first identified. For example, if an executive is seen as "trying to be a perfectionist" and the implications of this are not discussed with him, the executive's business talent may bring him to a higher point until senior management rejects him as a potential chief because he is "too inflexible."

THE FIVE STAGES OF CAREER DEVELOPMENT

Stage I covers the period from career entry to two or three years hence. Stage II begins when an individual is no longer viewed (by self or others) as a novice and is given a noticeable difference in responsibility, mostly evidenced by the opportunity to work fairly independently. Stage III begins when an individual is recognized as an expert in one's area of work and proceeds through middle levels of management. Promotion to the head of functional (e.g., finance, marketing) or operating management for a business unit of a corporation signals the start of Stage IV. Stage V includes the senior executive positions which have responsibility for the operating or staff functions of several business units or for the entire corporation. These are the chiefs.

People move through the stages of a career like they move through

[2]*Ibid.*

stages of their lives. Each stage presents new information and requires different behavior for actions to be approved and encouraged
by organizational superiors. During the first two or three years,
people focus on establishing credibility in their role. The second
phase begins when young people reach out to broaden their abilities
and knowledge. This step is a springboard for the more significant
career progress signaled by more responsibility and less supervision.
This second stage generally lasts the number of years needed to
acquire competence and knowledge in a functional area such as
finance, marketing, sales, engineering, manufacturing, or personnel.
For many people, this stage lasts too long to suit them. The third
career stage, however, is where most people remain for the duration
of their careers. This third stage ranges from the "journeyman"
individual contributor or specialist through the first and middle
levels of supervision, that is, actual management of the work of
others.

The Crucial Third Stage

Most executives who will be chiefs are spotted fairly early in their
career, almost always during the third stage. Two things typically
characterize these executives:

1. They are perceived to be very good at what they do; and
2. They communicate their ideas to anyone who will listen.

Individuals who become gleams in the eyes of senior executives
who pick chiefs are not reluctant to express their opinion. That is
generally how they come to the attention of more senior executives.
Their willingness to communicate their thinking probably is even
more responsible for the perception of their superior competence.
    While it is crucial for aspiring chiefs to say what they think, it is
just as important for others to probe their statements for specificity,
knowledge, depth, and other aspects of opinion that should comprise the opinions of chiefs. People who communicate their ideas
convincingly are generally assumed to know what they are talking
about—even though they may not. Executives who speak with conviction are rarely challenged. They should be. Questions such as the

following should be asked: "Can you give me several examples so I can understand the consistency of your point?"; " I don't understand what you've said. Can you say it differently?"; and "You said that 'always' happens (or 'never' happens), and that 'everyone' feels that way. Could there be exceptions to such inclusive (or exclusive) conditions?"

It is during the third stage, as supervisors and managers, that a good platform is available for aspiring chiefs to say what they think. For those who do, and who are perceived to be more capable because of it, the informal sorting out process begins. After all, if they don't say what they think, how can they expect to have influence? The executives who are judged to be potential chiefs also begin to *know* they are. Nobody tells them anything. They just know that their management acts differently towards them—by listening, asking for opinions, and generally being more cordial than is the case for their peers. People responsible for selecting chiefs must take care not to assure a chief-aspirant's self-fulfilling prophecy for the wrong reason—such as self-confidence manifested by speaking with conviction but without substance.

Stage Four: The Threshold

What happens now to these potential senior executives? Do they sit back and let time and events take their course? Will they intuitively do the right things to develop an even stronger candidacy? Do they need help to develop? Should senior executives assume that career progress will automatically provide the right knowledge, skills, and experience? In virtually all cases, the aspiring chief wants career advice and direction. Career discussions of good substance or high value, however, are very rare. Only exceptional supervisors have the ability, personal style, and initiative required. In most cases of career discussions at middle and senior levels, an astute aspiring chief learns more from omission and inference than by direct discussion. A clear description of career alternatives, the match between the candidate and the requirements of senior executive positions, career goals, and the probabilities of reaching these goals are usually absent from a career discussion.

As a result, some potential chiefs do not take enough control over their own career on the assumption that their organization will manage it for them. Lack of initiative in this aspect of career planning should be a signal to those who select chiefs that an individual may be too assumptive or insufficiently anticipative for a senior executive position. For example, typical of the expectations among those who pick senior executives is one expressed by an executive vice president of a major consumer products company: "He's just sitting back and waiting for someone to tell him that he has been made a general manager. He ought to be pounding on my desk and telling me why he wants the job and asking what he has got to prove to get it and he's not doing this. I don't want to give a job like that to anyone who won't let me know that he really wants it for the work, not just for the prestige."

ACTIVE CONTROL OF THE CAREER PATH

Aspiring chiefs should be aware that those who select them will be more attracted to candidates who actively communicate their curiosity and ideas about their next assignments. Taking more active control over one's career is not simply instinctive. If it is done well, it is the result of considerable reflection and intelligent planning.

Training candidates to do this effectively will help a great deal, as illustrated later on in this chapter. The advantage of actual training in career discussions is that it increases the chances of having outstanding candidates who know how to manage the ambiguities of career planning. Further, most candidates need help to develop their ability. In fact, most organizational superiors probably need even more help to discuss careers constructively with candidates. This kind of knowledge is not usually acquired through experience, which is why most executives neither give nor receive useful career discussions. Training will address this effectively.

CAREER DISCUSSIONS WITH POTENTIAL SENIOR EXECUTIVES

More than most anything, potential senior executives are hungry for information or signals that let them know if they are on the track and on time. Many executives ask their organizational superior for a career conversation. Unfortunately, most potential chiefs do not know how to ask about the issues and most of their organizational superiors are not much help.

There are two kinds of career discussions for potential senior executives. One focuses on the short-term and the other on the long-term. The short-term discussion is easier because it should deal with what a potential senior executive must accomplish and demonstrate over the year or two ahead. The long-term career discussion for candidates for senior management is more difficult because it focuses on issues involving alternative goals and paths, the obstacles to the goals and the probabilities of achieving them, and on the competition.

It should be noted that a number of organizations (e.g., AT&T, IBM, General Electric, and Citicorp) turn over the tasks of career planning and the screening of chief candidates to corporate staff groups. These staff groups develop preferred career paths for each of the various functions. When an opening is anticipated or occurs, the staff group screens or identifies the best candidates and gives the information to the senior executive who makes the final choice. This process is generally limited to the selection of middle and senior executives.

The role of staff groups in helping identify and screen candidates is well-known within the companies that have them. In these companies, candidates often initiate contact with a member of a staff group to explore career options, timing, and probabilities. This action is overt recognition that useful career guidance is not likely from one's operating management. In one sense, it is also tacit acknowledgment by an entire organization that executives are not able to effectively discuss careers with subordinates because they lack information, career control, and/or the ability to conduct a discussion.

Short-Term Career Discussions

The short-term career discussion must be based on what a potential chief can probably control or accomplish within two years. The short-term career discussion need not touch on goals or timing beyond one or two years.

The discussion should be a very tangible "here is what you should accomplish or demonstrate," focusing entirely on the near future. It should have two parts: (1) a clear review of what senior management needs to know about the potential chief, that is, abilities, depth of knowledge, drive, scope, flexibility; and (2) a discussion that will enable a potential chief to answer what senior management "needs to know" about someone before considering them as a candidate for chief. Again, the focus is on what can be accomplished over the next one or two years.

Long-Term Career Discussions

The long-term career discussion is an especially important element of prediction. When a senior executive discusses long-term goals, career alternatives, and timing with a candidate for chief, he or she should use the conversation to help assess intellect, vision, and flexibility. Individuals reveal a great deal about these qualities during conversations that focus on how their strengths can contribute to organizational objectives. Listening to and probing the ideas and perspectives of a chief-candidate should identify anything else that a senior executive needs to know as well as provide more comfort about how well the chief-candidate is known: A chief-candidate's values—for example, power, financial reward, personal accomplishment, contribution—can be ascertained; his or her attitudes toward various aspects of business climate or toward other senior executives can be determined; the nature of relationships between the chief-candidate and other senior executives can be clarified. This balance of comfort/discomfort should result in questions and decisions which increase the accuracy of predictions about a chief-candidate's performance. Without this discussion, too much information remains unknown and prediction will be less accurate.

In summary, a candidate for chief should expect several things from a long-term career discussion:

1. An exploration of career alternatives;
2. An understanding of his or her potential for growth;
3. Direction;
4. Straight feedback;

5. Better defined goals; and
6. Clarity.

Similarly, the executive who counsels a potential chief should also have some expectations from a long-term career discussion: (1) better understanding of the candidate's vision, depth of thinking, and flexibility; (2) identification of what he or she "needs to know"; and (3) an understanding of the experience which must be provided for the candidate over the next two to three years at a minimum.

The Senior Executive's Role in Career Discussion

Long-term career discussions are not easy. Executives who conduct them have problems because they are often not sure what to say and do not know how to avoid ambiguity or how to avoid making premature commitments. While the senior executive should take the initiative in these career discussions with subordinates, this initiative does not require doing the thinking or all the planning for the potential chief.

The role of the senior executive in career planning and career discussions is defined by the following:

Prior to the discussion, encourage the candidate for chief to think about career goals, alternatives, and a plan.

Explore career goals and criteria to evaluate progress towards those goals.

Discuss the reality of the candidate's goals and talents versus organizational needs.

Explore and speculate about the probabilities of certain goals.

Advise the candidate how well he or she is meeting performance criteria directed at the primary career goal.

Obtain and provide information related to the candidate's goals if the conversation indicates.

Take the risk of giving the candidate opportunities to demonstrate abilities.

Do not avoid career discussions at any time, nor postpone them too long when a candidate asks for one.

Follow up on the conversation and subsequent actions.

PRIOR TO CAREER DISCUSSION

A senior executive must remind the candidates for chief that they also have an important role in career planning. Since the elements of this role are generally not understood, the candidates often do not fully prepare for or clearly communicate their objectives. Prior to a career discussion, a senior executive should ask a candidate for chief to do the following:

Identify the primary and alternate goals

Identify the experience required

Be flexible in thinking about preparation for alternative career goals

Do a realistic appraisal of:

Self

Organization

Aspirations

Competition

Prepare to communicate these ideas

Identify the individuals to whom the ideas should be communicated

Identify risks which may be necessary and prepare to take them

GUIDING A CAREER DISCUSSION

In addition to assuring the content of a career discussion, senior executives should follow a procedure that will help the discussion to move in the right direction. There are several steps—called "learning points"—that should guide a senior executive in this discussion:

1. Prepare for the discussion with career information and available knowledge of the candidate's goals and abilities.
2. Ask the candidate to discuss his or her career objectives, alternatives, plans, and timing. Listen carefully.
3. Discuss the preparation and experience required to meet the stated career objectives.
4. Discuss possible obstacles and other information which the candidate should explore.
5. Ask the candidate how he or she thinks you might assist.
6. Summarize your understanding of the discussion and set a specific follow-up date.

Following these steps will increase the likelihood of a constructive career discussion from which better predictions can be made. The quality of this discussion, however, will increase dramatically if both the senior executive and the candidate are trained to discuss long-term career plans. Although some companies train executives in discussing careers, it is rare to find organizations where the *subordinate* executive is trained in how to approach this issue.

TRAINING FOR CAREER DISCUSSIONS

Many companies provide formal instruction to managers in discussing careers with subordinates. A number of them use a training process called "behavior modeling."[3] Behavior modeling provides models of good manager-employee interactions on specific issues, guided practice in handling these discussions, and reinforcement for doing it well. Behavior modeling is one of the most effective methods for teaching management skills involving interactions between executives and subordinates.

Most management training, however, typically focuses on teaching skills to the superior, not to the subordinate. Since superior-

[3]M. Sorcher, and A.P. Goldstein, "A behavioral modeling approach in training," *Personnel Administration*, March–April 1972; A.P. Goldstein and M. Sorcher, *Changing Supervisor Behavior*. New York: Pergamon, 1974.

subordinate interactions involve two people, it makes a great deal more sense to train both parties to effectively handle their role in a discussion. Career discussions certainly fall within this framework.

Senior executives should ensure that they are trained to guide an aspiring chief through a career discussion. Both of them should feel that the conversation has accomplished their intentions for it. Similarly, senior executives should insist that aspiring chiefs learn how to initiate and contribute to a discussion about their own careers. With both sides trained, the discussion will be more useful for the aspiring chief and will provide the senior executive with more predictive information. Further, the career plans are much more likely to test what the senior executive needs to know.

Behavior Modeling

Behavior modeling training starts with a short film or videotape showing a manager following the learning points. The participants then practice career discussions with each other in a variety of simulated interactions, using the learning points as guides. An instructor and the participants critique and verbally reinforce good simulations of career discussions. Within about three hours, a group of 10−12 executives can learn to become very effective in handling a career discussion within a wide range of situations.

To illustrate the value of training both the senior executive and an aspiring chief, four examples are reconstructed from interviews with both senior executives and chief-aspirants after their career discussions. Two examples cover the discussions of individuals who have not been trained and two examples demonstrate what can be learned about a candidate for chief when both superior and subordinate have been trained.

Not Trained.   The first example is a career discussion initiated by Dan, a 43-year-old personnel executive, with Paul, his direct organizational superior, the human resources vice president of a multinational high-technology corporation. Dan was on the corporate staff of the company and highly regarded by his peers and his boss as an exceptionally competent manager. During the last year, his major priorities were to become more familiar with the union contracts and labor issues, revise the compensation plan for salaried employees, and become more familiar with areas of vulnerability to sex or age discrimination in each division of the corporation.

He was smart, knowledgeable, ambitious, and very likable. Dan knew Paul was going to retire in three years. Dan wanted to be absolutely sure that he would not lose out as Paul's replacement to one of two other well-regarded personnel executives. Dan decided to ask Paul about it. He made an appointment with Paul, but did not tell him what he wanted to discuss. As a result, Paul was not able to prepare for this conversation. He later wondered if Dan was unfair to him.

Dan: I've waited to talk to you about this but thought it best not to wait anymore. Frankly, I'm concerned about not having a specific timetable for my own career. I know that you talked about retiring in three years and I assume you are still planning on it. I'm also assuming that I am the most qualified guy to replace you. Can you tell me how you see the situation?

Paul: Look, Dan, you've caught me by surprise. Not that I'm surprised that you are interested in my job, but I really was not prepared to talk with you about it. At least not with a timetable or guarantee. What is it you want me to say?

Dan: Paul, I'm 43 years old. In three years I'm going to be 46. I think that beyond the age of 45 a person becomes less attractive to other companies because they won't have them as long as they would like. Some companies feel that the spark goes out when he's close to 50. Now I don't think so, but I know that other people do. I'm concerned about what will happen if I find myself in a situation where I am passed over for the job I am most prepared for and best qualified to do. I'm talking about the personnel VP of this company.

Paul: Dan, you know you're outstanding in my book. You are highly qualified, ambitious and would no doubt be good in the role. But I can't make any promises. You know that. In fact, I don't even make the decision. My boss does. You also know that. Of course, I make recommendations but he doesn't have to listen to me. He doesn't always.

Dan: Then I think I should talk to him. I know how things work around here and I know that the replacement decision is not made by the outgoing executive. But you can certainly influence his decision. You know me better than anybody does, certainly better than he does. You also know how I compare against the other two guys who may also be in the running for your job.

Paul: Hey, Dan, I have three years to go. I'm not a lame duck yet. Don't treat the situation like that. I know you want to know where you are going and when you are going to get there but I cannot give you a timetable. What you ought to be thinking about is how you can do your job so well that you'll impress everyone with your ability to do mine. If you let your impatience drive you, somebody is going to interpret it as immaturity.

Dan: Come on, Paul, that's not fair. You know what it's like when you're aiming for a tough goal and there is competition out there with you. I think I'm the best around but I want to be sure that others see it that way too.

Paul: I told you I know you're good. No one ever said anything different. But you've still got a lot to learn. That's why you're assigned to three tough projects.

Dan: Paul, I'm concerned about being passed over. If I am, that means I'll never have a shot at the personnel VP job again. I won't be happy staying at my level for the rest of my career. And it will be too late for me to go out and find a job in another company. I need a commitment.

Paul: Look, Dan, I understand how you feel, but you must understand my position. Let me tell you this. You are my first choice. If you continue to perform, I think you'll get the job. In fact, I'm pretty sure you will, but I can't give you a contract on that, you know that.

Dan: Thanks, I appreciate that. Suppose I talk to your boss to make sure he sees it that way too?

Paul: If you do, you'll put me on the spot. But that's up to you.

Dan: Well, you're putting me on a bigger spot. I've got to keep my options open.

Paul: What do you mean by that?

Dan: I don't know yet but I can't close my eyes to anything that may come along.

Paul: Of course, that's up to you. That would be a mistake.

Dan: Well, I guess that's all we can say about it now. I was hoping for something more specific.

Paul: I don't have a crystal ball. I can only tell you what I think should happen.

This was a very frustrating conversation for both Dan and Paul. Dan did not get the commitment he wanted and Paul lost confidence in Dan's maturity and perspective. Paul also felt that Dan was pushing him too hard and much too soon. He was even sorry he told Dan that he thought he would get the job, because he had some second-thoughts based on how Dan handled the conversation.

During the few months following this conversation, Paul kept some distance from Dan. Dan resented the coolness between them and decided that his chance of becoming the next personnel vice president was not as high as he originally had thought. It was evident to Paul that Dan was acting badly and he concluded that petulance was not a good quality for a personnel vice president, especially one who would have to lead the company's labor negotiations. Dan's aspirations to become a senior executive were derailed when he was at the threshold of a chief's door.

Trained.   The second example is a career discussion between Judy, an advertising vice president, and John, the president of a prestigious advertising agency. Judy was 38 years old and had been with the agency eight years. Her career with the agency was successful. She was very creative and maintained the confidence of all her clients. John respected her and wanted to be sure she continued to be productive.

Both John and Judy were trained in a company program to discuss careers with their supervisor and their subordinates. Two weeks after this training, John decided to take the initiative and have a career conversation with Judy. He wanted to be sure that she understood his confidence in her and that she continued to develop along the right track. John also wanted to find out if he should take a chance on giving Judy more responsibility. He knew she was devoted to her husband and children even though she had a strong need to work. She was outstanding at her work but he was unwilling to give her more responsibility if her business interests and time would be diluted by subordinating the demands of work to her private life. John admired Judy but was unwilling to broaden her scope unless he was convinced she really wanted to work harder. For this reason, John made an appointment with Judy and asked her to do some thinking about her objectives, the kind of experience she would like to get, and her sense of timing. Judy said she would be glad to do this and would get ready for the conversation, which they agreed to tape. An abbreviated transcript follows:

John: I thought it would be a good time for us to get together. I know that you're interested in your career and I am too. I've done some thinking about the kinds of things you're interested in. I've also done some thinking about your strengths and how you might capitalize on them in the future. [John used the learning points for a career discussion to guide his remarks.]

Judy: Thanks, John. I appreciate your willingness to do this. I've looked forward to this conversation and I've done some thinking about it as well.

John: Judy, why don't you tell me about the kinds of things you are thinking about, your own goals, what you see as alternative strategies towards your objectives, the timing of various steps, and whatever else you'd like to cover.

Judy talked at length about her career objective, that is, to be the senior creative executive in the agency. She also described why the title and responsibility were not enough. Judy said she wanted to bring in several specific clients in two industries that were not now represented in their agency. She showed a strong value-orientation for personal accomplishment and the satisfaction of teamwork with other executives. Judy said that if she could not reach that career objective within four years, she would look for a position as a marketing executive in one of the agency's client companies. She felt that this career alternative would offer her a good opportunity for working closely with others toward the accomplishment of challenging business objectives. John listened carefully and took notes on what she said. He was totally surprised at the clarity of her career objectives and her strong work-orientation.

John: Judy, that's very helpful to me. I was not aware that you wanted to reach that high. My impressions were that you were satisfied with your position and would not be interested in responsibility past the next executive level. I always thought that you were unwilling to go beyond that because I know how strongly you feel about maintaining a good balance with your home life. After all, raising children and being a wife are jobs by themselves. I'm glad to get better information then I assumed.

Judy: Well, I never thought much about it until we had the training on career discussions. That got me thinking and I realized that I could balance my personal and business life. I want to work and I want to take on more responsibility when I'm ready.

John: To move in the direction that you would like, let's talk about the ways in which you should be broadening your scope and deepening your abilities. After all, I'm not the only person you have to impress. For example, I think that two areas that you should spend some time in over the next year are. . . . [John described the areas in some detail because they would provide other answers to what he and the board would need to know about Judy before moving her up to senior management.]

Judy: Okay, I think that's a good idea. I can do that but I'll need your help to clear the way. For example, one problem will be . . . [Judy described a problem she anticipated].

John: I'll do everything I can to help. There may be some other obstacles in the way. One problem is the risk of distracting you from your primary responsibilities. You can't let down on those. I think that you should consider some ways to avoid distraction. Otherwise, you won't make your primary objectives and that won't help your credibility.

Judy: I think you're right. Let me think that one out and I'll come back to you with some ideas.

John: Judy, while you're thinking about that, think about some other ways in which I might be able to help you. This should not be the last time we talk about this and I would like to get together with you again in a month or so.

Judy: Okay.

John: My understanding of our discussion then, Judy, is that you are interested in the [senior account executive] job in the agency. That's a reasonable objective and you seem to have all the drive, interest, and basic talent to get there. You need to broaden your abilities in the areas we talked about and you've got to figure out a way to build your skills in these areas without diluting your major activities. Let's get together on the first of October and see where your thinking has taken you.

Judy: Okay, John. Thanks very much for your time and your interest. It makes me feel good and you know you can count on me. This has been a very encouraging discussion. It also made me think.

Note how John carefully followed the learning points for a career discussion. It is easy to do that and it made a tremendous difference in the outcome. Judy was also prepared for the discussion and was able to contribute actively to it. She had anticipated the questions and was prepared to discuss opportunities, obstacles, and a plan. Judy was able to focus on the issues in a way that made it easier for John to feel he had learned what he needed to know.

The president learned some things about Judy that he did not know previously. He got a better sense of her ambition and willingness to do what was needed to handle more responsibility. Importantly, he also understood that Judy was interested in more responsibility for reasons of personal accomplishment and for the satisfaction of working well with others. These are different values than, for example, wanting recognition from others or financial gain. Understanding Judy's values enabled John to have more confidence in his prediction of how she would handle herself in the job she was aiming for. If he did not know this, John said he would not have recommended her subsequently for that position even though she was talented and energetic.

Not Trained. Frank was the 45-year-old controller of his company's largest and most profitable division, which was grossing about $3 billion annually. He had a Wharton MBA and was experienced in all phases of financial management. Frank had a record of consistent accomplishment and was respected for his judgment even in the areas outside finance. He had been in his present job for three years. While Frank reported to his division manager, he had functional accountability to the corporate vice president for finance, Tom, who was also responsible for the career progress of the division controllers. Tom was 60 years old and had to prepare a successor to himself. Frank was one of several candidates he was considering. For this reason, he decided to talk to Frank about his career objectives and to learn more about him. He telephoned Frank and asked him to visit corporate headquarters. The conversation was reconstructed from interviews with both men a day after the discussion.

Frank: I'm glad to see you, Tom. We haven't talked for a while.

Tom: Frank, I wanted to get to know you better. In particular, I wanted to ask you about how you feel about your job and the company.

Frank: Boy, that comes out of left field. What's up? You know I like what I do and I like the company. I've always thought that I had a career here and I still think so.

Tom: Are we treating you right?

Frank: Of course you are. Naturally, I'm interested in my future. What's in store for me? I've been in my job for three years and it's a good job. I'm not learning anything more in it, however. I'm ready for new responsibility, but I'm not complaining.

Tom: What did you have in mind?

Frank: Well, to tell the truth, I'd like to come to corporate head-
         quarters. I can use some more exposure to the interna-
         tional side of things. I'm ready for a move, Tom.

Tom: You've only been in your job for three years. You still
         have a lot to learn.

Frank: Like what?

Tom: You need to learn more about leadership. Managing
         other people is more than just knowing about taxes and
         accounting. You have to get along with all levels of
         management.

Frank: What do you think I've been doing for these years? I know
         those things. Are you trying to tell me something?

Tom: No. I'm just telling you that you have some things to learn
         here. I also wanted to know how you saw things and what
         you thought might help you.

Frank: More exposure to corporate financial matters would help
         me most. I've been around a long time and I know the
         financial issues in the divisions like the back of my
         hands. I've handled a lot of tough problems and I haven't
         made any big mistakes. I've made very few mistakes. It's
         more than a lot of other people can say in my business.

Tom: That's probably true.

This conversation continued aimlessly for about an hour. When
Frank left Tom's office, he was puzzled about why Tom asked him to
stop by. He found the conversation to be particularly unsatisfying
and he wondered where he went wrong. On the other hand, Tom
didn't learn anything about Frank. In particular, he wanted to know
how well Frank would be able to influence the CEO and the board on
complex financial issues that required a lot of interpretation. He also
wanted to know whether Frank was strong enough to give functional
direction to the other division controllers, who were seasoned executives in their own right.

It was Tom's experience that the ability to influence upwards on
financial matters and assure compliance to corporate financial poli-

cies among the division controllers were the two things that mattered most in the position of corporate vice president of finance. After the discussion, Tom said that he did not learn much about Frank's ability to manage upwards and he did not understand why. This attempt at a discussion of career objectives provided the senior executive with absolutely no information on which to make a good prediction.

Trained.   Alan was vice president of marketing for a medium-sized company. He had been with the company for 16 years and in his present job for five years. He traveled worldwide about 50% of the time. The executive vice president of the company to whom Alan reported was going to another company as its president. Alan wanted to succeed him.

Alan was aware that the financial vice president, who previously had 10 years of solid marketing experience, was also a probable candidate for the position of executive vice president. In any case, Alan wanted to know where he stood because if he did not get that job, he thought he should look for opportunities in other companies. After a national sales meeting attended by Bob, the company's president, Alan asked Bob if they could spend some time talking about Alan's future in the company. Bob agreed and they scheduled a meeting.

Bob also told Alan that he hoped the training in career discussions given to all executives by a consultant would help them to have a constructive conversation. Alan said he would do everything possible to make it constructive. They also agreed to tape the conversation. An abbreviated transcript follows:

Alan: I appreciate your taking the time to talk with me about this. I know we were both trained to do this kind of thing, but I haven't done it yet. Maybe you have, so you have a head start on me.

Bob: No, I haven't either. You're my first one. Let's hope it works.

Alan: Well, I'm going to follow my learning points. But this time it isn't a role play.

Both men chuckled about the situation and Alan kidded Bob about role-playing, but it seemed to draw the tension from the situation.

Bob: Alan, I've done what I could to prepare for this discussion. I know you are interested in more responsibility and I assume you know there is going to be an open executive vice president position.

Alan: That's right. That's what I wanted to talk with you about. I am certain I can do that job. My whole background has prepared me for it. I've always gotten results, I know everyone in the company, and I think they respect me. I'm ready to take over when the job is vacant. I also know that you'll need to fill my job and I'm prepared to carry dual responsibility until you do. If you want my recommendation for the best choice for my job, Victor is far and away the best qualified. He can walk into it today and he'll be off to a running start. I have every confidence in him.

Bob: I understand that. Victor is good and he probably can do your job well. Are there any alternatives to Victor? Are there any other jobs in this company that interest you aside from the executive vice presient?

Alan: No. There is only one.

Bob: You know, Alan, we have a very active board. There are several key stockholders and our board does a lot to represent their interest. They also have some very definite ideas about the way things should be run in this company. The executive vice president is a logical successor to my job and it would help me if I knew what direction you would take the company in and what changes you would make.

Alan: [Alan described in detail his ideas about business opportunities and his vision for the company's growth. Bob asked him to explain the reasons behind each opinion and he arrived at his conclusions.]

Bob: That gives me a pretty good idea about your thoughts for this business. Tell me, how would you handle the situation if you continued to feel strongly about [Bob described an issue] and the board opposes you on it?

Bob was especially interested in whether Alan would depart from the personal and business principles he expressed when faced with the risk of conflict. He wanted to learn how Alan balanced expediency with principle. He also wanted to learn the limits of Alan's flexibility. Bob asked a lot of questions to probe these points. Alan answered Bob's questions in depth and seemed to be prepared for most of them.

Bob: I think you ought to learn more about the workings of the board and the projects assigned to me and to the executive vice president over the last two years. That will give you a better idea of the board's thinking and their expectations. I'll get that information to you. The reports are in my file. Is there any other information that you would like to help you understand the role and expectations for the executive vice president.

Alan: Not right now, I think those reports would help a lot.

Bob: Okay. Let me sum up our talk. You're interested in the executive vice president's job. I also have a much better idea of your vision of the business and how we ought to be working and what directions we ought to go in. I was especially interested in your observations about line extensions. Those are interesting ideas. After you have read the material I send down to you, let's discuss your reactions to it.

Bob felt he had learned a lot about Alan. He found him to be incisive, prepared, and single-minded about the executive vice president's job. Previously, Bob had thought that Alan enjoyed business traveling too much to give it up. In fact, Alan often took his wife and sometimes added on a few vacation days. Bib did not expect Alan would feel as strongly as he did about another job. Bob concluded that Alan's energy would be a fine asset and he predicted that Alan would put new life into the company's operational leadership. On the other hand, Alan knew how to convey his objectives and was confident enough to initiate this difficult conversation with his company's president.

CAREER PLANNING

Career planning for potential senior executives should be based on the *behaviors* that will most probably be predictive of effectiveness in even more responsible positions. In their book on organizational behavior, Wexley and Yukl[4] discuss leadership. Their perspective sums up much of the research in this area:

> After the failure of the trait approach was realized in the early part of the 1950s, many leadership researchers began to study leader behavior (what leaders do) instead of leader traits (what leaders are). Leader behavior can be related more directly to the process of leadership and the requirements of a managerial position than can abstract traits. Also, a behavioral approach is more consistent with the discovery that leadership can be shared by several members of a group and does not necessarily have to be concentrated in a single person.[5]

On the same topic, Campbell said:

> Planning is a matter of probabilities, which means that sometimes your plans will turn out and sometimes they won't—you will save yourself a lot of grief by realizing that sooner rather than later. Nothing is a sure thing, and any plans that you make for the future have to deal with uncertainty. Once you realize that, several other conclusions are apparent. First, there are probably things you can do to raise your probabilities for success. Second, you had better have some alternatives in case your first plan doesn't work out. Third, any given plan can fail, and you had best prepare for that possibility.[6]

Career planning must account for behavior as well as probabilities. Both senior executive and subordinate executive should assure that this is the case so that predictions or expectations about future success are less assumptive and better directed. A Citicorp senior executive suggests the following framework to career planning:

[4]K.N. Wexley, and G.A. Yukl, *Organizational Behavior and Personnel Psychology.* Homewood, Ill.: Irwin, 1977.
[5]*Ibid,* p. 145.
[6]Campbell, *op. cit.,* p. 32.

My basic advice would boil down to: identify an area where you really have an interest, because that's probably going to be the area where you'll do your best and most effective work.

When I think of traits that will help throughout a career, I would say the first one is curiosity—to find out why something is, how something works, and where the pieces come together. Because if you don't have the basic curiosity, it is very hard to come up with improvements, or to integrate your knowledge, or to really stand out for an unusual contribution.

Second, I really admire a high standard of excellence. I admire the craftsmen who can make a beautiful piece of furniture—or perform with the American Ballet Theatre, for that matter—because they represent a high level of achievement as opposed to just being satisfied with a passable approach.

The third trait I'd mention is to be an effective team player. In any large organization, there are a range of jobs, some heavily dependent on the cooperation of others, some less so, but all to some degree dependent. There isn't the real world validation of the notion of being absolutely brilliant or absolutely creative if there is no way to communicate with, and collaborate with, your fellow man.

That's not a special statement about Citicorp or about business generally. The people who really contributed to this world have all been people who have not only brought something special, but also delivered it to the rest of mankind.

— 5 —

Testing Potential Candidates for the Chief Position

CASTING FOR THE ROLE

Those responsible for finding potential chiefs are quiet about their work. They do not dress in hunting clothes to impress others with the seriousness of their work or wear high boots to wade through tall tales. They do not carry maps or airline schedules because they generally do not have specific itineraries and they are not even sure where they ought to go. They never take a sleeping bag because they do not stay long enough to sleep anywhere. They do not carry binoculars because they do not want to give a clue that they are looking for someone. They conduct their search sometimes casually, often surreptitiously, rarely candidly, hardly ever systematically, but their mind is always on the prowl. More than anything else, they are casting agents—but for some reason they never think of themselves this way.

The analogy is a good one. Selectors of chiefs know the part they want filled. They understand what it should accomplish in the scenario. They can describe the different facets of the main character, and they know how the main character must relate with the other actors. The actor must have presence and convey the substance of the script. Most of all, the main actor must play his or her part in a way that people will pay to see him or her in it. If the main actor is weak, it will be difficult for the production to be successful. For a play to be successful, people must buy the product conceived and staged by its financial backers. Good casting is crucial, and those responsible for it must take great care in the tryouts.

MANAGERS OR LEADERS?

The wanderings of corporate casting agents take them down different roads. The crossroads have signs and the signs are sometimes not even noticed or often ignored. There is one sign, however, that should never be ignored. It says, "Go this way to find a manager and that way to find a leader." Abraham Zaleznik, of Harvard University, has so clearly drawn a difference between managers and leaders that the selectors of chiefs and aspiring chiefs will find immense value in examining his article[1] on the topic. Zaleznik's conceptual framework is very useful to position the testing of candidates for senior executive positions.

Zaleznik suggests that controlling and directing work and relationships in an organization is not the same as using imagination or creativity to move a company from one place to another. According to him, the perspectives of managers are determined by the traditions of the past while the perspectives of leaders are developed from their desires and their images of the future. Managers seek to limit risks while leaders look for opportunities where the rewards are as high as the risk:

> For some, especially those who become managers, the instinct for
> survival dominates their need for risk and the ability to tolerate

[1] Abraham Zaleznik, "Managers and Leaders: Are They Different?" in Harvard Business Review (Executive Book Series), *Executive Success*, pp. 123–139. New York, John Wiley & Sons, 1983.

mundane, practical work assists their survival. The same cannot
be said for leaders who sometimes react to mundane work as an
affliction.[2]

The following comparisons between leaders and managers is based
on Zaleznik's article and an article by Craig Watson. These comparisons provide an excellent framework for setting up ways to test and
evaluate potential chiefs:[3]

Relations with Others

Manager	Leader
Relates to others according to their role.	Relates in more intuitive and empathic way.
Prefers high probability of winning and low probability of losing.	Willing to risk losing if rewards for winning are high.
Communicates to subordinates indirectly, using signals instead of message.	Communicates directly.
Plays for time.	Impatient.
Perceived by others as inscrutable, detached, manipulative.	Attracts strong feelings of identity.
Conserves what is traditional and current.	Exerts influence in altering moods and expectations, in establishing specific desires and objectives.

Goals

Goals arise out of necessities.	Goals arise out of desires.
Goals are deeply imbedded in history and culture of organization.	Goals focus on need for change.

[2] *Ibid.*
[3] *Ibid.* See also Craig Watson, "Leadership, Management and the Seven Keys,"
The McKinsey Quarterly, Autumn 1983, pp. 44–52.

Goals

Manager	Leader
Impersonal and passive attitudes toward goals.	Personal and active attitudes toward goals.
Strategy assumes more importance than goal.	Strategy is the means to a goal.
Identifies threats and opportunities.	Defines superordinate goals such as product leadership or being #1.
Focuses on strategy, structure, systems.	Focuses on style, staff, skills, shared goals.

Conceptions of Work

Continues things, tradition.	Seeks change, new ideas.
Instinct for survival dominates their need for risk.	Seeks risk where opportunity and reward is high.
Acts to limit choices.	Act to open issues for new options.
Needs to coordinate and balance continually; aims at shifting balances of power toward solutions acceptable as a compromise among conflicting values.	Develops fresh approaches to long-standing problems; project ideas into images to excite people.
Delegates cautiously.	Delegates freely; faith in people.
Analytical, methodical.	Intuitive.
Maintains control over ideas, prefers to manage people and process.	Encourages entrepreneurial autonomy.
Reactive to ideas, responds to them.	Active instead of reactive, shapes ideas.
Cautious continuity of current or known methods.	Changes the way people think about what is possible, desirable, necessary.

Sense of Self

Manager	Leader
Identifies totally with organization.	Works in organizations but don't belong to them.
Conservator and regulator of events and things.	Change agent, excites people and arouses and mobilizes expectations—without which new thinking or new choice can never come to life.

Why Some Tests Fail

Zaleznik's observations may in large part account for why some executives rise to fairly high levels in a company but then surprise their chiefs because they are unable to provide the required leadership. The processes of developing business strategies, dividing responsibilities, dispassionately balancing the different needs of people who do the work, and negotiating differences of opinion among them, *are psychologically different* from trying to excite people with a new idea, communicate the advantages to them, and urge their personal involvement and sharing of risk.

Chairmen and presidents often look for successors who have both courage and intellect. Because of the accomplishments of many executives, they are given opportunities to do new things which require more of leadership than management—and they often do not come up to expectations for leaders. If chiefs expect their successors to behave more like Zaleznik's notion of leaders than managers, then it is essential to test them in these dimensions before going too far in the preparation of the wrong executives.

Search for a Leader

It is interesting to consider these dimensions in the context of one search for a CEO—the 1980 selection of the CEO of Rubbermaid Inc. What is so remarkable is the match between the characteristics desired for the CEO position and the qualities of the man selected, Stanley C. Gault. While Gault is one of the most highly respected

CEOs in the United States, perhaps more than anything Rubbermaid found a CEO with great personal flexibility to support his business acumen. As reported in *The Wall Street Transcript* (May 31, 1982), he addressed the company's weaknesses with depth of intellect, speed, and diversity of action. The article reports that

> Gault has produced higher earnings for Rubbermaid by pruning unpromising operations, making an astute acquisition . . . and taking advantage of the recent dip in petrochemical prices to increase margins on Rubbermaid's plastic and rubber products.

The article also quotes an industry analyst:

> The company had just got to a crossroads and had to be run as a larger corporation than a small business. Stan is perfect for that.

Fortunately for Rubbermaid, the selection committee responsible for finding a new CEO knew how to cast the difficult part.

EXAMINING THE CYCLE OF ACCOMPLISHMENT

Progress through the corporate structure depends upon accomplishments which are recognized by the addition of responsibility. At various points in their careers, potential candidates for senior executive positions are judged on how they have managed their responsibilities. The central piece of these judgments is how well they have met their personal objectives and how well their organization has met its goals. Since most companies set objectives on an annual basis, there is plenty of evidence over two or three years to determine consistency of performance.

Those chiefs who observe and judge performance are almost never aware, however, of the full impact of a potential chief's management or leadership style. They are buffered from that by organizational distance, inadequate sources of information, and subordinates who do not like to communicate unattractive characteristics or unpleasant information about potential chiefs who are meeting their business goals. Some potential chiefs reach organizational goals but create such a threatening or disapproving climate that the best people leave and only the mediocre remain. For example, in some situations, goals are sometimes reached because of an aspiring chief's tenacity and his willingness to drive people so hard that they would quit if they could find other jobs. In other situations, a potential chief brings in results for several years but his organization begins to fall apart from the pressure he puts on it. At these times, the critics speak out—but they are too late.

As potential chiefs show continued success with meeting objectives, they are recognized for their results with added compensation, praise, opportunities to take on even more responsibility, and promotions. Unfortunately, this accomplishment-recognition-more opportunity-promotion cycle does not fully account for the difference between good management and good leadership. In fact, the cycle predicts that good leaders automatically emerge from good managers—but they do not consistently do so.

Too many chiefs who select other senior executives assume that the management of people and resources is the same as leadership. It is not. Leadership characteristics, however, are not always better than management abilities. Both are required to be an effective chief. A wise leader is usually aware of his management shortcomings and he builds his staffs to insure the inclusion of good management practices.

This cycle falls apart for many executives who are good managers but poor leaders. The cycle of good leadership is manifested by successful innovation, a cohesive management team, and enthusiastic self-assurance at all levels—in addition to meeting business goals. These symptoms are readily observable if a chief takes the time to look for them. They are not present in a cycle of accomplishment that is about to slow down.

WHEN THE CYCLE SLOWS DOWN

Two reasons probably account for most of the slowdown in the accomplishment-recognition-promotion cycle for an executive: (1) the inability to manage one's image, and (2) the inability to be more than a conservator of a company's resources.

The first involves inattention to developing an image which one's chief will approve. The second involves the failure to broaden accomplishments from the management of people and resources to include the exercise of leadership, that is, leadership to excite, create, demonstrate courage, explore, and apply new ideas. Senior executives who are involved in succession planning, and those who aspire to become a chief, should be very sensitive to these two ways of interrupting the cycle.

The following examples of disappointment from two U.S. headquartered corporations are interesting because they involve different reasons for failing the test for eventual CEO candidacy. The selectors in each case ignored the signs that could have protected their companies against the problems created during the testing of the CEO candidate. Further, both organizations were subsequently deprived of the considerable talent of these executives. One executive resigned in anger and the other stayed in the company but turned his back on work.

The First Situation: Managing Impatience

Poor Judgment.   In the first situation, a general manager in a high technology engineering company had a history of fast promotions based on the high profits and technological advances of the operations he managed. The executive was an articulate and ambitious man in his middle forties. As a general manager, his ability to assimilate complex information quickly and take his organization to its next success was noticed by the top two or three people in his company. In business review meetings with his organizational superiors, he was outspoken and did not hesitate to criticize the corporate culture for its conservatism and unwillingness to use its great resources in other fields of opportunity. When challenged by his boss to support his dissident opinion, he produced folders of carefully organized material and reports to add credibility to his position. The information was so well-organized that it was difficult to refute. It was clear that this potential chief was very smart, could run a profitable business, and was willing to take some risk.

The chairman of the board and CEO of the company was advised of this executive's management ability and progressive opinions. He arranged for the executive to put on a business review for him, covering the previous three years with special focus on projects for the next five years. The executive not only showed how his own management decisions brought the business far forward in three years, but he described in great detail an exciting array of alternatives for growth in all parts of the company over the next five years. Further, the executive went through the organizational charts of key management in each part of the corporation and indicated who should be given more responsibility for handling some of these new ideas and who should be removed because of their inertia or obsolescence.

The chairman concluded that the executive was indeed a man of vision, conviction, and ability. In fact, he decided to give him more responsibility to begin to test him as his potential successor. He arranged for the executive to be promoted within three months. The promotion included responsibility for a large piece of the technical development business. After two years, the potential chief had significantly accelerated technical development to the point where the work force was having difficulty keeping up with contractual obligations. Business was very good.

At subsequent business review meetings, this executive became even more vocal and candid about the direction that the company should take. His somewhat flamboyant personal style spilled over into interpersonal interactions with executive colleagues, and they bristled at it. Nevertheless, his business vision could not be faulted.

At about the time he felt he was the most probable successor to the chairman of the board, his candor took a more critical tone regarding the corporation's leadership. Most of the criticism was personalized and directed at the most senior executives in the company, including the chairman.

Backlash.   The chairman was angry at the executive's occasional rude manner in meetings. Also, the chairman was told about the critical remarks, At first, he felt that he did not want to interfere with somebody who was doing so well. After a time, however, despite his confidence in the business acumen of this candidate for chief, the chairman confronted him and insisted that he stop his attacks on the leadership of the company. The candidate for chief was barely apologetic, repeating his opinion that the company needed more progressive leadership and that there was no time for delay. In fact, he counted on the company's board of directors to shield him from any adverse reaction that the chairman might want to take. He even thought that raising the issue like this at the board level would hasten his promotion.

In his discussion with the board, the chairman pointed out that the candidate for chief had certainly been successful, but at great cost to the company. Too many of his bright executives had left for other companies because they felt overwhelmed by him. His businesses were run by equally ambitious and aggressive individuals who were changing the character of the company from a reputable image to one that was looking for "big hits." The chairman summed up his position with the board by saying that this formerly very promising candidate for chief had shown that he would not run the company the way that had made it successful.

Disappointment. The candidate for chief was advised by the chairman that he would receive no further promotions in the company and that in the future he had better express his views about its operations in ways that were less likely to generate nonproductive dissent. Shortly after, the former candidate for chief resigned. It is of interest to note that he has moved several times since his resignation.

Prediction. The chairman could have predicted the behavior of the executive based on the way he operated as a general manager. While it would have been inappropriate to stifle him, it would have been appropriate to counsel him about the difference between the management role of the general manager and the implications of visibility and personal impact of an even more senior executive. The major reason why the cycle of accomplishment-recognition-opportunity slowed down for this executive was because he did not recognize the difference between managing people and resources versus managing his image. Based on this executive's behavior and comments when he was a general manager, it should have been easy to predict his behavior when his actions were reinforced by promotion. Anticipating this might have saved an action-oriented, progressive senior executive for the company.

The Second Situation: The Wrong Management Style

Bureaucracy. In the second situation, a brilliant, aggressive Ph.D.-trained scientist in a chemical and plastics company found early in his career that he could accomplish more if he could manage the work of others instead of just his own projects. He showed a lot of interest in the other projects in his organization and made concrete suggestions for their improvement, even when he had no responsibility for them. His ability to quickly reorganize resources and people to get a better focus on problems was noticed by senior management. The general manager spoke highly of the scientist at human resources review meetings and recommended the scientist as his successor. When the general manager was promoted to another organization, the scientist became the general manager.

As general manager, he reorganized the entire operation. He changed roles, responsibilities, and goals. He became intimately familiar with the projects of each part of his organization. When a conflict came up between subordinate executives, he arbitrated the issues and negotiated between parties until a compromise agreement was reached. He was also determined to maintain the company's traditions of hard work, absolute loyalty to one's management, never exceeding the budget for operating expenses, and endorsing the theory that "cream rises to the top" (i.e., the opinion that people do not have to be given experiences to help them to develop because if they have the ability to grow, they will do it without help).

For several years, this general manager ran a business that turned in healthy profits. He was invited to business review meetings at the company's corporate headquarters and he made an impression with his sense of urgency and dedication to efficient management. His record resulted in his name being added to a list of candidates for the corporate presidency.

To test him further, he was promoted to a position which gave him responsibility for the corporate acquisitions activities. This corporate group was comprised of top-flight specialists in law, finance, marketing, and the physical sciences. The objective of this group was to find small companies, ideas, or products that could be acquired and grown into large businesses. When he moved into his new office, the candidate set up a series of meetings with his new staff to review their current work and plans.

Two weeks after these briefing meetings, he called a meeting of his entire staff and asked for their help in reorganizing their work to set up better priorities. While the staff did not necessarily agree with the need to change priorities, they cooperated fully with him. The reorganization was an exercise in participative management. Every function was required to formally approve an acquisitions project before it could go beyond the very early exploratory stage.

Taking Out the Fun. Participative management, however, does not preclude conflicting objectives within a group. The candidate for chief arbitrated these differences. Compromise after compromise was reached. Good acquisitions prospects became scarce because everybody felt that they could no longer follow their hunches without the consensus of all the functions of the acquisitions group. They agreed only on the safest prospects, all of which had very little room to grow into large business entities. Within one year, the morale of the acquisition staff was so low that they made jokes about hiring a staff comedian to cheer them up at the end of each day.

When the corporation's top management (president and chief operating officer (COO)) inquired about the acquisitions' prospects, they learned that the executive's careful management style was responsible for its inactivity. The COO personally met with several of the more senior acquisitions staff and learned that the group was managed more as a democratic bureaucracy than as a group of curiosity-seeking, treasure-hunting, opportunistic professionals. This was clearly attributed to the executive managing the group.

Unfortunately for the scientist-general manager, neither the COO nor the president agreed that this style of managing, which was well-suited to running many of the company's on-going businesses, was suited for an executive whose function should be to lead a corporation in new directions with vision and self-assurance. This executive was subsequently transferred to head the company's new research center. For this company, the plan to test a potential chief in an aspect of a role similar to that required of an actual chief revealed a characteristic that would have been very damaging if it was not detected.

In both the cases outlined, the self-fulfilling prophecy of accomplishments leading to an expectation of continued success was interrupted—in one instance almost accidentally and in the other consciously. The illusions of self-fulfilling prophecies are potentially too dangerous to be left to accidental exposure. They must be deliberately tested.

COMPARING BEHAVIOR AGAINST VALUES

When an executive's behavior pattern departs from the company's principles or values, it suggests a willingness for expediency that should be fully explored. Certainly, a large or continuing gap between the principles a company stands for and the behavior of an executive raises questions about personal integrity.

Most companies identify strongly with certain values or principles, which they express as beliefs or goals. For example, one category of value centers on a company's products or services, such as products which are the epitome of quality or the leading edge of technology; other categories of values might be responsive customer service or meeting the health or safety needs of people. Perhaps the most important category of values is the one that centers on the management of people or the ways of working and interacting in a company. Examples of such values include: the amount of responsibility or confidence delegated; an emphasis on creativity or risk; a willingness to depart from tradition; responding to minority or subordinate opinions; concern for the self-esteem of employees; and the career development of employees.

One of the first things that ought to be done when planning to test an individual's potential to be a chief is reviewing the values or principles communicated by the company—explicitly or implicitly—to its customers and employees. The potential chief's behaviors should be reviewed in light of each of these values. Current and past supervisors and performance appraisals are often a good source of this information. Specific examples, however, must be sought because it is too easy to generalize or assume without facts to support a conclusion. Halo effects can cause misrepresentation. It is sometimes helpful to get help from a staff specialist or consultant in the process of comparing or identifying personal behavior for its congruence with company values. Guidance of this sort will guard against conclusions which are not adequately supported by evidence.

An illustration is the case of a company that expressed great support for innovation and career growth for employees. A manager who had a strong record of accomplishment and was well-liked by his organizational superiors because of it, would be an obvious candidate for senior executive levels. The test of value-behavior comparison was not applied. If it was, it would have been apparent that this manager was not suited for a senior executive position because of his opposition to career planning; he believed that companies have no responsibility to help employees develop in their careers.

Without the compatibility of personal and corporate values, corporate leadership cannot be effective. Corporate chiefs should urge systematic comparisons of individual behavior, based on a pattern of examples, with company values.

HOW LARGE CORPORATIONS TEST POTENTIAL CHIEFS

Corporations use a variety of methods to test the candidacy of potential senior executives. Three characteristics of the testing processes are common to most organizations:

1. The testing is primarily experiential, typically based on what an individual has achieved in progressively more responsible management roles (but not usually leadership roles).

2. The testing is not systematic or even planned much in advance for an individual; in most companies the predictive goal of the testing is often missed because the testing is based on what an individual is doing in a current position instead of what the corporation needs to know about him or her.

3. Criteria which are dependably predictive are rarely used; when criteria are used, they take the form of a checklist more than a set of operationally specific behaviors that fully describe dimensions such as business judgment, personal effectiveness, the nature and scope of intellect and integrity.

Most corporate chiefs and executives responsible for succession planning agree that better guidelines are needed for the succession process. They are especially concerned about the identification and adequate testing procedures at lower organizational levels because they have little or no control over the process. Senior executives in companies noted for sophisticated succession planning systems vary in their opinions about how well their processes generate promising candidates for chief. Within the same company, but in different divisions, attention to the testing of potential chiefs ranges from casual to compulsive. In one large computer company, the corporate staff executive responsible for succession planning feels that they test potential chiefs in so many situations that these executives are over-exposed. The problem, he says, is that "they are substantially stronger than they appear. Nobody is without soft areas and our testing yields so much information that we sometimes run into trouble."

Conversations with the CEOs and other senior executives in different industries revealed some extreme differences on testing for chief potential. Some focus on moving a number of individuals to different positions under different managers, others focus on only a handful of people. Some companies test candidates in a functional funnel—a series of steps in an area of functional expertise such as finance or engineering. Other companies transfer individuals across functions and depend on support staffs and outside programs to provide functional expertise. The common theme across all the companies and all the phases of testing is how well the potential chief can organize and motivate a cohesive team. Some of the most typical testing practices are described by several corporate CEO's and other senior executives as follows:

A Utility Company—Long before a person becomes an officer we intentionally give him many job opportunities. We want to see how he supervises. We don't always groom somebody for a top job in his area, either. When somebody [a senior executive] leaves a job, we often don't move his back-up into the job but we will make a cross-functional pick—for example, customer service to engineering or taxation to finance or any of these to each other. We let them supervise early. We move people quickly into key jobs in areas they're not trained in—and we send them to banks or universities that run courses in their new areas. We also bring people along to sit in on meetings for somebody they're probably going to replace although they may not know it.

A Hi-Tech Company—We have a program of early identification for the target of general manager positions. Our approach is multiple-filtered. We look at 8–10 dimensions and collect critical incidents in each (i.e., examples to illustrate behavior patterns in a dimension). The dimensions include strategic planning, decision making and interpersonal leadership with examples of positively-anchored behaviors.

Another set of filters we use are the Strong-Campbell (a vocational interest test) and a biographical index. A third filter is the assessment center and the fourth filter is a review of all previous filters.

All material is reviewed by a committee of officers who review 40 or 50 people annually. Less than a quarter of them make it through this filter.

One of the things we have is a preoccupation with cognitive functioning—people who are extremely bright—but we caution people on that because extreme brightness may be a problem.

Right now we're changing from a highly centralized review and testing process, because it bogs us down, and we're giving operating divisions primary responsibility and complete freedom for developing their own identification and testing processes. The corporate management development staff will provide succession planning guidance.

A Computer Company—Our early identification scheme gives people a high dose of accountability working for a manager that is highly respected. People are also given exposure to subsidiaries of our company but most of the testing comes out of interaction with people whose judgment is respected, like general managers and heads of subsidiaries.

We also have a corporate committee comprised of our most senior executives who have a great deal of knowledge about certain people and they will recommend or sponsor people who might otherwise not be considered for jobs of general manager and above. The pattern we try to look for, because it is pretty predictive of our successful top executives, is a tremendous commitment to a career and a strong work orientation. We often find these people have had uneven personal and academic backgrounds—broken families or financial difficulties when they were young—which caused them to learn and cope with the self-assurance to manage problems and develop the abilities to operate autonomously.

This process is also making women more visible.

A Photographic Equipment Company—We've only had this in effect for four or five years but what we try to do is move them from one area to another, to different but related functions like engineering to manufacturing, but still under the same operating vice-president. They're tested to do the job and judged in comparison to how other people have done the job. The problem is that we get a rating of an individual but it depends on the chemistry of the rater and the ratee.

But the biggest reason that the testing isn't working out well is over-rating, especially of very articulate people who make good presentations. They get rated higher than the individual who is equally good or better but may not communicate as well. Our testing favors the quick-tongued—which is why I think assessment centers may help.

An International Bank—The people responsible for deciding who and how to test for the most senior positions are the chairman, vice-chairman, and president. For other senior positions, the heads of our two major operating departments are included.

The process is fairly loose and informal. The criteria are principally in-depth knowledge of banking and conclusions based on observations of a person's success over a period of time. But the banks are fairly clique-ish and some people don't fit in. We look for people who are very smart financially, socially polished and who communicate well.

We move a very small number of people around to different areas to test them. We put them in an alien environment under a different manager. We're only testing four or five people for senior executive positions at any one time. If they have a high degree of success, they're protected in the future and regarded as a prime candidate for our most senior positions. Our thrust is carrying forward a select and small number of people.

For the rest of the people, very little is done except within their own departments. They are cared for primarily by the department heads and very little thought is given to beyond where they are now. We try to keep them happy with growth inside their department and maybe some outside courses.

One of the things we look for when we test are the individual's interpersonal skills and whether they are able to build and motivate a team of winners. Some people who are technically very bright and able to handle complex financial matters lack the intelligence to handle people well.

People who aspire to be a senior executive in the bank must demonstrate that they can produce earnings for the bank— client success. This requires them to demonstrate interpersonal skills and canniness. It is drive, initiative and creativity that does it, not sheer brilliance.

Typical among people who don't make it through the testing are individuals who are very bright but can't manage people at high levels. We've also been blinded by the ability of people to manage financial matters and we push them up the ladder without testing them. They fail because they can't manage people. Another common failure is the executive who has been brought along and promoted beyond his capacity by another executive who moves up. Lack of history or experience with people accounts for a lot of failures because we haven't tested them in the right jobs.

A Clothing Company—We've not been able to figure out how to avoid the Peter Principle where you promote people into jobs they can't handle. We make a lot of mistakes and need to find a better way of testing.

A Communications Company—When selecting a potential chief, we want to test him or her to see if it will work out. We look for mental ability and self-objectivity. I'm also surprised at how many managers are as inflexible as they are, particularly if they're successful. If they've got a strategy or way of working, they usually won't change it. We've got to find out in a test.

CRITERIA AND WHAT YOU NEED TO KNOW (OR SHOW)

Checklists.   Some companies have put together an extensive list of personal characteristics and management abilities which they use as criteria to test whether an individual is good enough to be a candidate for chief. Senior executives responsible for these decisions review each candidate against the list. If an individual is not perceived to possess a desirable quality such as leadership ability, executive caliber (which is usually not defined further), or tough-mindedness (which is often a euphemism for a high degree of skepticism or an unwillingness to consider opinions which are not in the mainstream of corporate thrust), he or she is removed from consideration. Often, these decisions are as arbitrary as the criteria. A major problem of checklists is that the terms used as criteria are often defined differently by different raters, thereby minimizing the validity or predictability of the rating process.

Most aspiring chiefs are familiar with criteria of this kind. Many executives find it to be an easy way to describe somebody because it usually involves checking a box. The process is not much more than a placebo for anxiety about management succession decisions.

Other companies use their lists of criteria to make development recommendations, especially for individuals who are still viewed as potential chiefs. Often, these attempted remedial actions are shallow. For example if an executive is judged to be a good candidate for chief but lacks necessary communication skills, an oral presentation course is recommended. If an executive is rated as outstanding in most respects except for aggressiveness, an assertive training program is recommended. No thought is given to the reasons why communication skills fall short or why an individual may be insufficiently aggressive.

There are reasons for personal or performance inadequacies that cannot be corrected in a training program. Besides, by the time an executive is considered to be a candidate for chief, selectors should not be confronted with individuals who have shortfalls that can be corrected by formal training. Staffs involved in early identification and management development should have screened for these behaviors and skills earlier in a potential chief's career.

Questions. Questions, instead of checklists, should be used to raise issues about candidates for chief. The answers should be based on the evidence extracted from reliable observations and information, not on hearsay or second-hand opinions, no matter how credible the source. Further, the answers should provide two kinds of information: (1) a specific description, including examples, of a level of performance or nature of behavior; and (2) a list of those aspects of performance or behavior about which there is a need to know more (e.g., a candidate for chief may be personally creative but there is a need to know whether he or she can maintain a climate for innovation on the part of others), or a candidate for chief may have a strong record of accomplishment but there is a need to know if he or she can motivate an executive team to perform well when there are unusual business pressures on him or her. Using this method, the predictability of information about candidates is largely determined by the specificity of the questions and the articulation of what selectors need to know.

An example of the questions used effectively by a consumer goods company illustrates how questions can provide information that gives reliable direction for testing the candidates for chief. It is also apparent that the focus is on actual performance, not on assumed ability or potential. Judgments about a candidate's potential for chief are made after performance and behavior descriptions are obtained and the need to know issues are identified. Table 5-1 outlines this information.

Sample of Behavior Observations.

It is easy to be behaviorally specific about performance. It is probably easier and less time-consuming to accurately describe an individual than it is to find words to soften, shape, suggest, disguise, or intimate what an observer actually sees. Specificity in performance appraisals was covered in Chapter 3. This section focuses on behavior relevant to leadership, not on the accomplishment of assigned projects or tasks.

Executives who write descriptions of potential chiefs might ask themselves, "What do I mean by that?" and "How do I know?" and then submit the answers to those questions. Examples of more specific and useful statements than the original ones have been taken from actual descriptions of potential candidates for chief:

Less Useful Information	More Useful Information
The candidate does not delegate well.	The candidate does not manage his organization through others and consequently his standards are not conveyed to his immediate staff. He gives assignments and instructions directly to more junior managers and his immediate staff spends too

Table 5-1. Need to Know

	Demonstrated Competence at a Superior Level in Current or Past Assignments	Indicate what Development Steps are Needed Based on Current or Past Performance	Not Demonstrated or Observed
Operating Results			
Describe performance against financial objectives for each of the past three years; refer to obstacles, accomplishments, and lack of accomplishment which could have been controlled more effectively.			
Commercial Know-How			
How does the individual:			
Serve as a resource person to whom others in top management go for advice?			
Answer even the most difficult business questions soundly and fully?			

Table 5-1. (Continued)

Demonstrated Competence at a Superior Level in Current or Past Assignments	Indicate what Development Steps are Needed Based on Current or Past Performance	Not Demonstrated or Observed
Keep informed of the latest developments in business area?		
Translate technical or business knowledge into practical, workable projects or plans?		
Planning & Organizing		
Does the individual:		
Formulate effective policies and priorities?		
Monitor his progress toward objectives and adjust plans as necessary to reach them?		
Take all available information into account when making decisions?		

Set a clear course of action for himself or herself?

Set a clear course of action for others?

Plan ahead to anticipate obstacles and contingencies?

Allocate and schedule resources to assure that they will be available when needed?

Establish reviews and follow-ups and monitor these carefully?

Accomplishment

Does the individual:

Accept challenging assignments and added responsibilities willingly?

Seek challenging assignments and responsibilities?

Strive to achieve organizational objectives beyond what is expected or required?

Table 5-1. *(Continued)*

	Demonstrated Competence at a Superior Level in Current or Past Assignments	Indicate what Development Steps are Needed Based on Current or Past Performance	Not Demonstrated or Observed
Push persistently to overcome difficult obstacles?			
Motivate others to accomplish independently of him?			
Organization Commitment			
Does the individual:			
Identify with the company's overall goals and objectives?			
Offer constructive criticism about policies and decisions formulated by higher management?			
Support the policies and actions of top management?			
Abide by organizational rules and policies?			

Comply with directives and preferences of top management?

Refrain from criticizing (in a backbiting way) viewpoints and individuals in top management when they differ?

Communication

Does the individual:

Communicate ideas and opinions in a clear and concise manner?

Share information required by other units of the organization to achieve their objectives?

Disseminate complete information to others of company policies and objectives?

Provide complete, reliable, and prompt information to superiors?

133

Table 5-1. *(Continued)*

Demonstrated Competence at a Superior Level in Current or Past Assignments	Indicate what Development Steps are Needed Based on Current or Past Performance	Not Demonstrated or Observed
Report progress towards objectives and organizational issues truthfully?		
Organizational Acumen		
Does the individual:		
Seek further knowledge about the operations of other organizational units in the company as a whole?		
Maintain a smooth working relationship with associates in other organizational units?		
Coordinate effectively the efforts of several units to achieve overall objectives with maximum efficiency?		

Training of Subordinates

Does the individual:

Assure the proper orientation and training of new employees?

Guide and assist subordinates?

Recommend or develop training to meet subordinates' needs?

Follow subordinates' progress in their training and development?

Have a good track record for developing other executives?

Delegation to Subordinates

Does the individual:

Show an appropriate willingness to delegate?

Table 5-1. *(Continued)*

Demonstrated Competence at a Superior Level in Current or Past Assignments	Indicate what Development Steps are Needed Based on Current or Past Performance	Not Demonstrated or Observed
Schedule and assign work among subordinates for maximum efficiency?		
Assign tasks to subordinates commensurate with their experience and abilities?		
Provide clear and complete instructions and explanations to subordinates when giving assignments?		
Monitor subordinates' performance closely enough to assure managerial control?		
Motivation of Subordinates		
Does the individual:		
Establish challenging assignments and objectives for subordinates?		

Encourage them to reach high standards of quality and quantity?

Give them stimulating assignments which stretch their capabilities?

Set an example of diligence, dedication, and organizational concern?

Address problems of inadequate or marginal performance promptly and directly with the individual(s) involved.

Developing Subordinates

Does the individual:

Conduct regular performance appraisals with subordinates?

Provide subordinates with performance feedback during or immediately following a major assignment?

137

Table 5-1. *(Continued)*

	Demonstrated Competence at a Superior Level in Current or Past Assignments	Indicate what Development Steps are Needed Based on Current or Past Performance	Not Demonstrated or Observed
Provide a subordinate with praise and recognition when performance is deserving?			
Analytical			
Does the individual:			
Evaluate alternative courses of action?			
Anticipate wide range of possible obstacles?			
Consider the side effects of decisions or actions?			
Exhibit well balanced judgment in arriving at conclusion?			
Innovation			
Does the individual:			

138

Correctly anticipate important changes which affect the job and capitalize on them?

Develop new solutions to all problems?

Apply innovative procedures to accomplish objectives?

Show a receptive attitude to suggestions for change in new activities?

Suggest original ideas in group discussions?

Crisis Action

Does the individual:

Recognize a problem as critical enough to require immediate attention?

Avoid creating crisis to use as a tool for managerial control?

139

Table 5-1. *(Continued)*

Demonstrated Competence at a Superior Level in Current or Past Assignments	Indicate what Development Steps are Needed Based on Current or Past Performance	Not Demonstrated or Observed
Properly evaluate various courses of action when confronted by unforeseen emergencies?		
Take charge effectively in crisis situations?		
Diagnose critical problems on the spot and quickly provide an effective solution?		
Behave deliberately and rationally under stress?		
Impact		
How well does the individual:		
Create a good first impression?		

Command the attention and
respect of other listeners?

Command the attention and
respect of other general
managers?

Show effectiveness in getting ideas accepted?

Guide a group toward task
accomplishment?

Stress Tolerance

Has the individual:

Evidenced stability to with-
stand pressures of work and
opposition to his ideas?

Show stable performance
under pressure?

Sensitivity

How skillful is he or she in:

Perceiving the needs of
others?

Table 5-1. *(Continued)*

	Demonstrated Competence at a Superior Level in Current or Past Assignments	Indicate what Development Steps are Needed Based on Current or Past Performance	Not Demonstrated or Observed
Reacting to the needs of others?			
Perceiving the impact of self on others.			
Decision Making			
What is his or her ability to:			
Weigh alternatives and make decisions in order to take a risk to achieve maximum benefits?			
What is his or her readiness to make decisions, render judgments, take action, and commit himself or herself?			
Management Control			
How well does he or she:			

Establish procedures to monitor or regulate tasks and the activities of subordinates?

Evaluate the results of delegated assignments and projects?

Use subordinates effectively?

Understand where delegation of responsibility can best be made?

Judgment

What is his or her ability to:

Develop alternative solutions to problems?

Evaluate courses of action?

Reach logical decisions?

Other Observations and Concerns:

Recommendations for Acting on Evaluative Comments (Include Timing).

Less Useful Information	More Useful Information
	much time clarifying the requests to their subordinates and too little time assuring that standards are maintained.
The candidate's impact on others is not always consistent.	The candidate is not sensitive to subordinates' need for support; he is abrasive with peers on a one-to-one basis but works well with them in group settings; he or she tends to be unnecessarily deferential to more senior managers.
The candidate is very creative and acts with a lot of energy on her own ideas.	The candidate is very good on conceptual issues but can transfer concepts to practical applications only if she works with others who encourage pragmatism. On the other hand, she is not openly receptive to criticism of her ideas.
The candidate is not inflexible but very tough.	The candidate is highly organized, unrelenting, and systematic on projects. Very intense but listens carefully and patiently to suggestions.
The candidate is a good manager of people.	The candidate has demonstrated a high ability to build and motivate a team of people; helps them to develop and present their own ideas; has gained great respect of even the best people in each department she has managed.
The candidate knows how to get things done, very results oriented and effective.	The candidate is an outstanding business manger because of strong analytical skills and exceptionally hard work. How-

Less Useful Information	More Useful Information
	ever, she is often so intent on driving her group toward an objective that she doesn't recognize that she is on thin ice. Needs to test ideas more fully before production run begins.
The candidate is a very polished communicator, with a lot of interpersonal effectiveness.	The candidate's speaking and oral persuasive skills are excellent but writing reflects the need to strengthen analytical thinking. Sometimes perceived by peers as too politically conscious of own image with upper management.
The candidate has a great capacity for work, high drive, and energy, more of a researcher than a planner.	The candidate's capacity and willingness to handle great work loads without signs of fatigue or carelessness, always maintains highest performance standards but is more mechanical than reflective in approach to work. As a result, sometimes has his entire department working on an activity that is not necessary and could have been avoided with more upfront consideration of alternatives and consequences for research efforts.

Sample Need to Know Observations.   A lot is learned about a potential chief from a framework of good questions, well-defined criteria, and a set of operationally specific statements. Predictions of probable effectiveness will be even more accurate if evaluators are aware of what they do not know about a candidate and try to get answers. It is very important to prescribe what one needs to know about a candidate for a senior position. Few organizations, however,

define their questions adequately and even fewer provide opportunities for a valid test.

Several examples of need to know issues and ways of testing are
indicated below. In each case, the executive responsible for the
evaluation followed up to assure that the gap in knowledge about the
individual was answered—either to assure that the strength existed
or to avoid a possible selection mistake because the characteristic
was overestimated on the basis of other strengths.

Need to know if he can manage as effectively in multi-national
environment, for example, Latin America or Europe. Transfer to
an international assignment with cross-functional responsibility
by July 19xx for two years.

Need to know if personally innovative. Give responsibility for
managing new product development area in a department where
progress has been slow in this regard. Will require 18 months to
measure results of his influence.

While a very seasoned executive in difficult problem areas, he
seems uninterested in managing people. Need to know if he can
manage people effectively and if he can organize and inspire a
team. Assign to organization where morale and team work are in
need of improvement. Consider attitude survey as a criterion.

Need to know if her own creative ability is intuitively sound (good
instincts) or if she is reflecting the ideas of others. She should be
forced to make decisions on creative issues before opinions of
others are sought and her decisions should be compared against
department manager opinions. Will need one year to test with
confidence and results.

Need to know if he can more effectively manage the ideas of others
instead of imposing his own analysis. Need to know how well he
listens to other sides or if he is too busy formulating his own point
of view. He must be coached and observed more carefully by
president in his present position. President should attend bi-
weekly meetings regularly to understand this.

Need to know if he can orchestrate success when left to himself
and not prodded into action. Can he orchestrate success when

things are not brought to his attention? To answer these questions, he should be lifted out of his current position and put in a new environment with a new set of problems to see if he is a strategist when left to his own devices.

Need to know if he is sufficiently mature, that is, does he have enough confidence in his own judgment to preclude shading of communications, inflexibility, and acting by the book—his book? He should be delegated full responsibility for all work in his area without the opportunity for frequent discussions with his organizational superior. This may make him uncomfortable but he won't be if he is the right person for the future.

Need to know if he has the necessary stature for the job. Specifically, how effective will he be when involved with government regulations and pricing. He should be given full operational responsibility for all functions, including marketing in the Far East.

Need to know if he can build something from scratch. He should be assigned to run the next small acquisition but he should be allowed to form his own team of key operating and support staff.

A review of these need to know statements should clarify the concerns that exist and why full confidence in an executive needs to be resolved. Answers to these questions, whether affirmative or negative, will make a senior executive more comfortable with his or her conclusion about the potential of a candidate for chief and more confident in the accuracy of the prediction. Chiefs should insist on advice which produces these need to know statements and recommendations.

LESSONS FOR ASPIRING CHIEFS

Aspiring chiefs will benefit by paying attention to the kinds of questions that senior executives should ask about them. It is easier to work toward tangible, more evident criteria than against ambiguity, contradictions, or assumptions. It is also important for aspiring chiefs to find ways to answer these questions as they ought to be answered. This may require some initiative on the part of the aspiring chief because one's organizational superior may not be aware of the questions to ask, much less how to judge the answers.

One way to take the initiative is to identify those areas and questions that an aspiring chief feels the most relevant to organizational growth. He or she might consider discussing these with their manager, along with the criteria by which progress or ability should be judged. There is some risk to this, but a valuable discussion may result—especially for aspiring chiefs who are in the dark about how to make their competence and potential evident to others.

In any case, it is usually better for organizational effectiveness if both manager and subordinate understand and agree on the criteria and conditions which determine an individual's potential to be a chief. The sooner this is understood, the better.

TAKING A RISK WITH CANDIDATES FOR SENIOR EXECUTIVE POSITIONS

It is sometimes necessary to take a more than usual risk when testing a candidate for a senior executive position. If an individual is very promising, but a chief is concerned with an aspect of knowledge, ability, or personality, it may be worth the risk of performance failure to test the candidate. Especially under these conditions, the test should enable the candidate's performance or contribution to be assessed separately from the performance or support of others, such as key staff. An executive's staff can cushion him by making decisions or taking actions on their own initiative. Conversely, poor staff can contribute to the failure of good executives.

If a risk fails, a chief will probably find that it is easier to repair damage that may have been caused to the business by poor executive performance than to give the fallen candidate a warm and dry shelter. Still, both the chief and the failed candidate share the responsibility for taking the next step. Of course, one alternative is to let the failed candidate do it on his or her own. Another is to give some help, not necessarily in the way of another job but in the way of direction. The conversation that follows was reconstructed by a chief after such a discussion:

Chief:	Ira, I think we should talk about the next step for you.
Executive:	Look, we've talked about what happened. I still don't agree with your decision but I can't change it. I'll work things out.
Chief:	What are you thinking about?
Executive:	Whether I want to stay or go. I don't expect your confidence in me will improve so maybe I should go.
Chief:	Ira, we tried you in a very complex situation. It needed someone to manage those mavericks. They're not like any one else in this company but they are what we need in that business. They also need somebody to keep order there with a soft hand. You do that very well. You always have. It's your strength. My mistake was that I hoped your relative unfamiliarity with the technical and regulatory affairs wouldn't get in the way. I thought you would be able to manage those things through your people, because they are the best in the business.
Executive:	Yeah, but it didn't work. They kept me out of the business and there is not one thing that an operating V.P. can do about that even if he is their boss. Not even me.
Chief:	It's clear, beyond any doubt now, that thorough knowledge of technical and government issues are critical to success as an operating V.P. We tried.
Executive:	I would have appreciated some back-up. Nobody on this floor gave me any. It was sink or swim. And my career objectives went down with the ship.
Chief:	You have other options, Ira. And you will have other opportunities. You're an outstanding manager and administrator and they are hard to find.
Executive:	In this company? Other options?
Chief:	Depends on what you want. I'm willing to discuss alternative possibilities here but I don't think you ought to try for another operating V.P. job. Your background is great but it hasn't prepared you for it.

Executive: O.K. What do you have in mind?

  Chief: I also think we should discuss some outside possi-
          bilities. Let's discuss both, you explore outside if you
          want, and then let's compare to see what's best for you.
          But remember, your abilities will be valued here—and
          needed.

In this case, the failed executive tested other inside possibilities
with his chief, but they agreed that he should explore his preference
for top operating responsibility in another business that would not
required deep knowledge of complex technical or regulatory issues.
In four months he found a new job and has had only good words for
his former organization and former chief. If the chief had not been
supportive, he probably would have a Trojan horse in his own
organization or an embittered former associate outside of it. The
chief took a risk. It failed. But the chief cleaned up.

Fortunately, all risks do not fail. However, win, lose, or draw,
risks are necessary to test candidates for senior executive positions.

BALANCING THE THREE ELEMENTS OF
EXECUTIVE EFFECTIVENESS

The research in the area of leadership suggests that an executive's
effectiveness is dependent on three things:

1. The nature of supervision (e.g., from a manager, corporate officer,
    or a board);
2. The kind of task to be accomplished (e.g., entrepreneurial, manag-
    ing a new or growing business, managing an established one); and
3. The environment in which the work is done (e.g., high pressure,
    frequent interaction with upper management, isolated from up-
    per management as in some international location, internally
    competitive, risk-tolerant, unstructured).

If any one of these three factors is changed, the outcome of leadership will probably change. For these reasons, prediction of execu-

tive success should not be independent of the way a chief will be managed, or the objectives and activities to be accomplished, or the environment in which the chief is expected to work.

Matching a Chief to a Staff

An important part of the work environment is a chief's staff. A senior executive with extensive experience in business and evident strength and skill in many personal characteristics and abilities will still have some shortcomings. It is important, therefore, to try and match a new chief with a staff that will balance—and not exacerbate—the chief's shortcomings. Otherwise, a shortcoming can become an Achilles' heel. It is worth the time it takes to evaluate and select a chief's staff.

The following three actual examples may help the selectors of chiefs to predict success with more confidence, assuming that actions can be taken to strengthen an executive's staff. In these cases, the information described below was obtained in a senior level assessment center process which added to and crystallized what was already known about the individuals.

Organization A.   The managing director of a medium-sized Asian component of a multi-national company is a very persistent man with strong analytical skills who works well in the absence of feedback. The assessment center exercises revealed that it took a lot of pressure to get him to turn the wheel when he was going in a direction and that he was very selective about who he took advice from. When he assumed a new position, for which he was highly recommended, he was in constant conflict with his organizational superior because he was managed very closely. He spent too much time chafing about meetings with his boss and his business revenues fell.

When the boss was replaced, the new boss decided to assign him a seasoned, mature, and wise assistant instead of managing him too closely. This mature executive was expected to be skillful in persuading the managing director to change direction before he went too far in the absence of feedback or information. The plan worked and the business has done well.

Organization B. The most promising candidate for a senior executive position in this company had a strong preference for a lot of things going on simultaneously. This meant that she might spread herself too thin. It also meant that she handled interruptions well because she found them stimulating. Sometimes this resulted in things falling through the cracks. She needed a lot of activity to keep her challenged and she had a high desire for status, although she was not egotistical.

She was a strong candidate for the position because of the business' need to accomplish a lot of things in a short time and because of her ability to excite and motivate a staff. The senior executives who felt she was the best choice for the position wanted to assure her success, but they also wanted to test her in the right conditions. Therefore, they teamed two staff executives under her to act as a brake on her occasional frenetic activity. The team has been an effective business organization.

Organization C. The president wanted to fill a senior position with a potential chief who was known as a dependable, distinguished, and mature manager. This executive was mildly introverted, introspective, had strong opinions on issues, and would not normally acknowledge opposing opinions easily. He was planful, hard-working, and set higher standards for himself than others expected of him.

The position to be filled required an executive who would take risks, and the president assumed that the potential chief's maturity and stability would help in this regard. The assessment center data, however, indicated a strong preference for traditional and historical frames of reference and an aversion to speculation and future perspectives. As a result, the president decided he would not be a match for either the new environment or the task, despite his otherwise fine qualifications or the presence of a good staff.

JUDGING A PREDECESSOR'S IMPACT

Every executive leaves an aftertaste. It is easy to forget it but it tells a lot about the enduring qualities of a candidate for chief.

When an executive assumes a new position, a lot of early time is spent learning what one's predecessor did. It is usually not until much later, perhaps four or five months, that the incumbent realizes what he or she actually inherited in the way of problems or solutions. A good part of what an executive does in the early days of a new position is to fix the problems he or she finds or to build on the platforms that exist. In either case, the impact of one's predecessor influences the incumbent's effectiveness.

Similarly, when an executive leaves a job, it is too soon to judge his or her impact, particularly if he or she has not been in the position long enough. The evaluation should wait until there is an opportunity to observe what has been the residue and impact inherited by the successor. At least two years is needed for individuals to make their own mark. Less than that will not enable a good evaluation. Assignments to test candidates for senior executive positions should not be so brief that the need to know issues are partially unanswered.

Chiefs should not succumb to pressure from aspiring chiefs who are impatient for their next assignment. Candidates must understand that time is required to determine the impact of their involvement. Further, they should not assume that moving to another position for another test is an automatic approval of their prior performance. That question will be answered by several months of observing their own successor.

THE GROUP EVALUATION

Potential candidates for chief must demonstrate their abilities beyond almost any doubt before they are considered actual candidates. Corporate procedures that evaluate candidates on a one-to-one basis tend to dominate evaluation decisions, for example, superior to subordinate, interviewer to applicant, observer to individual. The most common examples are the performance appraisal and the informal observation of how an individual performs. In the latter instance, there are many occasions, such as meetings, presentations, discussions, and lunches, where an individual conveys to others a lasting impression. Unfortunately, that impression is often incorrect and it is almost always incomplete.

There is so much personal chemistry involved in one-to-one observations and evaluations that the evaluations should be suspect. A custom-tailored suit, the "wrong" tie, a manner of expression, the use of jargon, the level of familiarity with a subject under discussion, and so on, can attract or repel an evaluator, whether the situation is formal evaluation or casual appraisal. Most corporate executives have a great many informal discussions about people in their organizations and say things like, "That new young woman in Ed's group is really sharp—I sat in on her presentation to the executive committee" or "He looks like a farmer. Somebody ought to take him shopping for clothes in a good store."

Compounding the issue of evaluation, most conclusions are drawn without dependable criteria to guide their direction or scope, without the opportunity to question or challenge them, and without the advantage of other points of view. For these reasons, a process called a "group evaluation" seems to be a better alternative.

Companies like AT&T, IBM, GE, Merrill Lynch, Chase Manhattan, and Kodak are aware of how important it is to get several perspectives on potential senior executives. This is why opportunities are created to transfer individuals to other parts of the organization, to other functions, and under different managers.

The group evaluation process is based on the perspectives of at least two or three evaluators, usually four to six evaluators participate. It is designed to integrate and/or organize the best aspects and characteristics of evaluative procedures in a practical and easily implemented way. It also generates extraordinarily rich information about people which does not typically appear in performance appraisals.

The Purpose and Structure.   The group evaluation is a discussion centered on a group of potential chiefs by two or three senior executives. It can be used as a part of a selection process or a development planning process.

The senior executives acting as evaluators must be familiar with the performance, personal characteristics, and abilities of the entire group. Not all of the evaluators need to personally know each of the executives in the group under discussion, but at least two and preferably three of the evaluators will know each one.

Anywhere from 6 to about 15 is the best size for the group to be discussed. Most group evaluations require about one day to fully cover six to eight people. The process crystallizes and surfaces issues, provides greater texture, integrates observations and reactions, and provides a better basis for understanding candidates, developing plans, and making succession decisions.

The Evaluators. The evaluators are senior executives who are familiar with the group to be discussed. In fact, each of the individuals to be evaluated should report directly to one of the evaluators.

The evaluators are usually comprised of groups such as (1) the general manager and two-to-four of his key staff (e.g., two operating vice presidents (engineering, marketing, manufacturing), a financial vice president, a human resources vice president); (2) the CEO and two executive vice presidents; or (3) an executive vice president and his key staff (e.g., a financial vice president, a research and development vice president, a manufacturing vice president, a marketing vice president, and an engineering vice president).

The Leader. A group evaluation requires someone to lead it. Usually, an internal human resources executive is the best internal person to lead it. Another good alternative is an external or internal consultant, preferably an industrial psychologist because of the focus on behavior, ability, and personal characteristics.

How Group Evaluation Works

Prior to the group evaluation meeting, the designated leader collects the names of the candidates to be discussed. Time is scheduled for the meeting, with a maximum of six-to-eight candidates for a one-day meeting. The leader should tell each participating senior executive that he or she will be asked to discuss the candidates and comment in sufficient depth on their accomplishments, ability, personality, and behavior.

The senior executive who will make the eventual selection decisions may also want the opinions of a few other people who may be familiar with narrow aspects of an individual's performance. These other individuals might include executives who work with a candidate only occasionally but closely enough for their observations to add solid information. They may be invited only for the part of the evaluation where their opinion is asked and discussed—there is no need for them to stay for other parts of the evaluation discussion.

When the evaluators convene, the discussion leader puts the candidates' names on a board and asks if there is any one else to be added. He also confirms that the evaluators are indeed sufficiently familiar with the candidates.

Categorizing.   The evaluators are asked to organize the names into three separate lists of approximately equal size, using whatever criteria they like. The purpose of this categorizing is to force comparative thinking. They are asked to do it by themselves at first, without sharing the criteria they will use.

The leader may also decide to add "anchors" to the list, by asking the most senior executive at the meeting for the names of two or three other executives who have previously moved through the positions currently occupied by the group under discussion. One or two may have been subsequently successful and one or two may have failed. These anchors sometimes help as benchmarks for categorizing the people under discussion. The anchors will not be discussed. They will only be used for purposes of comparison, which is sometimes useful.

After about 10−15 minutes, which is what it usually takes, each evaluator has categorized the names. The leader then asks them to describe the lists and then records the names on a board, without indicating criteria. After the three or four evaluators have described their lists, it is apparent that there are a few names that appear on the same lists and a few that are widely scattered. When the criteria for categorizing are then described, some of the differences are understood but some are surprising to the evaluators. The reasons and relevance of different criteria, if they are used, are explained by the evaluators.

The most common criteria include: "past performance," "future potential," "performance and potential," "individuals who have reached their ceiling," "individuals who need future proving," and "looks good but not yet proven."

What is surprising is that the initial reaction of some evaluators at this point is "We know all that already." What surprises them later is how the better information they have acquired during the day has changed their views and decisions.

Guiding the Discussion. The leader asks each evaluator to explain (1) why an individual has been placed in a particular group and (2) what evidence supports this opinion. Other evaluators are asked to question, disagree, add information, and to introduce any other issues they think should be considered. Evaluators should also be asked to compare the candidates against each other and against the questions.

This discussion, however, must not be freewheeling. If it is, it will not focus on the right things and it will wallow.

The leader should use a set of prepared questions, such as those set forth below, to guide the discussion in several important areas. The leader, however, must assure that the information sought emerges from the discussion. The questions, therefore, serve more as a checklist.

How Does He Lead?

What are his or her values (abstract goals, e.g., power, wealth, achievement, competence, creativity, tradition)?

Attitudes (e.g., toward the role of business leader, the company, other people in the company).

What are his or her beliefs (e.g., about how a leader should act, what can be accomplished, relationships)?

What is his or her degree of identification with a company versus personal goals?

Evidence of ethical conduct, integrity; when and how does he or she compromise; how has he or she conveyed his or her views about integrity (through actions, statements)?

How well has he or she introduced/supported minority opinion?

What is his or her flexibility in adapting to circumstances?

How well does he or she anticipate?

Evidence of interpersonal skills, tact, esteem for others.

Self-confidence.

Ability to gain confidence of others (what is evidence)?

What is his or her vision of where he or she and the business should go?

Hunger for success.

Evidence of perseverance, and durability.

Evidence of energy and activity level.

Fluency of speech.

Spokesperson.

Listening ability.

Assertiveness/dominance.

Decisiveness.

Evidence of emotional balance, ability to perform well under stress.

Evidence of initiative.

How Does He or She Innovate?

Flexibility regarding tolerance for ambiguity.

Can he or she bring together ideas or opportunities which were previously unrelated?

Entrepreneurship.

Analytical ability.

Conceptual fluency to perceive and understand novel ideas.

Personal courage.

Persistence.

Originality, creativity; evidence?

How has he or she used his or her imagination?

Evidence of curiosity.

How Does He or She Develop and Select Others?

Does he or she communicate his or her expectations to people?

Does he or she communicate his or her ideas to others; evidence?

Is he or she willing to explain his or her beliefs and expectations; evidence?

Does he or she have high standards for others; evidence?

What is his or her ability to evaluate people without halo and give them constructive feedback; evidence?

How good is he or she at selecting outstanding people (success versus mistakes)?

Is he or she a team builder; evidence?

Adequacy of a model for others.

Conceives career plans for individuals based on what they need to know and what they need to demonstrate their effectiveness; evidence?

Identify outstanding people he or she has developed directly or indirectly.

What is His or Her Business Competence?

In the past, what has he or she accomplished: evidence, history, pattern (both personal and business); how have his or her achievements been manifested?

What has been generated by his or her accomplishments, that is, both results and side effects.

What is his or her intelligence (all dimensions, e.g., abstract reasoning, deductive and inductive processes, integrating and sympathizing, judgment); give evidence.

Organizing and planning skills; evidence.

Analytical skills and conceptual fluency; evidence.

Writing skills; examples.

Task orientation; describe how.

Other

What is his or her ego like—does he or she take sole credit for successes, sense of humility and ability to learn from mistakes?

Optimist.

How does he or she respond to uncertainty, stress?

Sociability, social participation.

Thoughtfulness.

Social insight, empathy.

Very high personal standards; makes demands on self.

Personal health and vigor.

During the discussion of each individual, evaluators will consider "what if" questions. This will aid speculation and prediction of how individuals might behave in various situations. This discussion will also help to surface examples and evidence related to characteristics and issues identified in the above categories.

Certainly other characteristics and issues will arise during the discussions. The above categories and characteristics only serve to provide guidance to the discussion. It is expected that the evaluation of each individual will be based on different balances among personal characteristics and accomplishments.

Sample Group Evaluation Session.   Part of a tape-recorded group evaluation of several senior executives were transcribed to give a better feeling for the flow of a discussion. The leader used a set of questions to guide the discussion. In this case, Participant 2 was the chief who would make the final selection decision.

Leader:	What are [one of the individual's under discussion] most important values? What does he want out of life?
Participant 1:	More responsibility, achievement, recognition.
Leader:	Why? What does it do for him?
Participant 1:	He wants to show what he's done.
Leader:	To whom?
Participant 2:	To his wife, mostly, and his friends. Sure, he wants more responsibility but he wants to prove to everyone else he can do it.
Participant 3:	I don't agree. I think he wants to prove to himself that he can do it. His whole background points to that. He's not like [another candidate], he doesn't send memos around every time he's accomplished something.
Leader to Participant 2:	Can you explain why you said what you did?
Participant 2:	Well, he just seems to live awfully well. He's got a place at the shore, he's got a ski condo in Vermont, and he doesn't live in a bad part of town.
Participant 3:	(Laughs) You're right, but let's face it—we just envy him.
Leader:	Come on, living high doesn't mean he's trying to impress somebody else. Is there anything you've seen that makes you think his hard work is only for others, not for himself?
Participant 2:	I'd like to know what the rest of you have seen?
Participant 1:	Everything I've seen has been outstanding. He worked his way through college and got almost straight A's in computer science

programs—and that's not easy. He's always been interested in sports and he lives pretty simply so he can afford good addresses. But most of that has nothing to do with how he works. He's very smart, very helpful, and I count on him to solve problems. He's had a whole string of successes, most of them on 60 hour weeks. So it doesn't matter who he's done it for. He gets results and people like him.

Participant 3: That's the way I see it. He's also been able to push his group hard and they still like him.

Leader to Participant 2: Well, any reaction to these comments? Based on what you've heard and what you know, how would you describe his value system?

Participant 2: O.K., I admit my experience with him has been limited and I accept what the rest of you are saying. You won me over when you compared him to (other candidate). I'll agree he's interested in achievement against his own standards. I just hope they stay high enough. You convinced me.

Leader: Any reason to think otherwise?

Participant 2: I guess not.

Participant 1: Certainly not. He's always set the highest of standards for himself and everyone knows that.

Participant 3: I wish everyone worked as hard as he does. Our business would be better. He's as dependable as anyone I know and his ideas are better. Better ideas are what drive him. Let's not lose sight of his creativity.

Leader: Are you saying that breaking tradition with better ideas is part of his value system?

Participant 1:	It sure is. It's what separates him from most everybody else who is so afraid to stick their neck out for fear one of us will slap their wrist.
Participant 2:	What does that say for us?
Leader:	Let's stay with the subject. Can you give me some examples of his better ideas and what happened as a result?

It is important for the leader to be skillful and insistent in probing each area and question. Evidence must be sought to substantiate an opinion. As shown in the discussion, by the end of the discussion of an individual, views are often changed on the basis of the opinions and observations of other evaluators. Importantly, consensus on the potential of individuals is generally reached, differences are negotiated, and tangible plans to test people further are developed. There is a better thrust behind the testing because there is better understanding of the candidate and more confidence in the predictions of what a candidate can be expected to accomplish.

Excerpts from Group Evaluations.   A good way to illustrate the richness and value of a group evaluation is to review portions of the written descriptions that have been developed in several companies for candidates for middle management positions.

Example 1. Sid (Age 36, 7 years service with company)

The Market Research Vice President indicates that [the candidate] is unsatisfying to talk with because he is not close to the business. He does not have a strong marketing interest in the business although he is fast on his feet—but without depth. Finance does not think he follows through. When he might have an idea which he champions, he does not follow up. Personnel and R&D see him as a great conceptualizer but a poor implementer without follow-up. [All functional vice-presidents gave examples to illustrate their opinions.]

All in all, he does not seem to be interested in details. Timetables do not mean much for him. He is a pleasant person but cannot build a team or lead it. Administration and management are not his strength. His strength seems to be coming up with ideas.

He does well with what interests him but does not do well with areas which do not interest him. He is leading a project at the present time in which he is enormously interested and doing fairly well. He has very good relationships with people but this is quite different from his ability to motivate them. He is better at originating ideas than managing them. Perhaps he would be better in a position which did not require in-depth knowledge of the business. In our company, however, there are no such positions and he may be better off with a consulting firm where he can work from his strength, which is the generation of ideas.

Example 2. Bob (Age 29, 3 years service with company)

Engineering feels that Bob is very goal-oriented but does not know if he knows what he has after he puts an idea together. The engineering vice president also senses a lot of false starts on his part and does not see a lot being accomplished; he does not think there is much there. [Several examples were given to illustrate.]

Market Research interacts with him a lot and finds him difficult to deal with because he comes in like a bull in a china shop. His target also keeps changing and he tends to manipulate others to gain an objective. Objectivity is also lacking. The R&D vice president does not trust him.

The group did not think that Bob is very organized and it is difficult for him to set priorities. He is extremely tunnel-visioned and will not listen to other views.

If a task is laid out for him, including business strategy, he might do well because he is effective mechanically.

The question was asked about how good he is at marketing. He is not perceived to be a very hard worker and certainly not creative. There is no evidence of skill in developing concepts, although it was noted that he can probably recognize good concepts when he sees them. (Several examples given).

He does not want to talk with people about their ideas but wants to talk with them about his ideas. He treats all staff groups as adversaries who get in the way of what he wants to get done. He does not listen to other ideas but is very anxious to please top management. He sees cooperation with others as a weakness and is intensely competitive.

His perception of himself is not consistent with other perceptions of him. Despite good early impressions, Bob does not seem to be working out well. The early impressions seem to be based more on his personal agressiveness than on his ability.

Example 3. Jane (Age 31, 4 years service with company)

Jane has forced her way up into the personnel function. She is an outstanding business manager, has strong analytical skills and works exceptionally hard, sometimes even too hard. She must recognize that it is as important to focus on content as much, if not more, as on the process of selling. Sometimes she is too quick to close. She does not test her ideas fully all the time because she is impatient for action. [Several examples added.]

She has an ability to bring a group of people to action and can establish that she is the person in charge. She has extraordinary leadership skills and can synthesize a lot of points of view without threatening people. Jane also accepts bad news gracefully.

Jane is ambitious and gets high marks with her peers. One observation, however, was that she does not have a natural feel for writing. The personnel vice president gave her fair marks on this and feels that her strong analytical bent may be blocking out her instincts or perhaps she does not have them. He felt that Jane must be forced to write more clearly. It was also agreed that she should discuss a variety of alternatives before sending a memo and these should be reviewed with her manager.

It was agreed that if Jane ran into trouble, she would manage it well under any circumstances. She can be depended upon to motivate people. Overall, her greatest need is for more intensive training and practice in writing reports.

Example 4. Dick (Age 30, 5 years service with company)

Dick continues to impress people. The feeling is that the talent is there and that he has potential. He is bright, poised, grasps the creative process, and has good technical sense. He gets people to like and respect him but is still inexperienced and needs to learn many of the basics.

He is not as assertive as he should be and the feeling is that he may not be trying hard enough. The group wondered whether it was because of a lack of interest or the discipline to organize his thinking and activities. He needs to be pushed a bit by his manager. He also needs to know clearly what is expected of him to move to the next level. The next three or four months should see if it comes together. This must be a real test.

Example 5. Alton (Age 29, 4 years service with company)

Alton continues to grow. He has outstanding business confidence. He is the best that his manager has ever seen. He is a strong initiator, always well-prepared and works hard at whatever is assigned. It is always done well and on time. He is not easily intimidated and is an idea person. By nature, he is quiet and not a visible leader. He shows his leadership by demonstration. His assignment in manufacturing is a good example. He also deals with staff very effectively. [Several examples supplied.]

Alton needs a situation to practice selling himself and his ideas more aggressively. This is important so that he can become a more visible leader. He is ready now for promotion but must hit the floor running. His next assignment must be significant and provide stretch, but it must be under a good manager.

Example 6. Ben (Age 40, 7 years service with company)

Ben is an extremely hard worker, a good manager of people on his team, gets the job done, and has a high level of respect for other disciplines such as engineering and manufacturing. He was ranked slightly below (another employee) on his financial knowledge but the group agreed that Ben was nevertheless good quantitatively. It was observed that Ben has grown more in the last two years than any of the other operating managers. He has become very serious about the business and works well with his people as well as with other functions [examples supplied].

The group agreed that he knows how to get work out of staff areas when needed. There was some disagreement as to his conceptual ability. The financial director felt that he has some difficulty grasping new ideas the first time they are discussed but he could only give one instance to support this. The others in the group were able to give several other instances where this was not so; the financial director agreed that his impression was premature.

Two examples from senior manager group evaluations are included below. These evaluations were based on several dimensions which the company's president felt were the key criteria for executive success.

Example 7. Walt (Age 40, 15 years service with company)

How Does He Lead?   His most important values, according to his manager, focus on his own performance. Walt has very high personal standards which he does not impose on others. Nevertheless, he does have high performance expectancies for others and can become impatient when things do not move at his pace. Walt values loyalty very highly, commitment to a common goal, to which he is sometimes willing to subordinate his own belief about what is right.

His attitude toward his role as an engineering manager, other people in the company, and the corporation are positive and constructive. He has firm ideas about how leaders should act and about what can be accomplished. He tries to exercise his beliefs in interactions with other people. He is respected by his subordinates and has a reputation outside the company for outstanding leadership in engineering design groups.

Walt is flexible and does not get locked in prematurely or too firmly to the wrong position.

According to the vice president of development engineering, Walt is exceptionally sensitive to issues that could affect engineering schedules. He has long business vision and anticipates problems and issues even before they need to be acted upon. He is very strong in his ability to deal with strategic problems and with other people.

From a lab view, the vice president of engineering laboratories said that he is extremely consistent and able in his leadership, decisiveness and creativity. He knows the technology and the products. He confirmed that he does interact well with people.

Walt has a strong sense of identification with the company and does not let his ego get out of control. He shows every evidence of the highest ethical standards and is not afraid to introduce or support a minority opinion.

Walt is a good listener. This is evidenced by his ability to take an idea and react to it by plussing it up. He always responds constructively.

He is articulate and strikes a good balance of assertiveness with patience. At times, however, he will become impatient when an answer is obvious and others do not move into the same position with him. In these cases, he may intimidate others by pushing them, but this happens only occasionally. He is generally very well balanced.

The group agreed that Walt has an extremely high intellect. A couple of people were not sure that up to now he has been given a job which has tested his intellect. [This was subsequently planned at this meeting.]

How Does He Innovate?   He is very analytical and very good at bringing abstract ideas together. While his own personal ideas are not as good as his ability to build on a good idea, his own ideas are nevertheless on a higher point of innovativeness than the ideas of most others.

He has good value judgments and it is difficult to pull the wool over his eyes. Walt is very strong at setting an innovative climate and in stimulating others to think innovatively. He has shown good evidence of taking an idea from one place and putting it to work in another situation.

Walt has the courage to express his opinion and has a high level of conceptual fluency.

Walt's analytical skills stand out above all. He comes to things intuitively and then provides the analytical support for his conclusions. This kind of thinking is a good indicator of the ability to be creative.

How Does He Develop Others?   Walt is effective at communicating his expectations and his ideas to others. He has good selection and interviewing skills and his coaching and development skills are also very good. He sets reasonable standards and is a good evaluator of people.

Walt is probably a very good model for others and has the ability to help them achieve success. Several of his subordinates are evidence of this.

What Is His Business Competence? Walt is a very balanced executive with fine engineering experience in advanced operations. However, he has not been in situations in which it is easy to separate out his accomplishments from those of others. Nevertheless, everyone who has worked with him feels strongly about his abilities and his personal characteristics.

Walt exercises both deductive and inductive thinking appropriately and effectively. He integrates information well and uses good judgment when evaluating situations.

Walt is very well organized and shows outstanding ability in planning skills.

Other. The group agreed that Walt is warm and friendly although serious and businesslike. He should be somewhat more relaxed with others and it is expected his recent involvement on the two community service boards should help to do this.

Personal Development Recommendations. Walt should be provided with an opportunity to lead a major organization, which includes several functions. At present, it would probably be a major error to move him off his current assignment because there are several important projects that need his continuity to complete. There was, however, some disagreement about engineering being a good opportunity for Walt to show his abilities and an alternative was that he be placed in a multifunctional business that he can control. Another view was that we may run the risk of losing him if he sees himself stagnating. It was agreed, therefore, that he should be taken off his assignment but not for another year or so. Overall, Walt needs to demonstrate his competence to manage across functions. This will provide him with even more confidence in his own skill. [A plan was discussed and agreed upon at the meeting.]

Example 8. Art (Age 34, 5 years service with company).

How Does He Lead? [The executive vice president] observed that Art is only fair strategically, a fair motivator of people, less than fair in decision-making, average in growth potential, and fairly good in organizational relationships. He felt that he needs direction because he is not a self-starter. [Several examples were given to support these opinions.]

Art's primary values seem to be safety and service, that is, providing support to other people. He identifies well with the company and seems to work reasonably well with people although he is not a strong leader.

The group also felt that Art was neither stimulating nor inspiring, but he is responsive to requests. In fact, it was felt that he probably does many things because the organization wants it or expects it rather than because he feels that it is the right thing to do. For example, his over-responsiveness to other staff executives caused delays in completion of contractual arrangements with several major customers during the last two years.

How Does He Innovate? The group did not think he has a lot of confidence to take risks. As for personal courage, he prefers to play it safe and there is no evidence of his innovative abilities.

How Does He Develop Others? Art is a good evaluator of people but not as confident to make a judgment call as other people are. He knows that he may not be able to manage people through better ways and instead he tries to get a job done within fairly narrow bonds. He is expeditious rather than expansive. He does not look for new ways as often as he should and others do not learn how to be innovative from him. Also, it is not likely that he sets a climate which is very conducive to developing innovative behavior.

How Is His Business Competence? Art does a solid job, but not an outstanding or flashy one. He has good business skills, he is conservative, and he is a risk-avoider. A question was raised about whether he was over-organized but evidence for this was sketchy. Conservative is a better description.

Art is not especially assertive and there is not a lot of evidence of initiative on his part. He is methodical and deals better with tangible things than intangible ones. He does not have much vision but he is very responsive and he is a good lieutenant. His own standards are high and what he does, he does well. Art is also a good listener and he gets high marks from manufacturing for things like providing materials or support.

Art has not shown evidence that he is hungry for more responsibility and the group speculated that he might even prefer roles that would not put him into a risky or leadership position.

Other. [Art's manager] says that "the paradox of it is that Art wants to succeed but does not want to make a mistake and is not sure how to succeed by himself." He works best under a supervisor and takes good direction.

The challenge is to provide Art with a position where he does not feel at risk but where he can give evidence of his business skills.

Personal Development Recommendations. His last performance appraisal was very good and we need to find a place for him. Good lieutenants are very valuable and the group felt that everything possible should be done to keep him in an appropriate (and safe) role. [A plan was developed to do this over the next three years.]

Example 9. Ken (Age 36, 12 years service with company)

How Does He Lead? Ken's values are difficult to identify. He is somewhat inscrutable and seems to want self-respect in a good position as a member of a team. Other than that, it is hard to speculate about his values and personal goals.

He is not a great strategic thinker and does not show a lot of instinctive creative insight. He is stronger in his deductive thinking than his inductive thinking. [Several examples were given.]

How Is His Business Competence? Ken acts well on instructions and, if properly led, will do things well. He is usually flexible and is exceptionally well liked.

He does not show a lot of ability to anticipate nor does he show evidence of business vision or hunger for higher organizational positions.

How Does He Innovate?   A couple of people did not feel that Ken is personally creative, although they said he does create a climate for it to happen. Ken's manager disagreed. He said that he was not ready to say that he has no conceptual instincts. He though he might do very well in a business to which he related professionally because he has seen other signals of his abilities. [Several examples were given.] He feels he needs a better opportunity to judge him and that he has been very pleased and pleasantly surprised so far.

Ken has strong implementation and analytical skills. While [the vice president, finance] felt that he does not have an instinctive reaction to financial information, he said that his logical reactions are very sound.

How Does He Develop Others?   Ken communicates well with other people. He cares for the people who work for him, recognizes them, and gives them responsibility. He seems to have the ability to build a good team.

Other.   Ken is sociable, well-liked, and communicates well.

Personal Development Recommendations.   Ken's manager's confidence in him may be just the prescription for his growth. We should let him provide full direction in this case.

Using the Group Evaluation

Chiefs should encourage their staff to initiate a group evaluation process. This is a somewhat more structured way of doing what some organizations already do. It crystallizes and integrates. The advantages include: (1) the initial categorizing of names and the use of anchors to force comparisons; (2) the comparison of predictive criteria used by different evaluators; (3) probing for evidence and patterns instead of single events which shape conclusions; (4) better articulation of predictive criteria; (5) different opinions and expectations; (6) confidence in prediction based on thorough examination and consensus; and (7) better planning for testing and development.

Senior executives will find that they will quickly improve their evaluation skills as they become more involved with the process. An interesting way to determine the usefulness of this process is to compare the resulting evaluations with what has been said previously about candidates on performance appraisals or in other discussions.

FOR ASPIRING CHIEFS

There are many questions and criteria suggested in this chapter. Good responses to them are difficult to contrive. Aspiring chiefs who possess the qualities and characteristics necessary for senior positions should, however, learn how to communicate them.

At times, it may be important to take the initiative and to demonstrate the presence of these qualities, especially if one believes he or she is being tested. But it is equally important that the aspiring chief's manager knows how to look for evidence of these characteristics and how to interpret actions or statements.

It is worth repeating that occasional conversations with a manager, especially at the beginning of a new assignment, will help to get agreement on what is expected in the way of performance and personal behavior. This should not be left to chance. More deliberate and systematic attention to the nature of accomplishments and image by an aspiring chief will communicate senior executive potential more effectively.

— 6 —

Narrowing to
Key Candidates

THE MYSTERY OF HIGH PLACES

There is an old story about two drunks that reflects the mystery and wonder about how people reach high places. These two were sitting at the bar of a saloon after a night of drinking when one drunk raised his eyes, gasped in wonder, and pointed to the head of a moose mounted high on the wall. "What about it?" asked his friend. The first drunk replied, "Can you imagine how fast that moose was running when he hit that wall?!"

Likewise, there is also wonder expressed in the wide eyes of the many corporate veterans when they look up at high places in their companies. When a CEO replacement was announced recently, most of the company's senior staff did not know how the replacement got there. A senior and respected executive of that company kept track of the telephone calls and personal visits he received from other senior executives. None of them could understand how or why the successful candidate was selected by the board over two other men who seemed to be in possession of greater abilities. Among their remarks, all with shaking head or astonished gaze, were:

"Good grief! What happened to our values?!"

"I never dreamed the board would pick him—but maybe they were dreaming. I think it's a nightmare."

"What are they looking for? Where are we going?"

"On what basis does the board think he can run this place?"

"It's a mystery to me. What does he have?"

"Where's the match between the leadership we need and his abilities?"

"It must have been decided on a coin toss."

"Witchcraft! Somebody knows how to make voodoo dolls."

"This decision has got to shake the confidence of everyone in this company who thought we had a succession system that makes sense."

Mystery and vagueness about succession systems, and especially succession planning, is typical. Even in companies with reputations for highly organized management succession plans, such as AT&T, GE, or IBM, many executives do not understand how selection decisions are made for the highest position in the company. They are not even sure who is involved in selecting chiefs. They are aware, however, that management succession is a major issue and that it does get major attention.

Individuals who see middle management positions as stepping stones or career targets generally say they understand the criteria by which middle management selection decisions are made, even though the criteria may be poor. This is not the case for senior executive succession decisions. It might be helpful to understand how selection decisions are narrowed to key candidates.

Narrowing to key candidates is a more difficult process than evaluating potential candidates against a set of predictive criteria.

This is because most candidates display a high level of ability and it is more difficult to discriminate among them.

At Rubbermaid.   At Rubbermaid, headquarterd in Wooster, Ohio, the president has the responsibility for senior executive selection decisions, but the chairman and senior vice president of human resources are part of the selection process. Because of the size and managerial style of Rubbermaid, they know the candidates well and are able to discuss the fit of each candidate for the open position. While there is little opportunity for testing in the form of specific developmental assignments, they have watched the candidates perform on a day-to-day basis because of their involvement in the business.

There is, therefore, a constant development and evaluation process going on that aids in the selection process when a key executive position is open. Critical to this process is the operating general manager, who must make his promotable managers available on a day-to-day working basis with the corporate staff. Rubbermaid does take a unique approach to evaluating key candidates and it is described further on in this chapter.

At AT&T.   The narrowing process is somewhat different at AT&T. Prior to their 1983 – 1984 divestiture activity, the office of the chairman selected about 12 potential candidates from among 30 nominees. Each of these 12 potential candidates was assigned to a corporate "career planner." The "career planner" was a senior executive who would assure multi-functional exposure for the candidate in areas such as finance, marketing, or operations. The process was called the Executive Continuity Program. For example, before an executive was considered for a senior vice president position, he was required to have five to eight years of testing and development in various functions and with several senior executives. AT&T wanted at least three other presidents of telephone companies (which were AT&T divisions) to get to know each candidate before moving him up to greater corporate responsibility.

While some of the 12 or so candidates selected each year were subsequently screened out, there were about 45 people in the process at any given time. AT&T is currently analyzing its needs for the new corporate structure and strategies. In fact, it has begun to implement the Executive Continuity Program in the new structure to address anticipated management succession needs.

At Merrill Lynch.   At Merrill Lynch and Co., the chairman, president, and the four executive vice presidents get together annually for about three days to discuss 50 of the top executives. They raise and discuss questions such as: "How is he doing at his present job?"; "Is he ready for the next job?"; "Can he work independently?" They discuss whether an executive has ideas, how well he or she knows his businesses, and other characteristics and behavior which may predict success.

At Citicorp.   Citicorp has a well-defined and well-managed system of narrowing to key candidates for middle and senior positions. This system involves regular meetings between the levels of management to review key people in their part of the organization. These reviews extend from the bottom to top of the company and across all organizational functions.

Twice a year, the chairman and vice chairmen meet to review the key executives in each major business group. At this level, approximately 150 people who hold the most critical posts in the corporation are reviewed. In addition, each business group head, along with the chairman or vice chairmen, also reviews individuals who seem ready to become candidates for key positions as well as other outstanding performers at any level in the organization.

To prepare for these reviews, each business group head conducts similar reviews, covering some 1,000 executives, with their own division heads. Similarly, the division heads review key people in each of their businesses with their own managers.

The performance of almost every officer in the organization is considered during the process of preparing for these reviews. At each of these sessions, the executives are reviewed in terms of their career experience, personal strengths and development needs, career interests, and possible next moves.

A Different Approach to Narrowing the Candidates. The chairman of one financial institution has taken a novel approach to thinning out the candidates for senior executive positions. Since their business depends on exceptional cooperation among corporate chiefs, he assigns key candidates to areas of responsibility where they do not have much expertise. For example, the candidate who knows the least about technology is assigned to that area, and the candidate weakest on information systems is assigned to that area. In this way, a candidate's ability and willingness to cooperate with others is determined fairly quickly.

THE KEY CANDIDATES

Who are they? What do they have in common? What are their differences? Why will some fall out of consideration? After all the comparisons are made, is it possible to step back and confidently predict which candidates are the most qualified and which do not merit further consideration? Some of the answers and some of the pitfalls are covered in this chapter. Aspiring chiefs will find some trail guides here to steer their progress through an organization.

Most major companies, it seems, do set aside time on a regular basis to discuss the most promising candidates for senior executive succession. Nevertheless, the former chairman of a major U.S.-headquartered company, and member of several boards of directors, feels that the process is generally not orderly because of loose criteria and the need to improve the management of conflicting interests of those directly and indirectly involved in the succession planning process and decision.

Who Are They?

For the most part, the strongest candidates for chief are within an organization. They are known to the chairman, the board, the president, and the other selectors. They are all experienced, mature managers who have demonstrated their abilities and communicated their potential to the general satisfaction of the selectors. The promotion-from-within process itself, however, does not inspire satisfaction. Robert Lear, former Chairman of the F&M Schaefer Corporation, says that too many corporations "turn out uninspired, lackluster or mediocre appointments to the top post." He also feels that

> [M]any companies often neglect the early training of talented young executives with potential for advancement . . . [and they] may wind up with top people who do not have an adequate comprehension of the basic business or have mostly a specialized knowledge of one area of a corporation.[1]

According to an article in *Dun's Business Month*[2]

> [T]he unfortunate consensus of corporate officers and executive recruiters alike is that too many companies have not adequately developed systematic testing and career paths for talented, aspiring executives.

Nevertheless, says the article

> Whatever the theoretical pros and cons, fewer companies today search farther than their own backyard for CEO's. Only a major tremor in a company's foundations prompts it to look outside for a capable Number Two who can be groomed for the top post.

One of the implications of these observations is that contrary to the opinions of many chairmen and presidents, those candidates who become "finalists" in the competition for senior executive positions may include some distinctly mediocre talent. Too often, executives who are very good and very impatient will leave a company if promotional progress is slow. Good executives are always attractive to other companies. Further, many long-service executives become candidates for senior positions in their own company because they are "good soldiers" and not because they have outstanding executive ability.

[1]The Long Haul to the Top, *Dun's Business Month*, April 1984, p. 58.
[2]*Ibid.*

Key candidates for positions of chief, therefore, are not always as good as they need—or appear—to be. Familiarity with the long-service of candidates is the major reason that the selectors of chiefs are often comfortable with people who do not possess the qualities required to be successful as a chief. One survey of CEOs[3] highlights this concern:

> The DBM survey reveals that 7 out of every 10 of today's crop of Chief Executive Officers have served their companies at least 20 years, more than half their working lives; one-quarter have racked up 35 or more years with their respective firms. Two-thirds of the survey respondents have worked in only one industry, and more than 40% for just one company. . . .
>
> [T]here is an underlying allegiance in corporate America to the man who puts in his years for an industry, and, more preferably, one company.

It is interesting to note that a Heidrick & Struggles (a management search firm) survey reported in the *Wall Street Journal* (April 17, 1984) reveals that a typical CEO stays in his position for seven years, down from 7.9 years in 1983. Seven years is not a long time to be a CEO. Perhaps it is not even long enough for a CEO to have a full and constructive impact on the strategy, growth, or character of an organization. This relatively brief time span may reflect the dissatisfaction of chairmen and boards with the individuals selected. In situations where this is the case, the quality of key candidates who competed unsuccessfully for those CEO positions was probably also inadequate for organization needs.

Selecting Out

Narrowing a selection decision to the most qualified candidates is usually more a process of selecting "out" than selecting "in." By the time most candidates for senior executive positions are regarded as sufficiently prepared to move up to senior responsibility, probably all of the candidates are within the limits of acceptability. The

[3]*Op. cit., Dun's Business Month*, p. 53.

selectors are now seeking one or two more aspects of perspective, personality, experience, or ability that will remove a candidate from the final list. Their strengths are evident and their weaknesses are probed.

An example of a characteristic likely to remove a candidate from further consideration is the candidate's inability to negotiate in a crisis situation. Competent analysis and accommodation of different opinions is required at all times, but is especially difficult under time pressure, emotional pressure, or in conflict situations. Despite their obvious strengths, some of these candidates have never operated under the pressures incumbent in a senior executive's role. When they are placed in operational settings to confirm their potential for growth, the test will reveal their ability to manage effectively in a crisis. They may lose their temper, use poor judgment, scapegoat, demean others, or contribute to a worsening of the conditions that create the crisis—any of those reactions will cause them to be dropped from the list of candidates.

When an executive is excitable or flies off the handle, few people trust him again. George P. Hollenbeck, Director of Corporate Human Resources at Merrill Lynch & Company, Inc., says:

> People with senior executive potential must be able to participate effectively in crises. In our business, crises pop up every month and you must be useful to people solving the problem. If you're useful, you get to be a member of the team. You've got to understand the business and you've got to bring a cool head.

Another characteristic, the reluctance to share power, should drop an otherwise qualified candidate from consideration. This is usually not noticed until an executive is in a high enough position to be a key candidate for a promotion to chief. For an individual to be a key candidate for a senior executive position, there should be evidence of an ability to delegate authority and power. This is critical for any chief to operate well. One clue to an executive's willingness to share power, especially if he or she has been in his or her current position for at least two years, is whether he or she has identified or groomed his or her own successor. When a key candidate must be pushed by his or her chief to identify a backup, it is not a good predictor of senior executive potential. In this case, selectors should probe for clues to support this hypothesis. Confirming evidence should result in the dropping of a key candidate.

It is at the point in a succession planning cycle during which the number of key candidates is narrowed that selectors should identify questions or issues that could not have been addressed earlier. Behaviors and personal characteristics that do not visibly emerge until candidates are in significant and responsible positions, for example, should be explored. The unwillingness to share power, as mentioned previously, is one characteristic that will not be evident at middle levels of management. Other characteristics or behaviors that may not be evident until an executive has significant responsibility include: how well he or she negotiates differences; how effectively he or she can integrate and administer the work of several functions with multiple activities in each; how he or she establishes or changes an organization's climate to encourage stronger individual identification with the organization's strategy; and how well he or she exercises independent thinking to lead an organization.

The right need to know questions should be framed in order to bring these issues to the surface. Some questions that might serve the purpose include: What, how much, and to whom does he or she delegate? To what degree and on what issues does he or she expect to be fully informed? What is the decision-approval system for his or her staff or direct reports? What is the "division of labor" like between him or her and staff? What kind of recognition does he or she give to others for support? What are his or her relationships like with executives at his or her level? How well does he or she collaborate with other functions? Under what circumstances does he or she invite individuals from other functions to become involved with his work or problems? Selectors should take special care to look for evidence, ask questions, or engage in conversations to get answers to these questions. It should not be assumed that potential chiefs who possess the majority of preferred personal characteristics, abilities, or experience do not have serious deficiencies on these other points. The chances are great that most of them will. Unless they are screened more closely, some will get through the net and the wrong selection decision will occur—and the effects can be awful. This may account in large part for a lot of turnover at the top and a fairly short tenure in CEO positions.

WHAT MAKES THE DIFFERENCE AMONG KEY CANDIDATES

When narrowing to the key candidates, there are lists, litanies, and volumes filled with advice and research findings on what makes the real differences, that is, those qualities or characteristics that predict who will and who will not be successful. While the senior executives who select chiefs generally agree on a number of characteristics and abilities that they believe are predictive, very few of them express the same confidence and the same characteristics and abilities. For example, some say vision is most important, others say that motivating a team is paramount, and some predict success mostly from analytical ability. They will agree, when asked, that the other qualities are also important—but they do not typically look for those qualities or abilities on their own initiative. Many selectors focus on just a few aspects of personality, ability, or experience and tend to overlook or dismiss evaluating other characteristics because they do not know how to assess them or because they are unaware that deficiencies in some of them can be organizationally lethal.

Overriding these concerns, however, is the fact that narrowing to key candidates is an extraordinarily difficult task. It involves considerable ambiguity, the complexity of trying to match and balance an individual's behavior, abilities, personal characteristics, experience, and accomplishments with a different working environment, a new role, new tasks, and new interpersonal relationships.

It is of immense interest to see how the criteria for this narrowing and balancing process are perceived and implemented in different companies. Fairly representative perspectives are reflected by the following remarks:

> Candidates for senior executive positions need tremendous self-confidence. They must be tough, analytical-minded, a good data processor, inquisitive—and have the courage to say "Forget it" or "Tell us where we need to go." They must explore all alternatives with equal vigor.

> This is different from the characteristics of somebody we put into a mainstay business—in these businesses we have the world's best products, we're Number One in the market, we have slow to no growth and our quality of leadership and service is excellent. In these

cases, you want somebody who is thoughtful, steady, and who can manage a very large and a very slow-changing thing.

I want to know what somebody avoids—because they probably don't do it well.

We don't look at a breakdown of a candidate—We don't look at business competence, organizational acumen, interpersonal skills, financial abilities—The answer, in a sense, is none of the above. We look at integrity and brains. I draw a number of inferences on how his—or her—mind works, how verbal he is, how complex have been the situations in which he's been involved. What kind of league has he played in and how successfully has he competed? I put an emphasis on analytical skills.

I look at accomplishments and what a person left behind when they left the job—did he leave it better or was it a mess? Does he—or she—have a good sense of what people are about? One fatal flaw is that somebody doesn't have a rudder, a sense of direction and ability to steer.

Ambitious people must learn to manage staff and learn what staff can do for them. If they can't, they deny themselves a lot of help. They must be smart enough to surround themselves with outstanding people and have the confidence to say, "Follow me!" They have to be able to manage through up and down cycles, through growth and recession. They also need to manage in as many different situations as possible and with different kinds of bosses. They have to demonstrate they've been able to do all these things very well.

We sometimes mistake tough words for being able to handle confrontation. We sometimes mistake style for substance. We will never know enough to know with certainty what a person really has accomplished.

We sometimes assume that because a person has been through a lot of experiences, he has learned everything from it. We don't focus enough in what he has really learned on those jobs or what happened to him in them. *We sometimes generalize beyond an apparent success and sometimes mistake experience for learning.*

Theodore P. LeVino
Senior Vice President
General Electric

We're so public that each of our top people has to be trained to be public relations people—to handle the public.

> Robert E. Frazer
> CEO
> Dayton Power & Light Co.

Two years ago who the hell cared about Hong Kong, Korea, Japan? In our business they are now our major competition and you've got to know your competition. The most important things for a CEO are personal flexibility and knowing your competition.

> CEO
> Clothing Company

A potential CEO must know his business very well so he can participate in the solution of crises. He must also be perceived as active, as a doer—and he needs a vision to be good. He's got to be able to write his own job description—which is the uniqueness of the CEO position.

Vision! How can the President run the United States of America with so little detailed knowledge of the business?! What does he have? A vision! Yet there are people with detailed knowledge and no vision— no dream about what their part of the organization can become—and the organization wallows. . . .

> George Hollenbeck
> Director of Corporate
> Human Resources
> Merrill Lynch Company, Inc.

We need someone who can preserve our values—values like excellence, integrity, dependability, compassion, fairness, team play and responsiveness.

> Vice President
> A Communications Company

The most important ingredient for a CEO is vision—by vision I mean where the country, economy, industry and competitors are going and the ability to translate all of those facts into a direction for his business while at the same time managing the process for achieving short-term objectives. Though vision is really a long-range look and keeps the CEO out of the day-to-day running of the business, he still has to be able to periodically tap back into operations to make sure that the plan is really working and appropriately redirect it if necessary. A classic example of this ability is the vision that Stan Gault [Stanley C. Gault, Chairman of the Board, Rubbermaid] had for this company and the way he repositioned it and strengthened it for continued growth.

> Thomas W. Ward
> Senior Vice President
> Rubbermaid, Inc.

[O]ne of the most important criteria, if not the most important, is intelligence. Truly successful managers and businessmen have one common characteristic—they are usually very bright. The other ingredient that is an absolute must is honesty.

Given a high level of intelligence and honesty, the next two areas which I feel are critically important are the willingess to work hard and a sense of humor. Without these qualities, I question whether individuals can be truly successful by a reasonable standard in the long term.

> Robert E. Fowler, Jr.
> President and Chief
> Operating Officer
> Rubbermaid, Inc.

We need a CEO who can take people into his confidence so they feel better about him. That's the way you motivate people. They don't like aloofness and distance.

> Chairman
> A Diversified Consumer
> Goods Company

A CEO must also form and run a team toward objectives. . . . He's got to have a sense of urgency. . . and he must be a mature businessman

who can handle problems and adversity without getting rattled. . . .
We need to look at how he can manage tough issues.

> H. S. Richardson
> Chairman
> Richardson-Vicks Inc.

One of the hardest things to predict is whether someone's style of
decision-making will still be good tomorrow. All of our managers look
at leadership—and I know that's a broad statement. We look at who
does their job the best. The top candidates are all good but some are
better than others.

If a candidate has been a Sloan Fellow and spent a year at Stanford
or MIT, it's a pretty big plus in his favor. Most of our top people have
been Sloan Fellows.

We avoid blatant competition by keeping competitors in operating
jobs, not corporate jobs. That minimizes the horse race. We don't have
a firm set of standards but we just look for who does their job the best.
It's performance only.

> Vice President
> Aerospace Co.

The skills that differentiate the top performers from the rest would
include people management skills, leadership, charisma. . . . Experience helps build these traits, plus you can emulate other leaders,
observe their leadership characteristics, and then decide which traits
might be successful for you throughout your career.

> Senior Executive
> Citicorp

A view that suggests a distinction between managers and leaders
was expressed by another Citicorp senior executive:

In terms of policy and objectives and willingess to work out problems,
a manager has to demonstrate a leadership capacity. I'm not suggesting you torpedo the hierarchical management structure, but you have

to be willing to question, to get involved, particularly in difficult situations.

Occasionally, people get by as administrators. But generally one of two things happen as a result: (1) we don't do as well as we could have and (2) we might even have a disaster on our hands because an administrator is so preoccupied with pure paperwork, or numbers, that he or she really doesn't know what's going on.

When it comes down to a final decision, harmony and cooperation are not options—they are mandatory. Getting along with your colleagues—upwards, downwards, and sideways—is also very important. In an organization like ours, even the greatest geniuses can't operate on their own.

Also, in the final analysis, personal integrity is absolutely necessary. It cannot be compromised. Walter Wriston, Chairman of the Board for Citicorp, observes:

An obvious necessity throughout a career is personal integrity. Without that, you have nothing. The whole reputation of our organization is built on personal integrity.

Vision, integrity, and the ability to motivate a strong support team seem to be three of the attributes often sought by people who select chiefs. Neither the nature of an industry, nor its products, employees, or objectives seem to cause selectors to look for characteristics or abilities that are unique.

MAJOR FLAWS AMONG KEY CANDIDATES

It is difficult for selectors to identify major flaws among key candidates because these individuals have so many outstanding qualities—the same outstanding qualities that made them key candidates in the first place. Perhaps it is a sense of obligation to these candidates that causes selectors to be reluctant to acknowledge or probe for major flaws that usually become evident only when a significant level of executive responsibility is achieved. Research and observation in corporate organizations highlights these flaws:

Administrative incompetence, which is sometimes hidden behind an action-oriented and hard driving personal style or behind strong technical knowledge.

Premature activism, often seen in executives who act with little restraint and without reference to organizational or administrative strategies.

The inability to work well in a larger organization, because of difficulty in synthesizing and coordinating all the pieces and operating parts of the organization, or because they try to manage a larger organization as if it is a small one.

The inability to spot incipient problems or identify new trends or conditions.

The inability to set up a good support team.

Letting personal interests determine the focus and direction of an organization.

The inability to work with ambiguity, for example, working well without feedback or not capable of connecting apparently unrelated information with his or her expectancies or speculations.

Personal abrasiveness, especially in crisis or ambiguity.

Reluctance to cooperate with others.

Composure under stress.

No capacity to shift from the specific to the abstract, for example, using an event or condition to form the basis of a principle or policy that will enable a better response in the future to those events or conditions.

The inability to manage both the present and the future.

There are two practical ways to search for these flaws and to determine their depth. One way is to put the candidates into a situation (a "horse race") where they will compete with each other and demonstrate what selectors need to know about them. Another way is to carefully identify and evaluate what is known about the candidates and then to speculate and project how they will perform in a variety of situations.

The Horse Race

When two or three key candidates are available and the chairman or president is not certain who to select for chief, a staffing reorganization often puts the candidates into a race—each with operating responsibility for a segment of the business. The thinking behind this is that the best candidate among the competitors will emerge by producing the best results.

The advantage of this process is that it provides a rationale for the final selection decision that prior observation and analysis could not. Selectors can find certain comfort in this. A disadvantage of the horse race is that it creates adversary relationships that are not productive. Lack of cooperation, failure to exchange or share information, defensiveness, and competition for resources and affiliations do not enhance organizational effectiveness.

A horse race also highlights losers. The candidates who lose the race may leave the company. The reputations and self-image of the executives who worked for the losers are identified with them often suffer as well. Perhaps a better alternative to a horse race is better prior testing and a better analysis of what is known about the candidates.

An example of a horse race and its consequences is evident in the process involved in selecting Citicorp's successor to Walter Wriston. Three executives—Thomas C. Theobald, Hans H. Angermueller, and John S. Reed—were pitted against each other. Mr. Reed was selected in what appeared to be a highly competitive process. As reported in the *Wall Street Journal* (June 29, 1984):

> The contest was considered a typical Citicorp move to allow executives, each of whom was given an office near Mr. Wriston, to battle it out for the top spot. . . . The marathon also generated understandable tension within the bank. . . .

Mr. Reed, however, was very successful in addressing some of Citicorp's problems and needs. He also "more than his rivals . . .

seemed to share Wriston's restless creativity and determination to push Citicorp into new field. . . . More often than not, Citicorp has selected an innovator to lead it, someone who is interested in more than just banking" (*Time*, July 2, 1984). Thinking like his boss was also apparently a strong factor in Mr. Reed's successful candidacy. This point was emphasized in a *Forbes* magazine article on careers entitled, "Think Like the Boss and Take Chances" (July 16, 1984):

> How . . . did Reed get to the top? Hard work, intelligence and good fortune, of course. But he is ultimately a beneficiary of one other element in the decision. Wriston, in the end, opted for a successor who thought just like his boss.

Apparently, Mr. Reed won the case because he acted incisively to take appropriate risks and was perceived by Mr. Wriston to be predictably similar to him regarding his ways of working and his ideas for the future. Executives who find themselves in a horse race should take note of the importance and advantages of taking risks. Most significant business problems and needs require something more than routine judgement. Individuals who are willing to take risks are likely to be given more attention—and certainly more recognition and responsibility—when they are successful.

For key candidates involved in such a race, it is especially important to raise questions and project answers on issues such as the compatibility of their values with other chiefs in top management, potential points of difference or conflict with the board, their ability to build and motivate a team, the management of ambiguity (*not* its continuation), personal courage when under fire or in crisis, the exercise of power, and the ability to actualize the corporate strategy. These leadership perspectives and behaviors are not easily discerned in positions or roles below those occupied by key candidates. Leadership needs a context in which to become apparent.

Management skills, on the other hand, become evident at lower organizational levels, and they should be demonstrated before an executive becomes a key candidate for a senior executive position. Asking the right questions in the right framework will help bring clarity when comparing and evaluating the key candidates. This will reduce the need for a horse race.

A Framework for Prediction

Prediction is more likely to be dependable if it takes place in a framework that maximizes practicality and minimizes ambiguity. There must also be a way to bridge the past and the future. An important source of information for this framework is the assessment made in group evaluations, using an outline similar to that suggested in Chapter 5. Contemplation of future events and prediction of how an individual is most likely to perform should be based on how that individual has operated in the past. Without a strong bridge, succession planning will not be very predictive.

A practical framework for the selectors of chiefs includes a review of what is known about them, what we need to know, and ways to get answers. When this information is categorized as follows, it also gives clear direction on how to learn more about a key candidate in areas directly related to future effectiveness as a chief:

Personal Characteristics

>   What we know

>   What we need to know

>   Ways to get answers

Performance and Accomplishments

>   What we know

>   What we need to know

>   Ways to get answers

How We Feel He Will Conduct Himself in a Senior Executive Position

>   What we know

>   What we need to know

>   Ways to get answers

Organizational Implications

>   What we know

What we need to know

Ways to get answers

Getting Information.   The review of personal characteristics, performance, and accomplishments ensures that past behavior and demonstrated personal qualities will be the basis of projected descriptions, or predictions, of both how an individual will conduct himself or herself in a senior executive position and how the organization is likely to respond. To build on a framework of this kind, two or three people can usually contribute observations and opinions. Chiefs who are involved in succession decisions should also find someone to lead the discussion and assure that the right questions are asked, that the answers are as complete as possible, and that inference and assumption are not diluted by random speculation or personal bias.

The advantage of two or three senior executives participating in this discussion is that they can stimulate each other's thinking, question each other's opinions, and add to each other's knowledge of a key candidate. If one of the senior executives responsible for the selection decision leads the discussion, his own existing biases will prevent full and fair discussion—however unintentionally. An external consultant or respected internal executive might lead this discussion.

An Example of a Discussion of Key Candidates

Portions of the following discussion of key candidates by senior executives prior to a final selection decision illustrates how information is exchanged and considered. The purpose of this discussion was to review what they knew about the candidates—not to make a final decision. In this case, the president and a senior vice president discussed the candidates to replace the senior vice president, who was planning to retire in 18 months. The discussion was led by the corporate officer responsible for senior executive succession planning. In the following section, a written summary of the conclusions is outlined, within the framework for prediction described here.

Discussion Leader:	Let's start out reviewing what we know about Tom.
President:	Well, he's certainly a very smart guy, he's got a lot of interests, knows how to get things done and has a tremendous amount of personal energy.
Senior Vice President:	Yeah, I agree with that. He reads a lot of modern history and business magazines. He's as up-to-date as anyone I know in the history and background of the labor movement and the things that have blocked or helped its relationship with management. That's an unusual interest for somebody in his line of work but he says it's helped him to be a better manager.
President:	It probably has. That's one of his strengths. The people that work for him respect him. He knows how to motivate people.
Discussion Leader:	Is he good at motivating all kinds of people or is he more effective with some kind of people?
Senior Vice President:	That's a good point. The people he motivates best are self-starters, people who are independent. Anyone else seems to have difficulty working for him.
President:	That's right, he doesn't tolerate mediocrity for very long. People who don't do their jobs well don't last long in his businesses.
Discussion Leader:	Tell me about his judgment. Give me some examples of how you've seen him exercise it in difficult situations.
President:	His judgment is very balanced. I've seen him handle conflict on a variety of business issues. He is very smooth with other people and does not like poking them in the nose. Whenever possible he avoids conflicts and prefers to draw people into his thinking.

Senior Vice President:	Well, I don't know about that. I've seen him have difficulty when I would have expected him to coordinate different opinions with more skill. He's O.K. when things are running smoothly but he does not always act in a cool way when the pressure is on.
Discussion Leader:	Are you saying that he acts differently in crisis situations?
Senior Vice President:	Yes. He seems to get nervous when he's actively opposed by several other views, especially when those other views vary.
Discussion Leader:	Can you give us a couple of examples of that?
Senior Vice President:	[Two examples were given and discussed.]
Discussion Leader:	What are his major values?
President:	I'm not sure how to say this but he is always concerned about truth. He's also a stickler for accuracy. I guess that I have to say that his major values include truth and the importance of meeting commitments or keeping promises.
Discussion Leader:	Can you give us several examples of that?
President:	[Several examples were described and discussed.]
Discussion Leader:	How creative is he? What kind of business vision does he have? What has he done that's been different?
Senior Vice President:	He's not a terribly creative person—in a personal way, I mean. He knows how to react to a good idea when he hears one but he does not initiate a lot of new ideas on his own.
President:	Well, what about the reorganization of [business unit]. That took a lot of creative thinking. He developed a new business strategy, identified some new products, and convinced everyone else that was the direction they ought to go in.

Senior Vice President:	You're right about that. But he had some help with it. He had a good staff and they worked very closely together. I'm not sure how much of that was his idea or how much he was working with his staff's ideas.
Discussion Leader:	Seems clear that he can set a climate that can foster better thinking. But can you separate that from personal creativity? How well does he give good ideas to others that they can act on?
President:	That probably doesn't matter. As a senior vice president, he would be working more with other people's ideas than his own and he does that very well.
Discussion Leader:	Is he more conceptual or more operational?

The discussion continued in this vein for a while and then turned to a conversation about what they needed to know about the executive and how they might find the answers. One part of this conversation was as follows:

Discussion Leader:	You've always seen him speak with conviction and self-confidence. Do you know how well he communicates to subordinates when he has to pass on ideas that are not his own? Maybe they are his boss's ideas, but ideas with which he disagrees. Nevertheless, he knows that he has to communicate this to his people.
President:	That's a good point. I think you're asking how he communicates information that he doesn't agree with but needs to be passed on. That happens sometimes and a senior executive has got to be able to do that well. Otherwise, he can't be trusted to support policy and strategy as we expect him to do.
Senior Vice President:	I know he doesn't agree with the new incentive compensation plan. He said so in

very strong terms. But that is in effect now and he's got to tell his people what the program is like and he's got to support it. It would be wrong for him to explain it and then to say that he disagrees with it. Let's see how he does that.

President: When is he going to have that discussion?

Discussion Leader: Would it be appropriate for one of you to sit in on that meeting or to ask him what he said and how it went?

Senior Vice President: Very appropriate. I'll ask him to see me after he has a staff meeting. He's honest and he'll tell me what he said and how they reacted.

Discussion Leader: O.K. Is there anything else we need to know about him? Are there any gaps in our understanding of him?

Senior Vice President: No, I think we know him pretty well.

The discussion moved to a review of the candidate's performance and accomplishments.

Discussion Leader: Can you describe what you know about his accomplishments, especially those which have been attributed directly to him?

Senior Vice President: Well, not all of his business decisions have been good, but, in general, he has made good everyday decisions and has outstanding operational judgment. His business instincts are good and he has been able to stimulate good teamwork in all of the places he's worked.

President: I haven't seen any significant accomplishments but that's probably not a fair thing to say since he has certainly been involved with businesses and projects that have been very successful.

Senior Vice President:	He's an excellent planner and his plans generally work out. At least the short-range plans do. It's more difficult to look at long-range plans.
Discussion Leader:	Can you be more specific about his accomplishments?
Senior Vice President:	Sure, he has [the senior vice-president described several significant accomplishments in his current and previous positions].
Discussion Leader:	What else do we need to know about him?
Senior Vice President:	I want to know how well he will grow the business and diversity. We want to go in new directions and I would like to know how he's going to do it—and whether he can do it?
Discussion Leader:	What indications do you have that he's doing the right things now?
President:	He's doing a number of things now. For example, he [the president described several projects for which the candidate was responsible. He was questioned on some of these by the senior vice president and the two agreed about what else they wanted to know].

The discussion turned to ways of getting answers to what they wanted to know about this candidate. They also compared him to other individuals who were candidates for the senior vice president position. His candidacy raised some questions among them regarding his occasional reluctance to cooperate with others when he felt strongly on an issue. Some ways of getting answers to this point were discussed and planned.

The president and senior vice president then discussed how they thought the candidate would conduct himself in the senior vice president position.

Discussion Leader:	Based on what you know about him, let's

talk about how he would conduct himself in the senior V.P. position. For example, would his interest in the career development of managers continue and how would you expect him to emphasize this in his new role?

Senior Vice President: I expect he would continue to have a deep interest in the development of key people. I think he will take charge of an executive committee which assures that career development is not overlooked and that people get promoted or moved to get the experience they need. Based on what he has done in the past, I'd expect him to be very selective about the sort of people that assume more responsibility. He won't take-risks with people that are mediocre because he knows they don't perform well.

Discussion Leader: What kind of a climate will he set?

Senior Vice President: Oh, I think he will set a climate where people work well with each other.

President: I'm not so sure. He likes things to run well and doesn't like to hear complaints. I think that's one of the reasons he has been so interested in the labor movement and contract negotiations. While he hasn't actually done it, he is a very skillful negotiator. I think he'll have a climate in his organization that looks good from the outside but complaints will be suppressed because he discourages people from complaining.

Discussion Leader: Why is that?

President: Probably because complaints suggest an organization which is not running smoothly.

The discussion continued to review the characteristics of climate they expected the candidate to emphasize and to minimize. They also talked about the kind of people that the executive would probably select as his staff. They wondered whether the people on his staff would be candid with him and whether he would be isolated from real problems in the organization. They also considered how he would manage conflict within the organization and whether he would break with traditional relationships when that was required. After a while, the discussion leader led them into a discussion of organizational implications that would surround this executive's selection.

Discussion Leader:	What do you think would happen in the organization if he was selected?
Senior Vice President:	I don't think he would make any fundamental organizational changes and he'd work very hard to establish a cooperative climate.
President:	He probably would be very generous with compensation because that's one way to ensure good relationships and minimize discontent.
Discussion Leader:	Well, we need to know more about that. What organizational changes do you think he would make? Can you be specific? And how would he handle feedback which disagrees with his opinion?

The president and senior vice president discussed what they wanted to know about the organizational impact of this potential selection decision. They explored ways to get answers to the questions they raised and a plan was devised to do this.

At the end of this discussion (which addressed personal characteristics, past performance, accomplishments, how they felt the executive would conduct himself in the senior vice president position, and the organizational impact of that selection), the discussion leader summarized their comments into three categories (what they knew, what they wanted to know, and ways they intended to get answers to their questions). The entire conversation covered this executive and one other candidate in three hours. A summary of their conclusions and observations is outlined below.

SUMMARY OF DISCUSSION

Personal Characteristics

What We Know

Major values center on truth, personal commitment, and integrity. These are what drive him.

Does not always distinguish between friends and opponents in his treatment of them.

Speaks with strong conviction and enthusiasm.

Superior technical background and high state-of-the-art proficiency.

Not comfortable with ambiguity or organizational contradictions.

Draws people to him; has great personal magnetism; he gains their confidence.

Hungry for success.

Exceptionally bright and analyzes well without need to recycle ideas and information.

Polite, considerate and attentive upward and with peers; sometimes disdainful of subordinates who are anything less than exceptional.

Well balanced emotionally and in good physical health.

Good intellect, wide scope of interest, high personal energy; action oriented.

Knows how to motivate people who are competent and independent, others have difficulty.

Judgment is balanced and sound.

Prefers a smooth organization, without visible disagreement on issues.

Extroverted behavior in business situations.

Likes to work with ideas and handles concepts very well; expects others to execute against agreed ideas and plans.

Does not always handle pressure well, sometimes loses his temper.

What We Need to Know

Can he accept people whose value system is different than his?

Can he work with people who are different and engage them to gain consensus and maximize their contribution?

Ways to Get Answers

Note the people he selects and transfers over the next year.

Pay special attention to how he handles conflict and different points of view.

Performance and Accomplishments

What We Know

Has had excellent experience across functions, that is, engineering, manufacturing, finance.

As GM, has set strategy and direction for (operating business group,) has been very successful although not all business decisions were good, (e.g., three projects identified).

As GM, has stimulated several new lines and spinoffs, thus generating new businesses.

Not good at selection skills despite strong analytical abilities, (e.g., several selection areas identified).

Too impatient with lower level people and has permitted substantial differences of opinion on part of subordinates which have caused internal problems (examples given).

Good operating knowledge of core businesses but not of experimental ventures.

Sets exceptionally high standards for himself and expects others to meet their own objectives.

Operates well independently and can perform well without outside support.

Decisive, willing to control the situation where he feels it is required, sometimes tries to create outcomes.

Good everyday decisions and good operational judgment.

Good business and technical instincts.

Committed to management development of people in technical functions but no evidence of concern for careers of individuals in support functions.

His significant accomplishments have been attained in conjunction with other people.

What We Need to Know

Will he move the business into other areas?

Can he manage new ventures?

Will he deal with options and deviate from a direction when circumstances indicate he should?

Will he work with people who are different from him and will he work with people who can compete with him?

How compatible are his ideas for strategic directions with those of the board?

Ways to Get Answers

Note how he handles his businesses over the next year.

Review the plans he is now presenting and endorsing.

Talk to people who report to him and observe how he exercises general business leadership to people as well as technical leadership.

How We Feel He Will Conduct Himself in New Position

What We Know

Will not be overly interested in some staff activities, preferring to delegate leadership of them.

Will continue to have deep interest in career development of key people but probably not of middle-level people.

Not likely to make dramatic changes in organization direction or strategic plans; will continue on present course.

Will want a responsive staff and may replace people who do not provide the information or results he wants or who do not work in a fashion similar to his.

He will limit the number of people with whom he consults; as he gains confidence and consolidates his position, he may seek their advice less.

As a general rule, people further removed from him will not feel comfortable being candid with him.

He will not take high risks because he is comfortable with how he handles things.

He will want to have his own team.

He will know enough to take a business focus instead of just a technical focus and will put more emphasis on running a business than running a (technical) function.

He will be generous to management regarding compensation; will use money to motivate.

What We Need To Know

Will he surround himself with strong people who will be candid with him and who will challenge him?

Will he continue to be open as he becomes more secure in the new job?

Can he break with tradition if needed?

Will he miss the nuances of the business by delegating certain decisions to staff executives?

How will he work with corporate staff functions that do not report to him?

How far out does he think and plan?

Will his emphasis be more technical than strategic?

Can he deal with diverse personalities?

Will he engage opposition and look for common ground or will he try to negotiate differences and compromise?

How will he manage in bad times and crises?

How will he handle pressure?

Ways To Get Answers

Review how his plans work out over the next 12 months.

Observe how he staffs and works with his headquarters staff over the next 12 months.

Note the kind of people he selects and develops.

Personal conversations or general attitude surveys with employees in his organization.

Organizational Implications

What We Know

Will not make fundamental organizational changes.

Will create a flatter organization so he can be more involved in business decisions but will delegate support group decisions to other executives.

Will work hard to establish an optimistic climate.

Will be personally directive in career planning, which will probably result in more personnel movement within his organization.

There is a risk that some very good people will leave the organization if he does not take them into his confidence; if this occurs, his organization may suffer from a lack of strong managers at its top and middle.

What We Need To Know

What organizational changes will he make?

How will he focus on and improve his selection skills?

How will he get other executives involved with him more closely on decision making?

Ways To Get Answers

The president and current senior vice president should discuss these issues with him and ask him what he would do.

The current senior vice president should ask him for a plan, in writing, which outlines his organizational structure, recommendations for the next five years—along with a rationale as to how this structure would meet strategic and operating business needs.

AN INTERESTING ALTERNATIVE

Rubbermaid is a company respected for its business performance and management strength. This company takes extreme care in the selection of key executives. It uses an interesting and innovative alternative or supplement to other processes. Rubbermaid's approach is sophisticated because the thoughtfulness behind it is is appealing and because it is straightforward and easy to implement. This unusual approach to staffing was used by Rubbermaid's Thomas W. Ward, Senior Vice President, Human Resources, when

he was with the General Electric Company. He saw it used successfully there and it is now used at Rubbermaid.

First, the technique actually scrutinizes the performance of the
organization currently managed by a candidate. Next, the selector
(or the hiring executive) studies this information to determine the
nature of the match between the candidate and the position to be
filled; the advantages and risks of a match are carefully reviewed.
Third, an evaluation team is formed (in addition to the selector, or
hiring executive) to include one or two senior executive peers of the
selector, at least one peer executive to the position to be filled, a
human resources executive, and perhaps a former manager of the
candidate. Fourth, subordinate staff to the open position are also
involved in the evaluation process. Their opinions of the candidate
who may become their chief are obtained, and they exchange ideas
and perspectives with him. On this last point, Rubbermaid reports
that feedback from staffs, candidates, or hiring executives has been
unusually positive to this approach, and subordinate staffs have
developed a quick identification with their new manager because of
their involvement in determining the position specifications for the
evaluation process.

Rubbermaid's key candidate evaluation process can be outlined
as follows:

1. Evaluate performance of candidate's organization in the follow-
    ing areas:
    a. Performance against goals
        i.   How realistic were they?
        ii. How tough were they?
        iii. Were they met/exceeded:
        iv. What degree of control/influence did the organization
             have over the results?
        v.   Solicit views of subordinate managers.
    b. Special projects/programs
        i.   To what degree did the organization take on extra work?
        ii. How flexible/versatile was their response?
        iii. What impact did this work have on business results?

   c. Business environment
      i. Describe recent and current business environment.
      ii. How did the organization respond?
   d. Strengths/limitations
      i. What did they do best?
      ii. What did they do least well?

2. Evaluate current organization structure in the following areas:
   a. Effect on performance
      i. Strengths.
      ii. Weaknesses.
      iii. Does it use talent well?
   b. Key interfaces
      i. Are they well defined?
      ii. What are current relationships?
      iii. Are they satisfactory? Solicit views of peer/organization and staff interfaces.
      iv. Where are they working well/not well?
      v. Any new key interfaces likely to develop in near future—if so, what impact?
   c. Strengths/limitations
      i. Review 2a and 2b and summarize.

3. Evaluate current staff/people balance:
   a. What is ratio of mature to inexperienced employees? Is it right now and for the future?
   b. What is ratio of flow-through/long-term employees? Is it right now and for the future?
   c. Is current skill mix satisfactory?
      i. Identify strengths/weaknesses.
      ii. What will be the appropriate skill mix during the forecast period?
   d. Identify anticipated people changes:
      i. Promotions.
      ii. Retirements.

      iii. Other unplanned losses.

      iv. Lateral moves.

4. Evaluate peer organization performance/interface:

    a. Are roles/responsibilities still appropriate and properly aligned?

    b. Are there opportunities for role clarification/realignment or consolidation?

    c. Solicit views of peer managers.

5. Evaluate candidate's performance in light of:

    a. Management of assigned resources.

    b. Goals met or not met.

    c. Specific accomplishments.

    d. Appropriate match of his or her managerial style to business/ organization needs.

    e. Relationship to staff/peers.

    f. Summary of strengths/weaknesses.

6. Develop staffing needs based on following analysis:

    a. Develop and fine-tune position specifications. In addition to generic Position Guide description, identify and document the specific job to be done, highlighting key impact areas.

    b. Develop and fine-tune manager specifications.

      i. Using all data gathered, determine the skill/experience/ managerial style combination most appropriate to getting the job done.

      ii. Think through the proper managerial style match between the new manager and you, the hiring executive.

      iii. Does the situation call for a flow-through or longer-term selection?

      iv. Is this an opportunity to enrich the organization with a high potential talent from another organization?

    c. Selection of evaluation team and hiring process should be tailored to the specific situation.

      i. A recommended approach would be:

        A. Solicit views of subordinate and/or peer managers

as part of the initial analysis (steps 1, 2, and 3). This process provides a sense of involvement and identification with the selection process.

B. These views can be gathered individually and/or in group sessions. Usually, group sessions have netted valuable insights and high quality data.

C. Consider summarizing your views in a one-page "situation" statement which best describes the business climate, major work to be done, changes that are likely to occur in the next one to two years, etc. In short, *capture* the "situation" so that the evaluation team knows exactly what you are looking for and is not dealing with old information and/or erroneous perceptions.

D. A similar summary of "candidate attributes" is equally important. A carefully selected and prioritized list of attributes which best describe a skill, experience mix and managerial style of a candidate most likely to succeed in a particular managerial assignment is of great benefit to the evaluation team. Additionally, it may sometimes be beneficial to ask the team to concentrate on these key attributes during the interview process, especially as they relate to their own functions.

E. In most cases, especially at higher levels, the evaluating team should consist of the hiring executive, one or two peer executives to the hiring executive, the human resources vice president, at least one peer executive to the position being filled, and, if appropriate, a former manager of the candidate.

WHO ASSISTS THE SELECTOR?

Senior executives need help in developing criteria and questions, organizing them, identifying people to answer them, probing the answers, evaluating them, and, finally, putting it all together. Most companies have internal staffs and senior staff executives who provide these services.

Better questions might be: What do we know about the people who help in the process of selecting chiefs? What is their background and how are they prepared to do this? Are sufficient and diverse views brought to the selection process by those who assist with it? How does the quality of selection assistance affect the selection decision? How vulnerable are those who assist in the process when they express minority or divergent opinions on a candidate or on the criteria and information used to evaluate him?

Internal Executives. Senior executives must ensure that they receive information or advice that is not guarded or defensive. Human resources executives are usually a good source of support because most will be thorough about evidence to support opinions and willing to discuss opposing or divergent views. This may be unfair to them, however, because they find it difficult to subsequently work well with those candidates who are not selected because of this involvement in their evaluation and rejection.

Some other senior executives can often be helpful with knowledge of the candidates and their perspectives of them. Other internal executives may have biases which they do not control—intentionally or not—in the evaluation discussion.

Board Members. Involving external board members in the process can be very helpful if they know the candidates or can arrange to spend sufficient time with them on several occasions. Also, members of an executive committee of the board are more likely to be open to new information and able to evaluate all candidates without initial bias. It is especially important to separate reality from perceptions about key candidates—and this task is more difficult for those who have worked closely with the candidates for some years.

External board members have the advantage of distance but this must be balanced by interactions with candidates which enable understanding and insight. "Dog and pony shows," in which candidates make presentations to board members, can be misleading because they are highly controlled and rehearsed circumstances. This makes it difficult to discern intellectual depth and broad business knowledge from charm and communication skills.

External Consultants. An external consultant can sometimes add to a board's evaluative contributions because of his own experience and perspective. Still, an external consultant's observations and predictions about key candidates for management succession will be limited to those areas of his or her expertise, for example, personality, financial competence, and strategic planning. For this reason, care should be taken to select an external consultant for a specific, rather than a general, expertise.

— 7 —

Facing Resistance

FORCING A CHOICE

Since the selection of a key senior executive, or chief, is not determined by democratic or popular vote in a company, differences of opinion about the candidates must be resolved in other ways. In some parts of the world, differences of opinion about leadership are resolved by firing squads. In other parts, the firing squads get a lot of practice, but the differences are not resolved.

While some corporate chiefs may fantasize about the advantages of quick resolutions, most are realistically aware of the need for a consensus of opinion. Without consensus from the other senior executives who must engage, interact with, and depend upon the selected executive, the selection—and prediction—will be a mistake. Corporate chiefs cannot effectively operate independently from peer senior executives or even from board members. Collaboration and teamwork is required. There is no value in forcing a selection decision, even by a chairman or CEO who has the power to do it.

It is also inevitable that resistance to opinions about key candidates will occur. Each individual involved in a selection will have had different experiences with the candidates and will judge the candidates on the basis of their own experience. Differences should not only be anticipated when preparing a slate of key candidates, but the selectors should encourage the others involved in the decision to actively probe the rationale underlying opposing views rather than only preparing to fortify the rationale for their own choice.

Robert E. Fowler, Jr., Rubbermaid's President and Chief Operating Officer, tries to manage so that peers and subordinates feel comfortable in disagreeing with him. He says:

> There have been more than a few evaluations where there was legitimate disagreement over the best candidate to fill a key slot. . . . First, we go back and re-visit the job specifications to be sure we are in agreement on them. Then we sit down and talk about the task at hand.

> Finally, we talk about the environment, both inside and outside the company, in which the individual will have to perform. We then go back and compare each of the candidates again against this background. This is a far from perfect system but it has allowed us to reach a selection decision in situations where we started off virtually deadlocked on the candidates.

> From my own personal standpoint, it is rare that I would use power of my position to edict a selection. . . jobs filled this way invariably place the incumbent in an impossible situation which, more often than not, results in failure.

Seeding.   In many cases, the chief faced with making the actual selection decision may find it advantageous to begin to seed his rationale—without identifying his preferred candidate—with other executives from whom he expects some resistance. There is advantage to both sides. The selector has laid the groundwork for support of future observations—and resistance is often easier to overcome if there is time for a different point of view to become more familiar and less threatening. The probable resistor has had time to (1) reflect on another view and (2) more thoroughly contrast it with his own.

Even if resistance continues or is strengthened by time and thought, the selector may find that the reasons for resisting his choice have introduced elements that he had not previously considered. Seeding, or an earlier approach to anticipating resistance, will also accustom chiefs with different views on candidates to the process of reasoned discussion instead of abrupt confrontation.

Values.   If the selectors probe reasons for resistance carefully, they will probably find that it stems from different values, not from differences about what a candidate has accomplished. Selectors are more likely to balk at the "how" and "why" of a candidate's performance or history than the "what."

Although most all candidates for senior executive positions have a visible record of accomplishment, selectors will be uncomfortable predicting desired future behavior for some of them. They will attribute different values and motives to the candidates and expect (i.e., predict) less-than-desirable future behavior because of this.

External Impact of a Selection Decision.   Virtually all chairmen and CEOs are public figures in their communities. They serve on civic, educational, and charitable committees. They participate as board members in the affairs of other companies. They have a deep personal impact on the lives of people, many of whom do not work in their company. If a potential chief's values are not compatible with the obligation and need to serve public or community needs, even though he or she is exceptionally qualified to increase corporate revenues, it might be wise not to select this individual.

Sometimes selectors do not consider the broader and longer range impact on the image and competitive stature of a company when selecting a senior executive. Since many senior and executive vice presidents, as well as other corporate officers and general managers, will eventually become the CEO of their company, it is appropriate to question a preference for a candidate whose values or motives are incompatible with corporate policies and expectations.

William C. Friday, President of the University of North Carolina, posed an interesting issue to a group of CEOs at a conference in North Carolina (Center for Creative Leadership, CEO Forum, April 1984):

Looking ahead 10 years, what should a CEO do to ensure that your corporate interests work to support the needs of your state? For example, what is your responsibility to building the public school system in your state? How will you deal with this issue in your selection criteria? And what are we doing around the nation on some bigger issues—employment policies, the tax structure, the use of natural and human resources?

The CEOs did agree that they do have a responsibility and that they do want successors who can handle these responsibilities well. Selectors, therefore, should challenge the qualifications of recommended candidates to assure that corporate values of this kind will be enacted by the succession of chiefs.

MANAGING DIFFERENCES

Thomas W. Ward, Senior Vice President of Rubbermaid, says that an important part of the personnel vice president's role is the managing of the decision-making process for key candidate selection. He must assure, for example, that the individuals involved in a selection decision understand how each of them sees the candidates. One way to do this is to question the selectors on their impressions of a candidate before bringing them together to discuss opinions. Mr. Ward suggests that it is important to get as much detail and texture as possible from them before they get together to exchange views. This, he adds, will help to surface any "hidden agendas." As a result, unnecessary resistance is minimized.

THE EXPERIENCE OF RESISTANCE

A typical situation encountered by senior executives is best described by the conversation that took place. In this case, the chairman wanted C.C. to succeed the retiring executive vice president. The president disagreed. He prefered D.D. Excerpts of reconstructed dialogue illustrate the resistance experienced by both men.

Chairman: We've got to come to a decision on who's going to be our next executive vice president. The job is opening in less than four months and we've been discussing it for over a year.

President: I know. You want C.C. I'm telling you that he's good—but not good enough. He's an attractive, charismatic guy but he just doesn't know our businesses as well as he should.

Chairman: He spent his career in operating jobs, except for the last two years.

President: He's spent his career in operating jobs but they've been in our steady well-established businesses, not our tough businesses. He's had experienced staffs working around him in each one. He's worked for experienced people and he's had experienced people working for him. He's been protected.

Chairman: He hasn't made any mistakes. And D.D. has.

President: He couldn't make any mistakes because his organizations were so strong they wouldn't let anything serious go wrong. D.D.'s mistakes were not errors of judgment—he made some decisions which didn't turn out as he planned it. We can't expect anyone to be 100% right all the time. And none of his mistakes were serious—they were all part of calculated risks.

Chairman: D.D. doesn't have C.C.'s stature. C.C. has tremendous personal presence. Anyone coming into the executive vice president spot must be a back-up to you and we need somebody with presence, somebody who has credibility with the investment community, the public, the press—aside from long experience in our business. What we do and say is pretty visible.

President: I admit that C.C. has a lot of personal style. He just doesn't have enough knowledge of our businesses to develop a strategy that will work. D.D. isn't as attractive initially but he conveys a lot of strength and ability to the people who know him. He knows how to develop a business strategy that people will adopt. He's done it in each of the two top jobs he's had. He changed the direction of his last business and they've really turned around. C.C. has not developed a business strategy because he's always inherited one and he didn't change them. C.C. has been in three top jobs and he didn't change one thing in each case.

Chairman: He didn't have to.

President: So we don't know if he can when it needs to be done. D.D. can do my job. In a smaller sense, he's done it twice. He's strong, smart, and knowledgeable. People have confidence in him.

Chairman: You're dismissing C.C.'s accomplishments. He's got a fine record. Look, I don't want to force an executive vice president on you. You've got to want him because you think he can do that job and your job. You've been a great communicator. You've got an image. But you do depend on your executive vice president and group executives to run the businesses. You don't get involved in details. Why are you fighting this so hard?

President: Because I think an executive vice president has to be involved in details. He's not going to step into my job so soon. There's an executive vice president job to be done. We need someone who can do more than just talk about our businesses—Oh, I don't want to detract from C.C.'s abilities or experience but he just won't run them as well.

Chairman: We need a leader more than we need a high level operating officer.

Both chief executives felt frustrated. Neither was able to overcome the resistance offered by the other, even though both remained willing to discuss their differences. Neither man wanted to be perceived as stubborn or unwilling to listen. Their inability to reach agreement on a candidate could have been avoided—or at least confined to a shorter period of time—if at least one of them had taken a different path when he realized that he would face resistance to his selection preference.

CONVERSION VERSUS CONFRONTATION

In the preceding conversation, it does not matter who was right since a prediction can only be verified with time. What does matter is that neither executive stepped back soon enough to exchange opinions on the candidates with other people who had enough legitimate involvement or interest in the final decision (for example, board members and other senior executives) to give an open ear and balanced opinion.

When it is evident that a difference of opinion is an obstacle to a decision, it is time to solicit other opinions for consensus on one's points and position—but consensus should be sought through calm, reasoned discussions over time, going back to review ideas and views, and trying for agreement on common ground. These discussions cannot be rushed and time must be spent on them. The alternative is disagreement and resistance which often takes up just as much time and does not end up with eager support for the executive who is finally chosen. William M. Read, former Senior Vice President of Employee Relations, ARCO, feels that resistance should be overcome gently. He says:

> What's needed is a quiet sell. You have to talk with inside people in senior level positions who, because of seniority and age, are not candidates for the position you are looking at. You have to do the same with the outside board. It is important to be subtle in the distinctions you make among candidates because you don't want to oversell. This may take months but it's worth the time.

Mr. Read adds that one of the larger external sources of resistance encountered in selecting a CEO is the board's reaction to the candidates. He points out that key candidates who are more socially oriented are regarded more favorably because they are more visible. Therefore, a major problem that the chairman must resolve is how to sell the board on who is best because of ability—not sociability. A board often resists individuals who are not as familiar to them, despite other endorsements of their qualifications. Further, an internal point of resistance often faced by sponsors of a key candidate is

the chairman's perception of the candidate based on long ago experience with him. Sometimes this lingering perception may inhibit the
chairman from picking the most qualified person. In this event,
sponsors or advocates of a candidate should urge a group evaluation
to introduce a more balanced perspective.

John Carlson, Vice President of Haley Associates, a management
search and consulting firm, tries to anticipate resistance on key
candidate selection when he begins an assignment. At the beginning
of each search, he receives clearance to meet with the "jury members," all the people who will be participating in the hiring decision.
This serves a number of purposes: First, by determining how each
person is viewing the position to be filled and what they expect the
hiring decision to accomplish, a working consensus is formed at the
outset. Any glaring inconsistencies and misunderstandings can
then be reconciled. Mr. Carlson noted that well-qualified candidates
are not likely to remain interested in a job if they do not see a
working consensus.

A second reason for meeting with all the jury members is that they
represent the environment and culture in which the new executive
will be asked to succeed. Matching candidates with that environment is just as important as satisfying job specifications. Third,
when an internal candidate is under serious consideration, Mr.
Carlson emphasizes how important it is for the jury members to view
the internal candidate with better objectivity. This objectivity can be
gained by comparing the internal candidate to external candidates.
Favorable comparison against external candidates is an excellent
opportunity for the internal candidate to earn even greater support
from other executives, even those who may have previously resisted
his appointment.

SUPPORTING A MINORITY OPINION

Holding or communicating a minority opinion is somewhat different from trying to overcome resistance to one's point of view about a
candidate. The holder of a minority opinion knows that most others
feel differently on the issue. Predicting a key candidate's performance in a new job is, by itself, a judgment based on a lot of hunch

coupled with whatever evidence or history is available. Predicting the key candidate's performance differently than the majority of others involved in a selection decision requires more courage. It is easy to cave in to pressure on this issue—and it is important not to do so prematurely.

A sponsor, or participant in a selection decision, has an obligation to challenge majority opinions with which they disagree. In most cases, the majority of people involved in a selection decision do not know a candidate well enough to judge him accurately. Too often, for example, a key candidate becomes the majority preference because he or she has done one or two things well and a halo effect was created. William Read of ARCO cautions, "One of the biggest mistakes is picking somebody for a senior executive position because he's a good old Joe with a lot of service and he deserves some recognition."

One technique for increasing one's own confidence to hold and test a minority opinion about a candidate is to probe other opinions for specificity and to reduce generalizations. For example, asking the following questions will often elicit clarity, better information or even an admission that the minority opinion has merit:

Opinion: He cannot control his temper.
"Under what conditions has he become visibly angry? Have you ever seen him remain calm even when there's been a lot of pressure?"

Opinion: He is impatient with people.
"What else do you think might contribute to his occasional impatience with people—too many responsibilities, inability to delegate or over-delegation, not enough help from anyone, surprises outside of his control, the ineptness of others?"

Opinion: He is a poor communicator.
"Is he a poor communicator with everyone—subordinates, peers, upward? And on what kind of issues or topics—problem solving, seeking information, giving information? What kind of communication does he do well?"

Opinion: He does not have sufficient depth of experience.

"In what specific areas does he lack experience? How does this affect his ability to perform in the jobs we have in mind?"

Opinion: He is a strong leader.

"Can you explain how he leads? What do his people respond to? Who do you compare him with? Leadership has several sources— expertise, the power to reward or punish, the promise of long range satisfaction. Which accounts for his ability?"

Opinion: He has a lot of charisma.

"When you get beyond charisma, what other unique strengths does he have? What is the evidence for those? How does he compare with people who have less charisma but more ability in. . . ?"

This portion of a conversation among three chiefs (the CEO, his chief operating officer (COO), and the chief financial officer (CFO)) involved a selection decision between two candidates for the position of senior vice president of adminstration. The COO did not think that the candidate preferred by the CEO and CFO was suitable because he doubted the candidate's integrity. Rather than simply giving his opinion, he raised questions which the CEO and CFO had to answer.

CFO: Hugh has been around a long time. He knows us and we know him. Everyone likes him and he is a thoroughly responsible executive.

CEO: You know how I feel. I want him. I can trust his judgment and he'll take a load off me.

CFO: [Speaks to COO]. Why are you against us? Hugh is very solid.

COO: You both say he's solid. O.K., maybe he's got the experience and he certainly does know this place. I'll agree he works very hard and doesn't let things get away. He'll manage every administrative aspect well. But I've got to question his integrity—not as an executive, [but] as a manager. Have you talked to anyone who's worked for him about how they feel about him?

CEO: What do you mean?

CFO: That's awkward. We can't do that.

CEO: That's ridiculous. What would you say? I won't embarrass Hugh or myself?

COO: All you need to do is have lunch with a couple of the general managers who work for him. You'll find that not everyone likes him—there are exceptions. Ask them how Hugh supported them during monthly performance review meetings when [the CEO] challenged some of their numbers. Ask them if they felt they could depend on Hugh's backing if they agreed to take a calculated risk and it didn't work out. Ask them if Hugh ever contradicted himself, or changed his position mid-stream when [the CFO] raised questions about a general manager's funding of projects. I think you'll find that the general managers don't trust him because they couldn't count on him to be where he'd said he'd be. That's integrity as far as I'm concerned and there is a difference in the way he acts up versus down.

CEO: I didn't know that. If you do, then it needs to be checked out. I wish I knew that before because if it's true, he doesn't fit the job.

Probing for specificity is an effective and easy way to surface accuracy and to encourage people to listen seriously to a minority opinion. It does not happen often enough.

REBALANCING A POSITION

Rarely is a decision to select a chief made unilaterally and without advice. Chairmen, presidents, CEOs, COOs, senior and executive vice presidents typically seek others' advice and opinion on key candidates. They are, of course, aware of the importance of consensus and acceptance—and they are also aware that different views can be very revealing. Sometimes a unique insight coming unexpectedly from a solicited opinion completely rebalances the information collected up to that time.

A good example of an insight that rebalanced the selector's initial choice among the candidates was described by George Hollenbeck, Director of Corporate Human Resources, Merrill Lynch and Co. The selectors were impressed with the qualifications of a candidate in a series of responsible positions and predicted continuing success for him in a very senior position. However, one of the senior vice presidents who was asked about the candidate had a different opinion. He noted that the candidate had performed well up until then because his operating responsibilities were placed on a relatively long cycle compared to the decision requirements for the position to be filled. The open position, he correctly analyzed, demanded immediate reactions and decisions. The candidate characteristically took a lot of time to digest and ponder a decision. In fact, the strength of his reputation was based on how thoroughly he pondered information. Further, the candidate would never respond rapidly to requests for decisions, no matter how much pressure was put on him. The selectors immediately saw the candidate from a different perspective because the new information drastically changed the balance of information.

Perfection. No candidate is perfect. Few are even seen to be as good as the individual they will replace. Flaws or weaknesses often have more impact on a selection decision than strengths. When discussing a candidate's strengths, weaknesses, and needs, it is proper to request others to describe the relative importance of a strength or weakness in the context of an overall prediction. Where flaws are noted in otherwise strong key candidates, it is usually because they have emphasized the development of strengths in other areas. Nevertheless, some key candidates are found to have an Achilles' heel, such as a lack of integrity, a demeaning personal manner with others, inability to deal with ambiguity, or a poor judge of people. It is difficult to counterbalance such a failing, no matter how strong the candidate is in other areas.

— 8 —

Making the Best Fit

THE DECISION

Modern folklore suggests that the people who select captains of industry do so with great conviction in their choice. Not so. More likely, the decision is reached with some reservations despite many months (or even two or three years) of painstaking reviews of the candidates and their abilities. No alternative or "what if" is ignored as selectors screen candidates and issues.

While there is no photographic evidence of the immediate reaction of board members at the moment they make their final decision, it would not be surprising if a camera revealed each one slouching in his chair and looking at a different spot on the wall.

The reality is that decisions to select senior executives are made with a lot of deliberation. Even in companies with elaborate executive development programs, and with executives who have long service, the process resulting in the selection of a chief is not on automatic pilot. T.P. LeVino, Senior Vice President, General Electric, calls it an iterative process: "We don't sit down and say, 'Now we are going to make a decision.' We get different views and ideas until we realize there is only one decision that makes sense. It emerges with time and thought."

As Robert E. Fowler, Jr., President and Chief Operating Officer, Rubbermaid Inc., says:

When we get to the last two or three individuals in a senior executive staffing situation, we have already concluded that the . . . ability is present. The issue boils down to not whether an individual has the basic competence, but whether that individual will fit into our situation and whether that individual has the emotional and managerial background to do the task that is required.

PREVENTING REJECTION OF THE CHOICE

John Carlson, Senior Vice President, Haley Associates, has an interesting way of describing the selection process. He likens it to organ transplants. He says that matching a person's skills and experience with a job is relatively simple, like taking blood tests and tissue samples to match donors and recipients. The critical stages are the operation and the post-operative period. Incompatible styles, management chemistry, and culture account for more executive "rejections" than do shortfalls in technical skills and experience. It often takes time after the "operation" for new mentor relationships to take hold. Throughout this period, the hiring organization and the new executive must commit to an effective level of communication to promote a healthy transition.

This is a marvelous analogy. Selections do often fail despite a good match between a candidate and an organization's needs. Many selection decisions would have happier aftermaths if new chiefs and their organizations received better support during the getting-to-know-you period. The most appropriate source of support is from corporate staff executives who can counsel, advise, and negotiate among a new chief and members of his organization. Rubbermaid Inc., for example, has an assimilation program for new managers at all levels (described in Chapter 9) which dilutes the hazards of "rejection symptoms."

THE UNSPOKEN MESSAGE

The final selection of a candidate is more than the distillation of information. The decision sends unspoken messages to other executives and employees. Usually, the entire company staff knows the differences among likely candidates—whether or not they were aware of the actual candidates: some candidates are known for their demanding and tight-fisted management style; some for the breadth of their interests and experience; others for their deep technical expertise; and still others for their entrepreneurship.

The nature of the selected candidate's background sends signals to the organization. The signals and the reactions to them should be anticipated so that the meaning of a selection decision is not misinterpreted within the organization. Misunderstanding of the rationale behind a selection decision may result in energy wasted on the wrong reactions or insufficient support to the new chief's objectives or ways of working.

CORPORATE CULTURE AND EXPECTATIONS

Corporate cultures, like those of any society, are built on a network of opinions, ways of doing things, and relationships among people. In industry, a lot of attention goes into assuring that specific types of behavior reflect the company's view of the value of relationships, for example between management and employees or between management and customers. These behaviors include treating employees fairly, listening carefully to the concerns of others, initiating change to be on the leading edge of progress, giving responsibility or autonomy to employees, and cooperating fully with others.

Regarding culturally determined behaviors and values, Mr. Fowler, President and COO; Rubbermaid Inc., says his interest in talking with the strongest candidate for a senior position focuses on the "how" of his management style since the "what" has already been ascertained. He puts a great deal of weight on a candidate's values, especially those which address Rubbermaid's approach to management.

Many companies are eager to sustain their traditional culture. Some others are eager to change theirs. But the attempts to define and measure culture seem mostly limited to corporate communications and attitude surveys. In general, corporate chiefs assume a specified culture exists even when events and time have reshaped it somewhat. Perhaps a better way to describe a company's culture is in terms of the expectations of its top management and its employees. It is a company's expectations that actually define cultural behavior. Expectations cause behavior, conversely, behavior can be predicted from expectations. Expectations are also one of the most evident aspects of corporate tradition, or culture. A practical way to assess change in a company's culture is to ask its executives and employees about their expectations.

An example of cultural expectations in a company is General Electric's emphasis on technological progress. General Electric's corporate culture expects its management to emphasize state-of-the-art advancement, and many of its managers are evaluated on their ability to provide state-of-the-art leadership in their area. AT&T, on the other hand, is preparing to change its culture to adapt to the divestiture of the telephone companies and a more competitive environment. An excellent article in the *Sloan Management Review* (Fall 1983) by W. Brooke Tunstall of AT&T says:

> Clearly, the culture must be reshaped, adapted and reoriented to bring the value systems and expectations of AT&T people into congruence with the corporation's new mission and to prepare them for the competitive telecommunications battles looming ahead. . .as AT&T moves toward a more competitive environment, its management style must adapt accordingly.

CULTURE AND PERSONALITY

Senior executives are usually comfortable with their company's culture. This is not surprising, since they are an important reason it has continued. Even when there is a desire to change a culture, it is not a clean break from the past that is wanted, but some new behavior to make it easier to meet corporate objectives or follow a corporate strategy.

Many chiefs say that they want a "culture change" when all they really want are changes in ways of working. It is unrealistic to try to do this because the interlocking and pervasive network of opinions, relationships, and ways of working are extremely difficult for one or even several persons to change in a reasonable period of time. Besides, the chiefs who are powerful enough to try this usually do not want to do it.

A company's chairman or CEO may decide he or she wants to pick a senior executive who can significantly alter a company's culture because a change is needed to build morale or to move into new business areas. The nature of the task should be considered. A company's culture is as difficult to change as an individual's personality. A personality is comprised of a set of attitudes and beliefs that cause a person to think and act in certain ways. Attitudes, by definition, are predispositions to respond. They are very much like expectancies in this respect.

In the context of behavior modeling and attitude change, consider a pile of cannonballs heaped on each other to approximate the shape of a pyramid. Assume that each cannonball is an attitude, expectancy, or belief. If one of the cannon balls is to be replaced, the easiest cannonball—or expectancy—to replace is the one on the top. To change any of the other cannonballs requires a disassembling of the pile. Besides, each of the cannonballs is in some way connected to or supportive of others. The task becomes overwhelming.

Personalities resist dismantling. Corporate cultures also resist dismantling. In any case, it is equally difficult to do so.

BEHAVIOR CHANGE AND A NEW CHIEF

When a corporation's problems or objectives indicate that new behavior is required on the part of management and employees, these expectancies should be articulated as carefully as possible. It is practical to select a chief who can describe clearly how and what he or she will do to meet those expectancies. There should be an apparent and close connection between what a key candidate says he or she will do and the behavior change that is needed to turn the corporation in a better direction.

Corporate leadership can make a huge difference in the culture of an organization and the image it conveys. Some of the most dramatic examples of the effective leadership on culture are found in American politics. Some U.S. presidents, for example, Abraham Lincoln and Franklin Roosevelt, by sheer force of will, changed bedrock behavior in the U.S. culture. The result was a subsequent attitude change. In the corporate world, Lee Iacocca's leadership at Chrysler is a prominent example of this.

Selectors should not assume that a key candidate will change the behavior of others by a logical and persuasive appeal to their good judgment and attitudes. Attitudes, as indicated previously, are very difficult to change. It is more likely they can be changed by focusing on the behaviors a new chief will encourage. If behavior can be changed directly—by demonstration, urging, or even by demand—it is probable that the attitudes that supported the old behavior will decay because they are no longer reinforced. Instead, new attitudes will form to support the new behavior and the new attitudes will survive as long as they are reinforced—by verbal encouragement, personal accomplishment, recognition, or monetary reward. Selecting a new chief who is able to act in ways that encourage and reward behavior change is an effective way of changing an organization for changing times and changed needs.

INFLUENCE OF THE PAST

When selecting a new chief, the history of an organization must be remembered. Selectors inevitably look backward to learn and draw from the past. There is a tremendous premium on continuing what has been that can be either very helpful or very negative. The past cannot be ignored; elements from it are invariably brought into the future. Selectors must consciously and continually remind themselves, however, that the reality of the past may not be the reality of tomorrow.

As selectors move to a final decision, they should remember that a new chief will manage people and issues unlike those managed by his predecessor. The workforce and problems in most industries have changed. Many of the time-honored ways of leading an organization no longer work as well. Strategies and rules of leadership have changed. For example, the ability of a chief to share strategic leadership with his senior executives may be more of a requirement for success in the next 10 years than it has in the past.

Aspiring chiefs would do well to consider how the future of an organization might be different from the past. While the lessons of the past must be remembered, there are ways of the past the sometimes need to be changed. If the key candidate does not express his own views about what aspects of an organization's culture should be retained and what aspects changed, however, he or she may be regarded as a product of the past who is likely to continue tradition. In most companies, selectors will prefer a chief who shows promise of more flexibility. Key candidates who are viewed otherwise are not likely to be the final choice.

A STURDY BRIDGE TO THE FUTURE

Selectors want their final choice to remember the past. A culture has a strong hold on people. It has a heavy impact on how they will think and act. A major consideration of selectors is how the preferred candidate will avoid getting lost in memories.

Selectors ought to have some idea of the candidate's plans for building a bridge to the future. Thomas Storrs, former Chairman and CEO of the NCNB Corporation, feels that it is much better for selectors to look for generalized qualities of resourcefulness and imagination in the successful candidate "rather than pinning the selection decision to today's concepts of what you want—because there is a good chance you'll be wrong." He believes that, for the most part, selectors should "find a man for all seasons." The exceptions to this, Mr. Storrs says, are cases where selectors can foresee an immediate and specific task where specialized knowledge and skills are needed. At ARCO, the ambiguity in preparing for selection decisions is reduced, according to William Read, retired Senior Vice President of Employee Relations, because the chairman regularly communicates his plans for the future to key senior executives.

Decentralized and Distant. With less ambiguity about the future, a key candidate can tangibly describe how he or she will address the expectancies communicated to him. Selectors have greater uncertainty about the future when the successful candidate will be placed in a decentralized operation of business. When a business is distant or decentralized, the strength of a bridge from a corporation's culture to its future should depend more on communications than on close monitoring and hands-on support. Succinctly stated by one senior executive in a financial services corporation:

> When he (a new senior executive) goes out to a stand-alone business, we want him to wear a company T-shirt. But he's also got to remember where he belongs.

If the chief of a decentralized business does not remember where he or she belongs, it will most likely discourage selectors from advancing his or her career any further. A special hazard, then, for executives in decentralized businesses is the loss of identity with their corporation's culture. While communications to corporate staffs will increase understanding, steps should be taken to ensure the visibility of executives in decentralized operations.

HOW IT IS DONE

It is interesting to note how companies and individuals settle down to a final selection decision. The overriding emphasis is on reflective discussion. While there is also general reluctance to define the future beyond general expectations, final selection decisions are based on confidence in the fit between the successful candidate and the company's strategies and goals. The following observations are those of senior executives who are directly involved in the selection of chiefs. Each senior executive was asked, "When it comes down to actually making your selection, what really takes place and what influences you the most?"

IBM. The Corporate Director of Executive Resources, Don Laidlaw, has the staff responsibility for succession planning at IBM. Performance, he says, is the best predictor. For each key position there is an average of three solid candidates. The successful candidate for a senior position will have unusually broad experience and an excellent performance record. The selectors look for cross-functional and cross-divisional experience under a number of managers, as well as staff and line experience. Mr. Laidlaw says it is sometimes important to take a risk on someone who may be short of some experience. If the candidates had the support they needed, things usually turned out well. When they have not been successful, he feels it is often due to such factors as an imbalance in their experience—for instance, insufficient staff or line experience.

There are formal annual review procedures that occur down to the second level of management. For senior level jobs, the discussion of "best fit" takes place among the CEO, the vice chairman, and the president. For the next lower level, the division presidents are included. When final selections are discussed, senior executives zero in on two issues: the requirements of the job and the past performance of the individual. Nevertheless, even if a candidate has an outstanding performance record, they will be eliminated from consideration if he or she has not demonstrated excellent people management skills.

Aside from performance and experience, a most important criterion is integrity. The successful candidate is also trained at managing people and situations, beyond the management of functional matters. Experience outside IBM in executive development courses is also viewed as important. Typically, candidates for senior executive positions at IBM have attended an executive development program in public affairs, humanities, or general management at institutions such as the Brookings Institute, the Aspen Institute, or Harvard. In fact, the company encourages aspiring executives to get as many external experiences as they can.

The ability to get along with others is also important. Mr. Laidlaw indicates that IBM is not looking for consensus management, but for an executive who can disagree constructively. IBM also takes an additional and unusual look at candidates for more responsibility. The company has on-going attitude surveys which, among other things, seeks information from subordinates about their executive's ability to manage them.

When it comes down to making the final decision among the candidates, IBM selectors are just like their counterparts in other companies. They tend to pick people with whom they will be most comfortable—comfortable with their thought patterns and confident in their recommendations.

AT&T. AT&T is restructuring itself after the 1984 divestiture of the telephone companies. They had a thoughtful process of management succession in place before the divestiture, and there is every reason to expect AT&T will develop an equally careful process to accomplish its conversion from a telecommunications company to an information systems company.

To be a candidate for one of the top positions in the former Bell System, an individual had to be in the "presidential book." Candidates' names were entered in the book on the basis of recommendations from Bell System company presidents. The preference was for individuals who had multi-company experience with the system and who had the endorsement of two operating company presidents or equivalent.

The nominations were collected by H. Weston Clarke, Senior Vice President of Personnel for AT&T. He submitted them to the office of the chairman (which included the chairman, vice chairman, and three executive vice presidents) who decided which names to accept. Mr. Clarke points out that they had to go to considerable effort to make sure that the decision-makers were familiar with the candidates. To do this, candidates were invited to participate in corporate task forces or moderate at certain functions, such as corporate policy seminars. This provided the opportunity for interaction which will still be needed in the "new" AT&T.

When a senior executive opening occurred or was expected, the selecting manager asked the senior vice president of personnel for the names of potential replacements. The names were usually drawn from the presidential book. While the decision rested with the selecting executive, the executive could be influenced to select someone other than his first choice if, for example, his boss wanted to reserve that candidate for another position.

The process was repeated annually. Since most of the potential candidates for senior executive positions had participated in external development programs, the focus was on the internal experiences they needed and on an evaluation of their abilities. AT&T assumes that not all executives are proficient at evaluation or development and, therefore, several management experiences and evaluations are required over time.

AT&T's succession planning is somewhat unique. This is because AT&T feels that a concentrated development effort is required or aspiring chiefs will not get the broad exposure they should have.

Richard Campbell, AT&T's Director of Management Development and Education, identifies the following factors as having the strongest influence on determining the best fit: outstanding accomplishments; vision (as evidenced by strategic planning sense); the ability to pull things together that other people do not readily see; the ability to integrate; the ability to build, as demonstrated by the ability to take a function or operation to a better place; integrity (defined as saying what they think, not cutting corners, and treating people fairly); and the ability to deal with change, uncertainty, and ambiguity. AT&T, feels that outstanding performance, by itself, is not sufficient. For example, while AT&T almost always develops chiefs from within, a senior financial position was recently filled from the outside, perhaps because a different financial management was needed for the business and it was important to signal this change to other executives.

Mr. Clarke emphasizes the importance of paying attention to clues and signals when determining who makes the best fit. He says that there is sometimes a tendency to get "swept away by someone and ignore good information that is available." He described two situations where clues and signals were ignored—and it was subsequently regretted.

In the first situation, an executive was promoted into a senior position based on his experience, leadership, and personality. Unfortunately, this executive was at times so supportive of his people that their judgments and ideas were accepted without critical evaluation. While this was known in the organization, it did not preclude the executive's selection. However, it proved to be a serious deficiency in the more responsible position.

In a second case, an extremely successful and respected line executive was offered even greater responsibility if he would transfer to corporate headquarters. The executive was reluctant to leave line operations and relocate. Nevertheless, an especially attractive offer lured him to a corporate staff position, which he disliked intensely. The executive failed to recognize that he was being deliberately exposed to an area of staff work which would broaden him and enhance career opportunities. He did not enjoy it, and eventually left the company.

In both cases, if clues were not ignored, better selection decisions might have been made. Mr. Clarke says, "Our challenge is to make sure we don't overlook clues." Properly conducted group evaluations should help with this.

Final selection decisions, according to Mr. Clarke, also can be affected by the judgments of people other than the person making the decision. For example, in the process of searching for information about a candidate, a negative piece of information from someone will, in all probability, eliminate the candidate. Some behaviors that would eliminate a candidate include over-contentiousness and being too demanding on subordinates.

At AT&T, when a choice is narrowed down to two or three candidates, the candidates are invited to talk with the executive making the selection. Personal impact at this stage can override other issues. The final decision is often made on this basis.

Advice to aspiring chiefs within AT&T must include recommendations to look for opportunites, to increase one's knowledge of the business, and to try to do things not done before. Doing things differently—and better—increases personal visibility outside of an immediate organizational unit. As Mr. Campbell suggests, "People who manage your corporate function must have a high opinion of you. It isn't enough to have someone in a subsidiary organization think highly of you."

A successful candidate in AT&T, says Mr. Clarke, is someone who can "stick his head up out of the pack" and who appears to be in control of the situation he is in. Mr. Clarke adds that selectors say certain things about candidates who appear to be the best fit. Candidates, therefore, need to project this image. He says:

> A successful candidate at AT&T has learned to articulate what he is accomplishing in a way that shows he is well-organized and thinks things through carefully.

He is seen as somebody who is on top of a situation and who can organize people to attack a problem. We look for people who are seen as able to walk into a situation, take charge of it and move it.

Chase Manhattan Bank.   Chase Manhattan's annual corporate-wide review of succession plans involves the chairman and CEO, the president, the executive vice presidents in line positions, corporate functional executives, and the executive vice president of human resources. The less formal quarterly reviews, which are more useful for succession planning for specific executive positions, and for the discussion of the individuals who are identified as candidates, include the president, the executive vice president of human resources, and the executive vice presidents in line positions reporting to the president.

At the quarterly meetings, the senior line executives look down three levels in the organization to identify and discuss candidates for key positions that will open within the next 12 months. This kind of preparation enables faster decision making at the time an appointment must be made.

At a discussion centering on a selection decision, the president and executive vice-president of human resources listen to and discuss with the line executive at the sector level his recommendations for staffing a position at the group or division level. The recommendations must be made in a context of the position's specifications and the candidate's qualifications. Even in the event of the president's prior disagreement with a sector executive's recommendation, the discussion is open and candid. The final decision is made objectively.

Alan Lafley, Chase Manhattan's former Executive Vice President for Human Resources, feels that one of the difficulties that follows these discussions is subsequently developing the same degree of understanding of the candidates by the chairman and CEO since he is usually not as close to the situation.

CEO succession.   Mr. Lafley also believes that the CEO should not be the decision-maker on his replacement as CEO. His ability to choose a successor is often hampered by a lot of history and strong personal bias. He may not see or agree with emerging needs. Sometimes a CEO is tempted to pick the person he likes most or owes a debt to, or who is not a threat or who would not give him competition with the board. CEO candidates must present more promise than suggested by the observations, "He creates a good image for the bank," or "He'll represent us well." A CEO must offer a great deal more than image. In fact, there is a CEO at a major company who is something of an enigma to CEO-watchers and to his peers. While some people have wondered why he was picked, it is apparent that his leadership ability and his accomplishments as a business manager were given more weight than his lack of personal charm—for which he has been criticized.

Culture and fit.   Chase's culture, as that of any business, is largely determined by the CEO but also influenced by the nature of the business. These factors are what make a company different from others. In a bank, for example, a CEO usually develops for many years within its culture. Chase's culture, like that of most banks, is relationships-oriented because of the traditional assumption in banking that if people like you better, they'll do more business with you. But the banking and financial services industry has changed in the face of competition, technology, and government regulations. The important implication of this, for Chase and major banks, is the need to select senior executives who can move away from a singular "relationships culture" and operate effectively in a climate that demands insightful strategic skills and a strong sense of priorities.

Personal characteristics and fit.   Senior executives at Chase are selected from among candidates who have fine backgrounds in banking and high personal integrity. Yet, even when there are only two or three candidates for key positions, there are significant differences in ability, experiences, and accomplishments. Based on his experience and observations, Mr. Lafley comments:

> The successful executive must be willing to take risks, to make tough decisions—so many people who appear to have everything else lack these characteristics. Without these, leadership takes place in a vacuum. Not making a decision—or the fear of making it—is one of the biggest problems I see in candidates for senior positions. Physical stamina is also important in today's world—time changes and international travel, for instance, take a lot of energy.

There is another area where, in the final analysis, some executives fail miserably. They are terrible listeners and if they shut off the sources of valid information, they start to lose touch and the people in the organization close up on them. Sometimes they don't know it because some managers are very political and appear to communicate upward so well. Poor listeners get emotional, shut off bad news and nobody wants to communicate with them. We need to look for executives who know how to listen and don't shut people off.

It's also hard to predict how people will act with their peers as they move toward the top of the company. Some become better executives, some worse. These are some of the factors we have such a difficult time assessing; teamwork, courage, willingness to listen, relationships with superiors; but we need to predict the results when we pick someone for a key executive position.

Integrity and fit.   Integrity is one of the very important personal characteristics Chase seeks in its management. A lack of integrity involves devious behavior which results in losing the trust of customers, employees, and the public. Not surprisingly, candidates who are well-qualified in all other respects for senior positions are removed from final candidacy because their peers, subordinates, or managers simply do not trust them. Their intentions and promises are suspect.

Image and fit.   Mr. Lafley says that there are executives at Chase and in other companies who are respected for the breadth of their knowledge, their accomplishments and results produced, their ability to make decisions, and just about everything one seeks in an executive— but who do not possess the ability to demonstrate leadership and manage a situation. Instead, they are reticent about exercising their influence over others or using their personal power in situations where it could add to direction or clarity. This reluctance is perceived as a lack of leadership ability. No matter what other strengths, this perception will remove a candidate from final consideration for a senior executive position. Conversely, an executive who is a strong leader in this sense will not go far if he is too dogmatic, autocratic, punitive, and emotional. His immediate staff would be entirely frustrated with him even though others in the corporation, not as close to him, think he is an outstanding leader.

Strategic capacity and fit.   Balance between the strategic vision and executional skills of candidates has been a vital point of discussion among those responsible for executive selection at Chase. While there is a tendency to be attracted to strong strategic skills, despite a candidate's relative void in implementation—or vice versa—both attributes are needed in the top jobs. This has been a matter of some concern for the selectors at Chase, especially because strategic capacity—and how it is balanced with the ability to execute—can only be discerned when an individual has served in an executive role close to the top. To assess this quality, Chase selectors pay careful attention to how a candidate has developed and run a business unit. Executives who are good marketers often lose out because they are not good strategists. A strategic capability, along with the demonstrated ability to effectively execute, are critical criteria required of the corporate executive.

The selection decision and fit.   Mr. Lafley's experience at Chase confirms what he believes to be true in most companies: "You are probably lucky if you have a couple of well-qualified candidates for CEO. For a new president, maybe three candidates if you're fortunate. And for a sector executive, we're lucky if we have two or three good ones."

He describes the framework and flow of a selection conversation among corporate chiefs at Chase as follows:

> We spend a lot of time talking about what we are really looking for in the position and what the business needs are now and within the next few years. We discuss what we want out of the job and from the individual who takes it.

> We discuss what the predecessors brought to the job, how they perform it, and the results. And we compare that to what we want now. Unless you spend enough time talking about the position requirements, you may select the hottest candidate going in, who may be the worst possible fit for a particular position.

> Often, the conversation starts out with the president or sector executive discussing whether the intent is to leave the organization structured the way it is or if there is a need for some restructuring around the candidate. Organizational forms should not be cast in concrete—

we mold an organization structure to a candidate if it will give us the best overall result. Since we know the strengths and weaknesses of our people, we may need to mold an organization to fit them. It is important to recognize a candidate's weaknesses so you can know where you are vulnerable. We can compensate with other staffing or organization change to help assure that an individual's gaps are filled.

We talk about business needs, where the problems are, the results expected, and the measurements to be used. This tells us a lot about what we really want in the way of a person. Is a new strategy needed for the business? Are marketing problems a significant factor? Are we behind in executing cost control and staff reduction plans? Are significant staffing changes required?

Unfortunately, one area we often don't pay enough attention to is the compatibility between a new senior executive and his boss. Unless this is carefully considered, you may force-fit an executive into an organization without giving thought as to how he and his manager will work and live together. This is particularly important at senior levels. If it happens very near the top, you're in trouble and somebody's got to go out of the company. At levels below the group executive, however, you can move the person to another group within the company.

OTHER COMPANIES

The observations of other corporate chiefs add to the insights into how senior executives are selected. Some representative comments are included here.

Industrial and Consumer Manufacturing Company

In our company, more often than not, all the candidates are highly qualified or they wouldn't be candidates. It comes down to personal preference. Our chairman, vice chairman, and senior operating executives all make the decisions together on top jobs. Everybody agrees what they are looking for and the candidates are very well known to them. The process we go through is deciding who can do what is ahead.

You can't predict the future but you can see the next couple of years pretty clearly. If you can agree on tasks to be accomplished, then it's clear who the pick will be. It is rare, among our top 20 jobs, that there is a major disagreement about tasks to be done or the attributes of the candidates.

Industrial Manufacturing Company

A big part of our final choice comes down to who can manage the company in the way we want it. People can't be managed today the way we did it years ago. Our top management knows this and so do our first line supervisors. We're having trouble with middle-management on this and we need to pick top management people who can change this as soon as possible. That is most important to us.

Financial Services Company

The final question for us when we pick a senior executive is whether the assignment is a logical step in his career path. If it is, but he's good on the creative side and not as strong on the administrative side, then we make sure we can back him up where he needs it.

Electronics Company

I try not to run a contest when picking somebody. I try to start the evaluations early to give necessary signals to others so that they don't get their expectations out of line. I focus on the guy we want the most. We try to accommodate our second choice by saying, "stick with this for six months and we'll move you." What I do not want to happen is to have one clear winner on Monday morning and five or six losers.

At the start of the process, I also assess who I want to lose—maybe because he'll get in the way of the guy we pick.

I look for intuitive people who know something is good or bad when they see it. If you participate in 25 business reviews with someone, you'll learn how he operates. Good people, for example, can skim a chart and say "Baloney" or "That's genius." You want people who can look for and find the anomaly—someone who can get to the bottom of something fast. I get an impression of intellectual capacity from this. The individual must also be willing to risk damn near anything for winning.

Photographic Equipment Company

Each senior executive at our locations worldwide makes out his succession plans and identifies the candidates who seem to have the highest potential. The CEO reviews this material annually and goes into extreme depth at the top. He asks why, how, when. Thus, plans are laid for the next decade for every senior job in the company.

Industrial and Consumer Manufacturing Company

When we fill a key role, we think about where we are trying to take the business and what are the obstacles for us. We think about the changes we want to make and the things we want to continue. About two-thirds of the time we know where we want to go and about one-third of the time we need somebody to tell us about the opportunities. Its more difficult to pick somebody who will take us to new places.

We also haven't used data as well as we should. We form hypotheses based on what we know; then we try to get corroborative or refutational data from what he's done over the last few years.

Consumer Package Goods Company

We used to look for strong leaders. The values in this country have shifted from heroes to idea people. We still need strong leaders but they have to be innovators.

Engineering and Electronics Company

You've got to take a senior executive's team into account. We do this in several ways. If a team is very strong, you've got to pick somebody very strong or his key people will be looking around. On the other hand, if a team is weak, you must pick somebody who can face tough personnel decisions and attract subordinates. Other times you have to pick somebody who will develop a successor. These considerations help to make the final decision.

Bank

Boards play a relatively minor role in the selection of people below the top two or three people. Boards are concerned about the CEO's immediate associates and they depend on him to build his team. We would like to think this is all done with great deliberation and foresight but I'm not sure this is the case—as a former chairman. You frequently take the best of alternatives without saying you've picked for excellence. If you search for the ultimate choice outside the company, you may not have anything better and you might damage the company. It's not a question of the board saying, "Here's what we need and go find him." Rather, the board says, "We've got momentum so let's look inside to find somebody who has a high probability of success."

I know of a case where the company had a precise definition of what they wanted. They were looking for somebody to reshape the company. So they ran a search on that basis and ended up hiring a man who, I'm sure, will continue to run the company just as it's been run.

Financial Institution

The chairman (CEO) recommends his own replacement to the board, but it's unusual for the board not to go along with the recommendation. It depends on the relationship between the CEO and the board. A big chunk of the chairman's job is managing his board. The criteria for judging his replacement is how well he handles his budget and gets results against his four or five critical objectives.

Hi-Tech Manufacturing Company

When it comes down to it, it's gut reaction. How is he going to fit in with the organization? As president, I make many decisions about senior positions on gut feelings after I have absorbed all the data on the candidates. At middle levels of management, it is different because it's easier to match what you know about candidates with a job to be done.

Energy and Oil Company

The obvious candidate has managed his aspect of the business in the best way possible. He's also made a generally favorable social impression. We don't usually pick a dark horse. He's always a risk because he's relatively untested. It's a hard sell. Our current president, however, is very different from his predecessor. Even though he lacks the charisma you'd normally see in a CEO, he was picked because he handled the number of jobs very well. He doesn't make mistakes.

This type of selection almost becomes a crap shoot—it's tough to predict. For example, we can pick somebody who we know a lot about, but then later on his ego gets in the way. They all have powerful egos. Even though you've picked them for the right reasons, he is now in a spot where his ego grows. Sometimes it grows too big and he can't be controlled. That is something that needs to be anticipated—if it can.

Regarding egos, T.P. LeVino, Senior Vice President, General Electric, notes that a big ego, an absolute determination to win, and a healthy view of oneself is critical. Nevertheless, he says that a successful candidate for a senior position must have (1) a deep concern for people—part of which is picking and growing the best people—and (2) a strong staff. He adds that the most common reason for failure among the people selected is that the job is changed and they pick the wrong person. The lesson here is that care must be taken by the selectors to assure that they are accounting for changes in a job that have occurred since it was filled last.

"DEADLY" CHARACTERISTICS

There is a tremendous consistency among companies regarding personal characteristics that are disdained. Although many candidates for key positions exhibit undesirable behavior as they move through a company, their strengths, which are weighed more heavily in their favor, tend to obscure their flaws. This balance generally shifts, however, when a selection process is approaching the finish line. At that point, it is important to look at reasons why a candidate should *not* be selected. This is a defensive posture but it does reduce the odds of selecting a chief who has a damaging fault. In the final stage of selection discussions, therefore, selectors will review candidates with a less forgiving attitude. Any one of several personal characteristics can shred an aspiring chief's expectations of becoming a senior executive. These characteristics are, in fact, dead weights. Some of the heavier burdens include:

The inability to work as a part of a team, for example, to collaborate with and support others or to share power, praise, and recognition.

Political over-sensitivity, for example, not initiating or taking a position, never advocating or sponsoring anything for fear of damaging one's personal image, or a lack of courage.

Racing to the sidelines when potential conflict appears.

Abrasiveness, for example, challenging and disagreeing without tact or concern for others' self-esteem.

Being wrong at the top of one's voice.

Cracks in integrity, for example, not treating people fairly, devious intentions, actions that are inconsistent with corporate values and policies.

As one senior executive says:

Whether we like it or not, there is a whole set of personality issues that limit somebody's potential. It's hard to really define these things but we do talk about them and they are important. They are often more important than what somebody has done because they tell us what he will do. I guess it's chemistry. Some of the best executives we have just don't have my confidence because of the way they act sometimes.

THE SHOOTING THE MESSENGER SYNDROME

Selectors sometimes receive information that conflicts with their opinion of a leading candidate. One chief said that there is a tendency to shoot the messenger, which is why negative information is sometimes not passed on to a selector. A CEO described a situation where he selected a senior operating executive. Shortly after the executive assumed the role, the CEO noticed that his new operating vice president bent custom on personal propriety in office-social situations. The CEO asked why he was not previously informed of this. He was told that nobody had the courage to tell him something that he might have considered outrageous gossip.

Joseph C. Overbeck, President and CEO of Motor Wheel Corporation, a subsidiary of Goodyear Tire and Rubber comments:

> Unfortunately, my chair has a big impact and can inhibit people from saying what they think. It depends on the people on your staff. Most of my people are strong-willed and tell me what they think. If I am in the minority, I will take their advice.

> When I'm looking at a replacement for somebody, I look at personal work habits, experience and how well he has performed. For somebody who spends a lot of time with customers, his appearance and how he handles himself has a tremendous impact.

A POOR FIT

A former corporate chairman who is active on several boards says that boards are often lax in their responsibility. It is most difficult for a CEO to enter into the process of replacing himself, according to this former chairman. He feels that the CEO needs help because the criteria for picking a new CEO are probably different than the ones used to pick him. The decision needs objectivity. When asked by the chairman of another company to estimate the percentage of cases in which the CEO selection decision is done systematically, the ex-chairman said that it was not done well in six out of eight situations he had observed. When asked how frequently a board disagreed with the CEO's recommendations, the ex-chairman said that he only saw it happen once out of eight times.

A Good Soldier

The senior vice president of a consumer products company made an observation about loyalty that most selectors rarely communicate openly. This executive said that he influences a final decision based on four criteria. The fourth one adds a tangible reality to the thinking behind a final choice:

1. He must be good technically.
2. He must be flexible on how he deals with things.
3. His leadership must push for better ways to do things.
4. He must be a good solider and know how to give his boss what he wants.

In this senior vice president's company, the board selects the new CEO, with the outgoing CEO finding ways to give the leading candidate more exposure to the board so they become comfortable with his skills.

Depending on a CEO's Information

Thomas Storrs, the former Chairman of the NCNB Corporation, confirms that boards depend heavily on the facts that come to them through the CEO and they depend on what he tells them. Mr. Storrs adds, however, that communicating information to boards about key candidates for senior executive positions is one reason why the CEO job is dangerous. If the CEO's opinions are subsequently proven wrong, he is discredited to some extent. If it happens often, he is just discredited.

Richard C. Shepard, president and CEO of Linclay Corporation, a large, privately held real estate development company, tries to anticipate needs for his own succession and for senior vice president positions several years in advance. About candidates, he asks, "Who is he and who is he likely to be?" Mr. Shepard makes selection decisions on personal characteristics and not just accomplishments. In particular, he looks at "how an executive moves from executing and managing to strategizing and leading—and how he's reacted to crisis, in personal as well as business life." He is especially interested in how a key candidate handles pressure and adversity. One of the best sources of information and insight for him is personal communication. One and two levels below a candidate, he discusses how the organization is working and he observes how people below the candidate are reacting. For CEO succession, he discusses candidates only with the owner-chairman because they presently do not have a board.

Mr. Shepard says that the most significant criterion for candidates is their past, present, and predicted performance in picking, guiding, and developing key people. He points out that

> Chemistry with other key parts of the organization is also vital. Chemistry means that people fuel each other; they don't necessarily agree. For example, when we filled a CFO's [Chief Financial Officer] job from outside because an inside candidate had not grown up with the company, we picked a person who fulfilled most major criteria except he didn't have the desired level of real estate structuring experience but his chemistry was tremendous with everybody. As a result, even though he had a perceived weakness in structuring, the rest of the organization drove to teach him. I also look for integrity—including specifically whether he'll be open enough to talk about a problem or if he'll hide it.

He also cautions that a board should be aware of who aids the CEO in collecting and evaluating information about the candidates, since it is possible for information and recommendations to be shaped and influenced somewhat by the opinions of the evaluators. There is, after all, a difference between a reporter and a journalist. Since CEO candidates have usually had visible careers, the people who participate in evaluating them, such as other senior executives, human resources officers, and internal staff consultants, are likely to have formed impressions of them through previous interactions.

The chairman of a leading communications company expects his senior executives to be visible to employees. He watches closely for this. If a key candidate has not shown that he will "walk the floor" where employees work, he will discourage this executive's candidacy to the board even if he has the right experience and exposure across company functions.

LED TO WATER BUT NOT ALLOWED TO DRINK

It is not unusual for senior management to tell a key executive that his major priority is the solution or handling of a major business problem or crisis. Under these circumstances, the executive is often encouraged to be single-minded about achieving a solution—to the exclusion of attention to other matters, if necessary. It takes a fairly intense individual to focus almost exclusively on a problem and deliberately ignore or tacitly delegate other responsibilities which he had previously considered important. A typical case involves a large segment of a business that is suddenly declining fast in the face of competition and high operating costs. To repair the business, the managing executive is told something like, "You've got to fix the business. We're losing market position each day and each month we've declined more than the month before. The operating costs are also killing us. They're draining all our profits and we can't compete. Fix it."

With this mandate, the managing executive goes into high gear. He whips his marketing and sales groups. He cajoles the creative or technical people and he puts a tight arm on his financial people. Under heavy pressure, the organization turns itself around, stabilizes costs, and then heads into a upward trend. But, because it brought results, the pressure continues. People in the organization complain about it, but they are told that they still have a way to go. There is no daylight at the end of the tunnel because the managing executive does not want to risk a fall-back.

At first, corporate chiefs give high grades to the managing executives for fixing the problem. He is even considered seriously as one of two candidates for a senior executive position with more responsibility. However, when the corporate chiefs discuss performance and potential, they sometimes decide the executive is not well-suited to assume more responsibility. In an actual discussion among three corporate chiefs, the decision-making went like this:

Senior Executive 1:   Bob has done an amazing job in [location]. He pulled that operation out of the fire.

Senior Executive 2:   He did. And he managed to cut that business to the bone. He cut through fat and muscle also.

Senior Executive 3:   Bob did what we asked. He was so tough on everybody in the business that they all hate him. He may have gotten results but he is not liked out there.

Senior Executive 2:	We asked for results. We didn't ask him to cut the heart out of an organization. There aren't a lot of people there who like working for him. Some of our best people have quit.
Senior Executive 1:	I don't think that we needed to remind him about the importance of keeping a strong team. He should know that.
Senior Executive 3:	He may be an effective leader but he is no team builder.
Senior Executive 1:	We need a team builder to run technical operations. Bob hasn't shown he can do that. He seems to be an effective leader in very demanding situations but I'm not sure he would be so good in trying to grow something.
Senior Executive 3:	He sure hasn't raised my confidence in him.
Senior Executive 2:	Let's not dismiss him so fast. He may be tough on people, but what are his business development plans like for the next three years?
Senior Executive 1:	He doesn't have any. He spent all his time looking ahead for the next quarter.
Senior Executive 2:	What are those plans like?
Senior Executive 1:	Not very good. They're just a carbon copy of what he's done for the past two years. The fact is he's also done exactly what we asked him to do.
Senior Executive 3:	Hey, we need somebody who knows where to take technical operations. That's a long-term need. We need somebody who can see over the horizon. Can he?
Senior Executive 1:	I haven't seen it.
Senior Executive 2:	Nor I.
Senior Executive 3:	So we've got a guy who has done extremely well in a tough assignment but who doesn't know how to motivate a team and has no vision. Is that what we're saying?
Senior Executive 2:	We're saying he can't handle people. At least

he can't make them like it. They act out of
fear, not involvement. And the good ones
have left.

Senior Executive 3:   I guess that's right.

Senior Executive 1:   Too bad. He did well for us but we've got no
place to take him.

This is not an unusual case of the failure of success. Selectors of
chiefs, it seems, are inclined to favor executives who have demonstrated they can develop a business. There is not a lot of reward to
those who conduct salvage operations because of the human costs
incurred and the difficulty of finding evidence of vision in someone
who is fighting for survival.

POST-DECISION DISSONANCE

After the selectors reach a decision, they tend to look for support for
it. Seeking support is a way of reducing the dissonance, or psychological discomfort, that occurs when a selection alternative has
some negatives about it and the rejected alternative has some positive aspects. The need to reduce dissonance is normal. A few companies even use a consulting psychologist or management consultant
to evaluate the managerial capabilities of the candidates. Since the
candidates for key positions are generally all high in ability in
important areas, a psychological evaluation that confirms top
management's observations is helpful in reducing dissonance.

In other companies, dissonance is reduced by deciding how the
unsuccessful candidates will be handled. Whether or not all the
candidates are advised that they are under consideration for senior
positions, they will be aware that they were passed over when it is
given to someone else. For each candidate a company does not wish
to lose, it is important (1) to reassure that individual of his or her
value to the organization, and (2) to discuss plans for other potential
career opportunities. Nevertheless, care should be taken to assure
that a candidate is not a bridesmaid too often without becoming a
bride.

GUIDING A DISCUSSION

The opinions and observations of chiefs from various industries and companies highlights the fundamental issues that influence final selection decisions. It is apparent that selecting a chief is hardly systematic (as the screening of candidates tends to be in many companies), but it is judgmental, subjective, and certainly an anxious time for selectors.

It is helpful for chiefs to get guidance from an internal or external resource when assessing candidates. A somewhat structured discussion plan and an experienced discussion leader will prevent the final decision-making process from wallowing. In the discussion that follows, the CEO, senior vice president, and human resources vice president met for the purpose of getting consensus on selecting a general manager to run the company's North American operations. They had been discussing candidates for seven months and had narrowed the choice down from four candidates to two. They agreed they would make the selection at that meeting from the two remaining candidates:

Chief Executive Officer:	Let's try to finish this up by 11:00. That gives us three hours and we've gone over all the pluses and minuses on each candidate. What do you recommend?
Human Resources Vice President:	I'd like to get out for a round of golf and come back to a decision. This is a hard one.
Senior Vice President:	We're divided, it seems. I think Sandy is the obvious choice. He knows how to focus on problems and we do have problems at each of our plants that need to be resolved.
Chief Executive Officer:	You still think Sandy can do that? He can sure bring focus but

he doesn't bring much else that we're going to need. That job has changed. We need a delegator, somebody who knows how to motivate a bunch of people and then knows enough to get out of their way. Sandy gets in his own way. I admit he knows the technical side of our business better than anyone but he doesn't know how to delegate.

Senior Vice President: Well, Dick is better at handling people. He's got good chemistry at each plant. They all like him but I've still got doubts about his willingess to sacrifice himself to get the job done. It's going to take a lot of travel and he's not going to want to do a lot of that.

Human Resources Vice President: Nobody likes travel.

Chief Executive Officer: A lot of people do. I remember when I traveled 70% of the time and I did it for almost five years. The worse travel was between here and Japan.

Human Resources Vice President: That's a tough trip. I wouldn't be surprised to see a Concord on that run soon.

Chief Executive Officer: Look, Dick and Sandy are both good. One of them has got to be better for North American Operations.

Senior Vice President: Sandy knows how to anticipate problems. He is a problem finder. He's a very able administrator

	and has a lot of energy. Dick is not as good an administrator and doesn't use our systems very much. He takes short-cuts sometimes too often.
Chief Executive Officer:	But he knows how to delegate. He is also very experienced and we can make sure he focuses on the real problems himself. He can't leave them to anyone else.
Human Resources Vice President:	You both remember several years ago when. . . .

The human resources vice president reminisced about an incident that occurred six or seven years ago, involving an executive who over-delegated. The three men talked about the problems of over-delegation and how they were resolved. At the end of two hours, they were no closer to a decision than they were when they started. The decision-making process wallowed because of the personal agendas and ruminations of the participants. As a result, the human resources vice president suggested they get outside help to reach a decision, since they could not bring anyone else in the company into their confidence. They called a management consultant to lead the discussion.

Based on what the human resources vice president told the consultant, he decided to keep the conversation on the issues and not to allow any wandering. The consultant asked them to start out with a quick review of what they had previously agreed were the relative strengths and weaknesses of the two candidates. He summarized these on a blackboard which contained the comments in Table 8-1 after about a 30-minute discussion.

After listing this information, the conversation continued like this:

Chief Executive Officer:	That's the way we see them.
Consultant:	But you disagree about what is needed to do the next job?

Table 8-1. Comparison of Strengths and Weaknesses

Sandy's Strengths	Sandy's Weaknesses
Strong technically.	Sometimes abrupt with people.
Outstanding administrator.	Not personally aggressive, diffident
Very analytical.	personality.
Integrity.	Personal creativity.
Discipline.	Doesn't distinguish well between
High intelligence.	good and mediocre people.
Reliable.	
Doesn't get lost in details.	
Courage of opinons.	
Energy.	
Knows the business.	

Dick's Strengths	Dick's Weaknesses
Delegator.	Administrative skills.
Handles people very well.	Sometimes accepts subordinates'
Can motivate.	opinions without thoroughly
Curious.	checking.
Courage of opinion.	Personal ambition may not be high.
Good analytically.	
Broad perspective.	
Excellent business judgment.	
Good business instincts.	
Creative.	
High intelligence.	

Senior Vice President:	Yes.
Consultant:	What's your main point of departure from each other?
Senior Vice President:	Whether Sandy can work through others— by delegating—and if Dick will get close enough to problems to ensure their solution. It's a big area and we need somebody who can do both—delegate to others and focus on problems.
Consultant:	Do you all agree?
Others:	Yes.
Consultant:	Sounds like a contradiction to me. Exactly what and how do you expect him to delegate—and to whom? And what kind of focus should be given to problems that they are now getting?

In reply, the senior vice president carefully described the decisions and work that should be delegated. He also described what kinds of results should be obtained. The CEO described the difference between the focus they wanted and the present focus on problems. As they described their expectations and organizational needs, it became apparent to the consultant that they wanted more focus on problems because they lacked confidence in the business judgment of most operating staffs at the plants. He asked if this were the case, and, after only a one or two minute discussion, they agreed fully that they did feel this way. The consultant then asked whether the selection decision was difficult because of the poor qualifications of the two candidates or because of their concern about the competence of key staff at the plants.

All three men conceded that both candidates were very good. The human resources vice president said he thought, in retrospect, that they were probably overreacting to what they saw as deficiencies in both candidates. They thought that this might be their way of rationalizing not coming to a decision because of their doubts about plant staffs. With that statement, the senior vice president said, "Well, let's pick the guy who can hire and develop key people at each location." The rest of the conversation lasted less than five minutes.

Chief Executive Officer:	You're absolutely right.
Senior Vice President:	I think we've done it.
Human Resources Vice President:	I agree. Dick is the clear choice. His chemistry and people skills are what we need.
Senior Vice President:	I'll go with that. But let's make sure that he understands exactly what we expect of him. Otherwise we may not get the changes we want.

The differences made by modestly structuring a discussion will often force attention to the more important issues which delay a selection decision. An internal or external consultant can sometimes help by raising questions and hypotheses about opinions which mask the real source of concern.

INFORMATION FORMAT FOR FINAL DECISION

Information about key candidates should be summarized in a simple way to facilitate review leading to a decision. For this purpose, a listing of strengths and weaknesses may be too shallow. A detailed review will be too much.

It is probably best to use a narrative style because it enables qualifications and texture. The narrative should be brief, since its purpose is to guide a discussion. For each candidate, no more than one page is required. The narrative should contain some of the major questions raised and answered about a candidate. Since the candidate's experience background is usually well known to evaluators, there is no need to repeat it. Some examples of excerpted statements follow.

CEO Candidate

He is very flexible and durable. He has great capacity to accept differences among people and can work well with different kinds of people. He has a lot of personal optimism, which is reflected in his work with others. He offers creative solutions to problems because he believes in his ability to build on the ideas of others. While a question was raised about his ability to be sufficiently critical of subordinates because of his general supportiveness of them, the evidence shows that he is constructively critical at the appropriate time. His appointment would be a popular decision throughout the company.

CEO Candidate

His vision and entrepreneurial skills are very high. He knows exactly how the business should grow and he can describe it in detail. His business judgment and motivational skills are very good. In stressful situations, he remains cool and continues to analyze and contribute effectively. In spite of his limited experience in the company, he comes across as exceptionally qualified but a dark horse. Might be a big surprise if picked as CEO. Would have to prepare others in top management.

CEO Candidate

Very experienced in all aspects of a business. Well-known throughout the company. He is respected by people who work for him and knows how to establish a positive climate. He is an effective communicator and knows how to select good people and put together a strong team. One of the concerns about him is that he is too political and may let this influence his decisions more than the relevant facts. This may interfere with his judgment when pressured by strong subordinates. The CFO and two senior vice presidents are exceptionally strong. There is a question of decision-making balance that has merged.

Executive Vice President Candidate

He is action-oriented and impatient. Typically he gets good results and knows how to motivate people. Although he is a strong executive and does not hesitate to express his opinions, he is careful about the way he treats people. On operational matters, he does not always anticipate as well as he should, thereby reacting to problems somewhat later than necessary. His emphasis on action seems to overshadow anticipatory thinking. Selection in this case will be read by most as a new direction for us.

Chief Operating Officer Candidate

He is exceptionally bright, handles conflict well, he is decisive but flexible, energetic and very curious. He has great self-confidence and generates enthusiasm for his ideas among others. Although he is very demanding, he understands the importance of treating others well. His business vision is broad and not risk-aversive. He also conveys a great amount of statesmanship in most situations, which attract people to him. One of his major strengths is engaging others in discussion and getting consensus. His restlessness, on the other hand, sometimes leads him to explore opportunities that distract him from major priorities. Some counseling from the CEO may help here.

THE DEED IS DONE

When a selection decision for a senior executive position is made, there is typically a sense of relief. Selectors will often congratulate each other on a choice—and congratulations are deserved because of the energy and thoughtfulness that went behind the decision. Helping the new chief to move smoothly into a new role is an important next step. Some plan is now required to establish personal credibility as soon as possible and to become integrated with one's new team. The human resources or personnel function should help with this. The next chapter covers several things that will ease an executive's transition from candidate to chief and an organization's experience of going from one chief to another.

— 9 —

Informing and Preparing a New Chief

GETTING OFF TO A GOOD START

Getting a new chief off to a good start is not easy. There are a lot of adjustments to be made, especially on the part of the organization he or she will lead. Using the analogy of an organ transplant, the patient will need a lot of care to guard against rejection or even passive resistance.

Several things must be done, including:

Advising the new chief and explaining the reasons why he or she was selected.

Informing the other key candidates why another candidate was selected and what the implications or plans are for them.

Helping a new chief establish initial credibility.

Helping the new chief to be assimilated by his or her organization.

Giving the new chief support to build a cohesive team.

ADVISING THE NEW CHIEF

After a selection decision is reached, the next issue is timing: when to inform the successful candidate. This takes second place, however, to what the new chief is told. It is not enough to tell the new chief the date he or she will assume responsibility or what kind of organizational restructuring that should go along with it. A new chief should be given the reasons he or she was selected. He or she should understand how he or she is perceived, what strengths he or she is expected to exercise, and which shortcomings he or she is expected to overcome or compensate.

The selector, a board chairman, or the senior executive to whom the new chief reports, should very carefully review the corporate and personal values and behavior that the chief is expected to sustain and enact. These expectancies should be described to the new chief in the most direct way; several examples are as follows:

> We are moving into an even more competitive environment and you must be prepared to take risks where the potential rewards make it worthwhile. If we continue our conservative position, we will fail. You are expected to be more aggressive in the marketplace than any of your predecessors—and by a significant degree.

> I expect you to open up our markets in the entire Pacific. You will need to find outstanding managers who can run those markets but you will have to ensure that each one gets all the support he needs from our central staff. We should have a leading position in each market within five years.

> Our customers don't know us as well as our competitors. You must make sure they do—and very quickly. This will require a shifting of people and energy from the corporate activities of monitoring and advising to the line activities of meeting and making customers. You will be expected to find your own way to do this even though you've grown up in a system which was dependent on corporate staff support.

> The first thing you'll need to do is put a team together. You won't be able to tackle our priorities without strong inside support. It may mean reorganizing the senior staff. I also expect that you will have to bring in outstanding financial and marketing talent to do it. And you

will have to strengthen and use our management development systems. We need the right people who will ensure that our top four priorities don't stray from our corporate strategy.

ADVISING THE NONSELECTED CANDIDATES

A lot of people want to be a chief. They work hard and communicate their ambitions. For most of them, the path leads to disappointment. They followed the rules as best they could but they got lost—not because of their inability or because others lost confidence in them, but because the competition looked better or positioned itself better.

Few companies can afford to lose good people. When a candidate knows he or she has not been selected, it is natural for him or her to seriously consider looking for a new career opportunity outside the company. While some candidates do leave for other companies, others merely resign in place. Their motivation and interests slows down. An even greater danger is that other people will regard a nonselected candidate as a loser in the competition and, therefore, politically unattractive to be around. Since power is lost to an individual when others will not attribute it to him or her, the nonselected candidate's operational effectiveness is threatened, regardless of his or her desire to continue to work well. In all these situations, good people are lost to a company.

There are certainly situations where it is preferable for the nonselected candidate(s) to move elsewhere. For the most part, however, this kind of oversupply of executive talent exists only in the largest companies. If you lose somebody who is not going any further and who can do better outside, it should be accepted. It is difficult to retain people whose ambition exceeds a company's ability to fulfill it—or where there is disagreement on what they can do.

One reason it is sometimes preferred that a nonselected candidate resign is the concern that may explicitly or implicitly impede the leadership of the new chief. Another reason is that a nonselected candidate is often not at a career stage or age where another opportunity will occur in the company. In this case, he or she may block the growth of other executives who are waiting for a position which is a good testing ground for future candidates.

Candidates who are not selected should not be put into the position of losing too often. Nonselected candidates should be told the reason why the successful candidate was selected. They should also be told in advance of the official announcement of the decision. Sometimes it may not be desirable to make this disclosure too far in advance, but this is more a matter of courtesy, timing, and judgment.

It should be emphasized to nonselected candidates that the decision is not a personal reflection on them, but more a decision based on a contrast of some aspect of experience between them and the selected candidate. Most companies say that nonselected candidates handle these decisions well.

William Read, formerly Senior Vice President of Employee Relations at ARCO, observed:

> People handle it well. There shouldn't be any difficulty unless a person is overly aggressive and power hungry. We've never had anyone leave us because he was not selected for the top job.

Thomas Storrs, former Chairman and CEO of the NCNB Corporation, has this to say about a nonselected candidate:

> First of all, you have to make sure he doesn't think he's a loser. You should avoid a publicized horse race. The best way to work on a selection decision is long in advance of it—otherwise you will make sure your company will lose some people. And the nonselected candidate's people feel, "Our leader got kicked in the face." Get people to buy into the change before you hang it up on the wall. Long discussions are a good investment of time so people understand how you reached your decision.

A senior vice president of a financial services company says that their key candidates generally know they are in the running. He makes sure to give nonselected candidates personal feedback on the decision but he also feels, "You don't have to make a big deal about it because it's a free and open market."

The expectations of nonselected candidates that a company wishes to encourage and develop must be addressed and managed. Since neither the company nor the candidate look forward to discussing reasons for rejection again, career options within the company should be discussed. Ways of positioning the executives to be a candidate for other opportunities should be reviewed along with aspects of experience or skill that need to be gained or demonstrated. This is a very important time for a career discussion and a company should confront it. The company should, however, avoid over-exercise in control and direction for a nonselected candidate in an attempt to compensate for the unfavorable decision.

THE FIRST STAFF MEETING

New chiefs must establish their credibility and presence at the outset of their appointment. An important way of doing this is through an initial staff meeting and subsequent one-to-one discussions with subordinates. The following guidelines can be used and reinforced at any time. These remarks assume that a company's values will support them.

Credibility is a function of perceived expertise and trustworthiness. Both are required for leadership to be effective. New chiefs need direct guidance to establish their credibility. Otherwise, weak starts, early mistakes, indecisiveness, and ambiguity will affect everyone's performance. Preparation—not assumptions—will strengthen a chief's abilities.

A new chief should meet with his or her group immediately. There are four points of expectations to make:

Clarity

The expectation of open communication; the necessity and courage to express minority or opposing opinion on all issues and all directions; the maturity to seek opinion; the self-confidence to listen; the ability to obtain consensus.

Quality

The expectation of setting high standards of work; the relationship between difficult objectives and high achievement; the importance of trying new ways; the balance between willingess to risk mistakes and doing things better than before.

Direction

The expectation of meeting objectives; the continuing awareness of how each individual's responsibility supports—or can block—the organization's end-product; development of a sense of mission.

Recognition

The expectation of active support to employees; clearing the way for individual effectiveness; acting on their behalf for their career success.

What to Say at a First Staff Meeting.   Some examples of what to say on each point of expectation are indicated below. These remarks will help a new chief to structure that meeting more effectively.

Clarity

We're a team. Most of us will work together often. But all of us will depend on each of the others at times.

Sometimes we have information or an opinion to give. When we do, we should give it. And it must be done constructively, promptly, candidly. We must talk to the others.

We must listen to each other even when we don't want to. If someone thinks he or she can help you, you must listen. In fact, you must invite comment because it is not always easy for someone else to give an opinion. Don't let low self-confidence close your ears. We don't know what we don't know.

Ambiguity works like an anchor when you want to move in a direction. It often diffuses energy. Problems should be crystalized. Asking questions and getting opinions helps to reduce ambiguity.

We must understand how and why others in the business see something differently. We don't have to agree, but we must understand why they have reached different conclusions.

It takes courage to take a minority stand or confront a strong opinion. It is easier not to. Progress often requires departure from the conventional or the norm. A minority opinion is not always correct but we all have them from time to time and we typically repress them. Don't deprive someone else of your help. Have the courage to question, suggest, and disagree. Have the courage to listen and explore.

After you have talked and you have listened, work for consensus so you can all move as a cohesive unit. Cohesiveness requires communication—but it requires consensus, too. If you depend on each other, your individual image can be enhanced by the group.

Ask questions. Ask others if they have questions you can answer.

Quality

You know your area of responsibility better than anybody else. Decide what makes the difference between an easy objective and high achievement. Figure out what you have to accomplish.

It is a lot more interesting to try new ways. You will probably make mistakes but they won't be setbacks because you will learn from each one. You will accomplish a great deal more.

Without risk, there cannot be progress. Use your abilities to work toward difficult goals and have the courage to risk failing. With continued energy and curiosity, you will move around or through the risk.

I expect personal initiative on problems—and the selection of appropriately difficult objectives. And the application of the best management and technical methodology. I will depend on your judgment. There will be no substitute for it.

Direction

When our business does not meet its goals, the organization's profitability is compromised. Meeting goals is the principle responsibility of the business. Nevertheless, the end does not always justify the means and the urgency of goal achievement must not create problems that dilute accomplishment.

Let's be sure we all know what everyone does and why it is important.

Ask about business or organization meetings which summarize progress periodically or enable a step back to evaluate the quality and contribution of work.

Recognition

One of my most important objectives is your personal career success. I would not expect you to work hard without knowing that.

To get things done, you may want and need support in clearing the way. That's my job at times. Your ability to build a chain of successes will develop your image and expertise. I will work hard to give you support, direct or indirect, volunteered or requested.

Just as you can depend on me for support, you can depend on me for recognition. Your work will not go unnoticed and I will bring it to the attention of others whenever I can. Your personal abilities and accomplishments enhance our organization's strength and you will be identified accordingly.

While I cannot assure you of the career success you want, I can do everything possible to help you prepare for it. Effectiveness in your current role is a key. Whenever possible, I will be your advocate and sponsor. Growth and promotion ought to come.

NEW MANAGER ASSIMILATION PROCESS

A complement to the staff meeting is a process which will make the aftermath of an appointment easier to handle.

New chiefs often assume responsibilities for parts of organizations or companies with which they are unfamiliar. Even if they are familiar with the operations of an organization, they are strangers to many of the people that staff the organization. Un-

familiarity with each other will postpone organizational cohesiveness and good performance. There is a need to facilitate a
quick and effective introduction of a new senior executive into an
organization. The need may be with the executive's staff or peers.

The process of quick assimilation should convey early understanding of the chief's personal style, values and opinions, expectations, interests, and plans. It is also an opportunity to help the
new chief understand the environment, problems, and concerns
with which he or she will be dealing. There are four parts to the
process as it is used in some companies:

1.   What do we know about the new executive, for example,
     initial impressions?
2.   What do we want to know about the new executive, for ex-
     ample, expectations, how will the new executive run a staff
     meeting?
3.   What ought the new executive know about us, for example,
     how we operate?
4.   What problems and issues are going on around us, for ex-
     ample, relationships in manufacturing, relationships be-
     tween marketing and research and development?

The manager (or executive) assimilation process requires someone to manage or guide it. For senior executives, the most effective
person is the human resources vice president, who would assume a
consultative role. First, the consultant and the new chief agree to
conduct the process. The consultant explains generally how the
process works, the expected benefits, and the new chief's role in the
process.

The consultant meets with the new chief's staff (or peers) to
develop information for a discussion (the chief is not present):

1.   What do we know about the new executive already?
2.   What don't we know but would like the new executive to
     know?
3.   What concerns do we have about the new executive's coming?
4.   What should the new executive know about us?
5.   What problems will the new executive be facing?

The consultant organizes the information into an appropriate discussion agenda and reviews it with the new chief to insure clear understanding of the group's thoughts.

The senior executive, his or her staff (or peers), and the consultant next meet to discuss the information. The new chief responds to questions, and discussion is encouraged. Emphasis is on give and take, openness, constructiveness, and team development.

A follow-up list of action items is often developed. This list includes actions that the chief and his or her staff (or peers) agree to take at a later date, for example: individual meetings, planned tours, business reviews.

As reported by Thomas W. Ward, Senior Vice President, Rubbermaid, the new manager assimilation process is used extensively in his company—with excellent results. It is usually conducted within two weeks of an appointment to break down barriers to communication. It shortens the time required for a new executive to be assimilated, and it sets a climate of openness and willingness to confront issues. At Rubbermaid, the sessions are conducted away from the corporate headquarters. They are planned for a full day, ending with dinner.

A COHESIVE TEAM

If a new senior executive establishes his or her credibility through early staff meetings, one-on-one sessions with key staff, and a new manager assimilation process, his or her staff are far more likely to be attracted to the goals of the organization and their roles in it. A cohesive team cannot exist among the members of a staff without attraction to other individuals in a group and to its goals.

When selectors agree on a new senior executive, they should anticipate any points of conflict between him or her and other members of the staff he or she will lead. It serves no purpose to put a new senior executive in a position where he or she will spend his or her early days arm wrestling with key staff members whose values and ways of working interfere with the objectives that the new chief is expected to accomplish.

The new chief should be urged to confront problems of this kind quickly. While he or she should not be encouraged to bring in an entirely new staff, he or she should selectively strengthen the staff with individuals who have similar values and who can more fully support his or her objectives. Nevertheless, a new chief should not remove people who merely disagree with him or her. After all, other opinions are very important. Only executives who will not work well with the new chief should be removed. Disagreement on points among executives does not, by itself, suggest that they do not work well together. On the contrary, it is how they manage the different views that indicates the cohesiveness of a team.

Alan Lafley, Chase Manhattan Bank's former Executive Vice President of Corporate Human Resources, underscores the critical nature of a new chief's boss. He reminds senior executives that a new chief will fail unless his or her boss takes responsibility for his or her selection and assures that a team is in place to act collaboratively on corporate strategies and goals.

– 10 –

Summary

At this point, it is important to sort and compare the information and perspectives previously covered in terms of one's own experience or expectations. The chances of becoming a senior executive—or selecting a good one—are enhanced significantly if decisions and actions are guided by several key considerations. These issues cut through the entire process of succession planning for senior positions. They are:

Predictability

Mechanisms

Criteria

Risk

Familiarity

Predictability

Accurate prediction is the fundamental purpose of succession planning. Not only must selectors predict behavior and its consequences (i.e., business performance) accurately, but individuals who aspire

275

to be senior executives must determine what kinds of attitudes and behavior are most likely to make desirable things happen. Prediction of executive success is more dependable if continuous assessments are made of an individual's position in a situation against a well-defined outcome. Although future events or situations are often different than the past, prediction is improved by carefully describing what is desired or required. For example, when a senior position must be filled, selectors should go beyond an evaluation of a candidate's past record. Prediction must involve consideration of how an individual is expected to act in the range of situations that will be encountered—with special attention to prediction in situations where observations or direct information is not available. The predictability of performance (one's own or the performance of candidates) in specific situations, and not merely descriptions or wishing, should be the over-riding factor in selecting or becoming a senior executive.

Mechanisms

Most organizations have mechanisms, or processes, which support the selection of new employees, the early identification of "high potentials," the development of management ability, and the identification and evaluation of candidates for senior positions. Where these processes do not provide adequate numbers or quality of candidates, they should be repaired. In most larger organizations, these processes provide the rationale and strength for dependable succession actions.

Senior executives must assure the operation of processes which force attention to decisions about people who will run major portions of the business. When these mechanisms do not mesh smoothly or when one or more of them are taken out of operation or simply ignored, the hazards of executive selection can painfully rip an organization.

Individuals who aspire to be senior executives should become intimately familiar with the mechanisms that are intended to develop or judge them. It is essential, for better performance and better control of outcomes, to understand why, how and when these processes are operating—or should be operating—on their behalf. Without this understanding, a potential candidate for senior positions becomes more dependent on chance than on ability for achievement of his or her goals.

Criteria

Both selectors and senior executive aspirants should understand what criteria are most likely to influence selection decisions. Too many inadequately defined criteria are used, often resulting in the selection of the wrong people. For example, terms like leadership and tough-mindedness are so general that they mean different things to different people. Instead, the behavioral and conceptual components of desirable or required characteristics should be described in operationally specific (i.e., observable and comparable) language.

Selectors of senior executives should identify what they need to know about candidates but the should also say how they expect to give the answers. In some cases, situations will have to be created to get the answers because there are some personal qualities which cannot be observed in current roles, for example, how an individual responds to crisis.

Good questions are needed to articulate criteria and to probe their nature in a candidate. Several frameworks and guides for determining criteria, probing personal characteristics and exploring performance have been provided previously. Individuals who aspire to be senior executives should assure they understand the specific criteria by which they will be evaluated. They should also initiate action to improve the quality of the criteria by which they will be judged. Without these initiatives, selection decisions are likely to be made on the basis of observations and information that are not congruent with the candidate's expectations. In these cases, both the candidates and the organization will suffer.

Risk

For the most part, serious candidates for senior positions are all reasonably competent and experienced. While there are usually clear differences among them, it is also difficult for selectors to make a choice. One factor, however, brings attention to a candidate in a way that will distinguish him or her from the other candidates: willingness to take risks and the ability to be successful in doing so. Most progress requires change. Usually change requires some kind of risk because something novel or untested is introduced into a situation. There is also evidence that individuals who know how to take risks are more likely to attract more attention and confidence than others who approach problems or work in a more routine fashion. Candidates who aspire to become senior executives should consider the advantages of risk and should be prepared to act boldly. To do otherwise is to take another risk, that is, not distinguishing oneself.

Familiarity

There is so much evidence that familiarity is a most prominent factor in senior executive selections that it cannot and should not be put aside. As so many selectors say, "personal chemistry" is very important to the level of comfort they feel when trying to predict how a candidate will perform in a role. Unfortunately, familiarity and resultant comfort with it often causes selectors to overlook serious drawbacks in some candidates. It also results in the rejection of candidates who have the ability to perform in an outstanding way.

Selectors should, therefore, be especially careful to put aside their personal comfort with the candidate and to base their judgment on a more predictive evaluation of accomplishments in the context of what is required in the position to be filled. Individuals who aspire to senior positions, however, must be aware of the power of "personal chemistry" and they should carefully plan how to describe their work and communicate their thinking to individuals who contribute to selection decisions. Unless they can develop familiarity with their performance and abilities, it is not likely that they will be serious candidates for senior positions. Communicating effectively to others about one's accomplishments, objectives, and ideas is a critical issue in senior executive selection.

Suggestion

This material should be reviewed carefully from time to time, especially the key issues and the frameworks for evaluation. Selectors and individuals who aspire to be senior executives will find it will help to make things happen the way they should. The performance of organizations should benefit directly and measurably.

Index